THE WORLD OF UCL

NEGLEY HARTE, JOHN NORTH
AND GEORGINA BREWIS

REVISED AND UPDATED

First edition published in 1978
Second edition published in 1991
Third edition published in 2004
This edition published in 2018 by
UCL Press
University College London
Gower Street
London WC1E 6BT

Available to download free: www.ucl.ac.uk/ucl-press

Text © Authors, 2018
Images © Authors and copyright holders named in the
Picture credits, 2018

The authors have asserted their rights under the Copyright,
Designs and Patents Act 1988 to be identified as the authors
of this work.

A CIP catalogue record for this book is available from
The British Library.

This book is published under a Creative Commons Attribution Non-commercial Non-derivative 4.0 International license (CC BY-NC-ND 4.0). This license allows you to share, copy, distribute and transmit the work for personal and non-commercial use providing author and publisher attribution is clearly stated. Attribution should include the following information:

Harte N., North J. & Brewis G. 2018. *The World of UCL*. London:
UCL Press. DOI: https://doi.org/10.14324/111.9781787352933

Further details about Creative Commons licenses are available
at http://creativecommons.org/licenses/

ISBN: 978-1-78735-294-0 (Pbk.)
ISBN: 978-1-78735-293-3 (PDF)
DOI: https://doi.org/10.14324/111.9781787352933

Designed by Bobby Birchall, Bobby&Co
Printed in Belgium by Albe De Coker

Front cover image: View of UCL Portico (UCL Digital Media)
Back cover image: A view of the scene in the Front Quad during the
Bazaar and Fête in July 1909 (UCL Library, College Collection)

Contents

Foreword 6
Author's note to the fourth edition 8

Chapter 1   The Foundation: 1825–28   10
Chapter 2   The University of London: 1828–36   32
Chapter 3   University College: 1836–78   62
Chapter 4   The Admission of Women: 1878–1904   86
Chapter 5   The Gregory Foster Years: 1904–29   136
Chapter 6   UCL in War and Peace: 1929–51   180
Chapter 7   The Evans and Annan Years: 1951–78   220
Chapter 8   The Years of Expansion: 1978–2003   248
Chapter 9   London's Global University: UCL in the twenty-first century   290

Appendix 336
Further reading 340
Notes 341
Picture credits 342
Index 344

Foreword

From its foundation in 1826, UCL has embraced an innovative, progressive and critical spirit of which we are the proud inheritors today. We were the first university to make higher education affordable and accessible to a much broader section of society and the first to introduce university level teaching in many subjects. Our commitment to pioneering methods of teaching continues today through an intense focus and absolute commitment to excellence in research-based education.

Our 20-year strategy, UCL 2034, provides a framework for the next few decades that is firmly grounded in UCL's founding principles of academic excellence and research aimed at addressing real-world problems. For almost two centuries our staff, students and alumni have endeavoured to shape the modern world. To date no fewer than 28 Nobel Prizes have been earned by people who are, or were, students or academics at UCL. The university's leadership over these 190 years has benefited from a tradition of independent academic critique that is alive and well at UCL today.

In the twenty-first century UCL is truly London's global university, but from its very foundation UCL has been international in outlook. The very word 'global' was coined by our spiritual guide, and oldest resident, Jeremy Bentham. UCL has never chosen to rest on its laurels: this edition comes at a time of both ambitious redevelopment on the Bloomsbury campus and the establishment of an entirely new campus on Queen Elizabeth Olympic Park in Stratford. Such vision would not seem out of place to UCL's founders, whose bold decision to commission a grand, neoclassical design for the new university was roundly derided at the time.

I am delighted to introduce this thoroughly revised and updated edition of *The World of UCL*. I particularly welcome the greater attention paid in this volume to women's contributions to life at UCL over the past 190 years. UCL was the first university in England to admit women on equal terms to men. Equality and diversity are enshrined in our Benthamite origins, and promoting these values has been central to my period in office. I am also pleased to note that through UCL Press's innovative open access publishing programme, this edition will be available to a much wider audience than ever before.

Professor Michael Arthur
President and Provost
April 2018

Author's note to the fourth edition

This is a completely revised and updated edition of a book first published in 1978 at the time of the celebration of the 150th anniversary of UCL's foundation, when the College was home to barely 6,000 students. The second edition was undertaken in 1991 at the prompting of Professor John White, the then Pro-Provost, and Dr Stephen Montgomery, then the Director of External Affairs. The third edition was completed in 2004 at the behest of Dr Alisdaire Lockhart, the Director of Development & Corporate Communications, and Professor Malcolm Grant, the President and Provost. UCL today is home to 40,000 students and counting. It is embarked on some of the most ambitious developments in its 190-year history, including the establishment of an entirely new campus in East London. This new book was undertaken at the suggestions of Professor David Price, Vice-Provost (Research) and Paul Ayris, Pro-Vice-Provost (UCL Library Services).

Credit for the bulk of the research must lie with the book's original authors, Negley Harte and John North. As they have acknowledged in past editions, the book owes a strong debt to previous historians of the College, above all to Hale Bellot's *University College London, 1826–1926*, published in 1929. My task has been to draft an entirely new final chapter and to restructure the penultimate chapter, as well as to attempt to correct inaccuracies and revise certain earlier sections in the light of changed interpretations and understandings of past episodes and individuals. I have derived much satisfaction from adding new material on the role of women at UCL, as well as additional information on the considerable impact of the First and Second World Wars. I have also been pleased to elevate the place of students – a group that is curiously often omitted from such institutional histories – in the book. For this new edition, which has been completely redesigned, we took the decision to reduce the number of illustrations significantly in order to give more prominence to those selected.

The new chapter is based on documentary research and interviews with a number of key individuals at UCL. My thanks are due to: Michael Arthur, Tim Beasley Murray, Jonathan Bell, Cathy Brown, Celia Caulcott, Helen Chatterjee, David Colquhoun, Subhadra Das, Becky Francis, Mary Fulbrook, Marilyn Gallyer, Hazel Genn, Deborah Gill, Malcolm Grant, Lori Houlihan, Rex Knight, Paola Lettieri, David Lomas, John Mitchell, Alan Penn, David Price, Geraint Rees, Rebecca Reiner, Anthony Smith, Cengiz Tarhan and Mark West.

My particular thanks go to colleagues at UCL Press, especially Lara Speicher and Jaimee Biggins, as well as designer Bobby Birchall and editor Catherine Bradley; Colin Penman and Robert Winkworth of UCL Special Collections; John North, Gary McCulloch, Paul Ayris, David Price, Rebecca Reiner, Nicola Brewer, Subhadra Das, Liz Bruchet and Helen Downes for helpful comments on the draft; Mary Hinkley, Pauline Hubner, Amy Smith, Charles Harrowell, Peter Guillery, Faria Alam, Rebecca Spaven, Kristina Clackson Bonnington and Oliver O'Brien for their help with the illustrations, and Sarah Hellawell, Nina Pearlman, Natasha Walsh and Rachna Kayastha for other assistance.

Georgina Brewis
April 2018

CHAPTER 1

The Foundation

1825–28

> Unlike the modern civic universities which grew from some local patriotism, University College London grew from an idea. Originally that idea was based upon a belief in freedom of investigation without any distinction of creed or race or sex. That quest, which made University College the pioneer in modern university development in England, also led the founders to find a place in the College for studies which had previously been outside the university curriculum. The freedom to investigate was not an idle phrase: it meant breaking into new fields. This is still the central tradition of the College.

Sir Ifor Evans in UCL: A Survey, 1950–55 *(1955)*

What we know today as University College London (UCL) was founded in 1826 and first opened its doors to students as the self-styled 'University of London' in October 1828. London at that date was the largest city in Europe and almost the only capital without a university. The new institution was intended from the beginning to open higher education to people excluded from the ancient seats of learning in Oxford and Cambridge. Its first students included nonconformists, Jews, Catholics and others. Notoriously described by Thomas Arnold as that 'godless institution in Gower Street', England's third university prompted anxiety, contempt and curiosity among the early nineteenth-century establishment.

It is generally but incorrectly believed that Jeremy Bentham was the founder of UCL. This myth is sustained in a bizarre manner by the display of the body of the great philosopher of ethics, jurisprudence and government, 'in the attitude in which I am sitting when engaged in thought', as he instructed before his death in 1832. Besides the box with Bentham in it, UCL possesses over 200 more boxes full of his writings, a collection that has been called 'one of the most remarkable monuments to the mind of a single man in all its aspects to be found anywhere'. Prominently displayed in the Flaxman Gallery is the huge painting undertaken in 1922 by Henry Tonks, the then Slade Professor of Fine Art, portraying William Wilkins, the architect, offering the original College plans up to Bentham for his approval, while Henry Brougham, Thomas Campbell and Henry Crabb Robinson look on (Fig. 1.1). The 'Auto-Icon' has been in the possession of UCL since 1850,

Fig. 1.1 Henry Tonks' remarkable but completely unhistorical painting of the building of the College dates from 1922. It shows the architect William Wilkins offering his plans up to Jeremy Bentham for approval.

Fig. 1.2 The clothed skeleton or 'Auto-Icon' of Jeremy Bentham, sitting in pensive posture outside the Provost's office in the South Cloisters. The head is made of wax.

Fig. 1.3 An engraving of the Scottish poet Thomas Campbell (1777–1844), based on a portrait by Sir Thomas Lawrence. One of the founders of UCL, Campbell envisaged 'a great London university' open to the middle classes.

and occasionally attends meetings of the College's governing body. His most recent appearance was at a Council meeting in July 2013, the minutes recording that Jeremy Bentham was 'present but not voting' (Fig. 1.2).

In fact Bentham played no such personal role in the establishment of the College and was an old man of 80 when it opened. He did give his blessing and financial support to the venture, however, and the founders certainly owed a very considerable intellectual debt to him.[1] UCL was founded by what Bentham called 'an association of liberals' in which the leading roles were played by an improbable duo formed by a poet and a lawyer. Credit for the original proposal must go to Thomas Campbell, the now largely forgotten Scottish poet whose *Pleasures of Hope* (1799) brought him popular fame and a rapid entrée into London literary society (Fig. 1.3). In 1820, on a visit to Bonn, he was impressed by the religious toleration of the re-founded university there and formed the idea of establishing 'a great London University' for 'effectively and multifariously teaching, examining, exercising and rewarding with honours, in the liberal arts and sciences, the youth of our middling rich people'. In February 1825 *The Times* printed a powerful open letter on this

Fig. 1.4 The lawyer and politician Henry Brougham MP (1778–1868), another of the founders of UCL, in a painting by James Lonsdale.

subject from Campbell to Henry Brougham, another Scot. Brougham was a brilliant man, one of the founders of the *Edinburgh Review*, who had moved to London to seek commanding outlets for his versatility and energy in the law and politics (Fig. 1.4). First elected as an MP in 1810, he became particularly involved with the cause of

popular education, associating himself with George Birkbeck and the mechanics' institutes and founding in 1826 the Society for the Diffusion of Useful Knowledge.[2]

Brougham regarded himself as a Benthamite, as a believer in the utilitarian principle of 'the greatest happiness of the greatest number' – though it has been claimed that in his view the greatest number was number one. His extravagant style smacked of humbug to many, but he was a man who got things done. Under his direction Campbell's dreams of a 'great London University' were turned into reality. A second university which provided a model for UCL was Thomas Jefferson's carefully planned University of Virginia, which had opened in 1825 (Fig. 1.5). The

Fig. 1.5 The University of Virginia, founded in 1819 and designed by Thomas Jefferson, was an important model for UCL. Here it is seen soon after its opening in 1825.

University of Edinburgh was the most powerful model of all, familiar as it was to Brougham and many of the founding professoriate in London (Fig. 1.6).

When Campbell and Brougham began to organise a university for London, the only existing universities in England were those long established at Oxford and Cambridge – described by Bentham as 'the two great public nuisances ... storehouses and nurseries of political corruption'. Membership of the Church of

Fig. 1.6 The University of Edinburgh, familiar to Brougham and many of UCL's first Professors, was the most powerful model for the new College.

England was necessary for admission to the one and for graduation from the other. All nonconformists, Catholics and Jews were thus excluded, while many Anglicans were kept out by the social restrictiveness, the cost or the institutions' characteristic intellectual backwardness. The old universities were seen to be increasingly out of touch with a rapidly changing society. The population of England

Fig. 1.7 The portrait of one of the leading members of Council, Sir Isaac Lyon Goldsmid, presented to the College by the Jewish Historical Society of England.

doubled in the first half of the nineteenth century, and the combined effects of industrialisation and urbanisation were producing new social patterns with new pressures and demands. The industrial revolution necessitated an extended system of higher education.

The main appeal of the new university was therefore to the interests excluded from the established system, such as it was, and to the various new social groups. Isaac Lyon Goldsmid, a millionaire financier and later the first Jew to become a baronet, played an especially significant role (Fig. 1.7). He brought Campbell and

Fig. 1.8 A foundation medal recording names of the original Council, including James Mill, Zachary Macaulay, George Grote and George Birkbeck.

Brougham together on the project and ensured the considerable support of the Jewish community. The nonconformists were actively led by Francis Augustus Cox, the Baptist minister of Hackney, while a different dissenting strand was represented by the support of Zachary Macaulay, whose main work had been devoted to the abolition of the slave trade. Catholics were represented by the Duke of Norfolk and the Whig establishment provided a number of other titled luminaries. James Mill, the utilitarian philosopher and father of John Stuart Mill, actively represented Benthamism, and the various progressive influences rubbed shoulders readily with supporters from the City of London (Fig. 1.8).

As the result of a year-long series of public and private meetings chaired by Brougham, the College came into formal existence on 11 February 1826 with the signing of an elaborate Deed of Settlement. It was agreed to raise a substantial sum

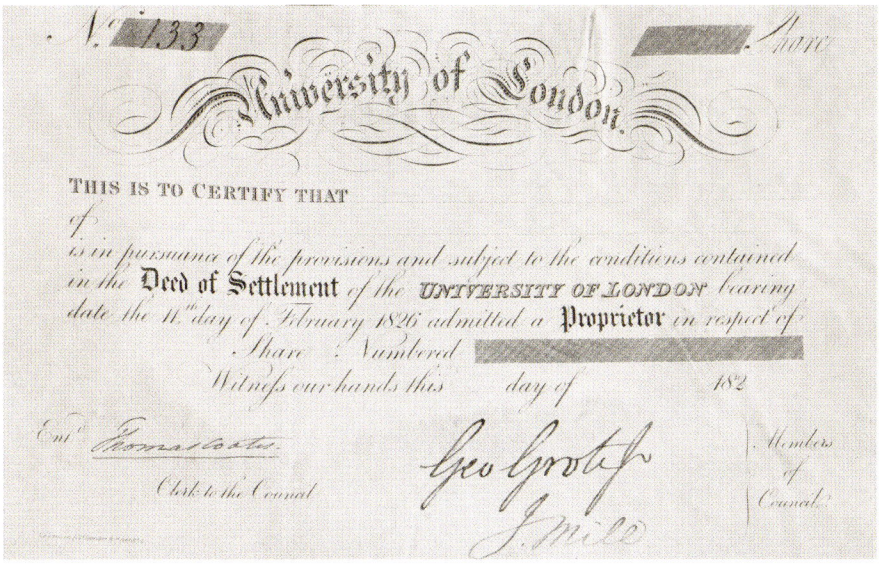

Fig. 1.9 A share certificate issued to the College's original proprietors.

of between £150,000 and £300,000 by the selling of shares of £100 each (Fig. 1.9). From among the 'proprietors', as the shareholders were called, 24 men were to be elected as the Council, the all-powerful body which was to control the University's property, appoint the Professors and regulate the education of the students. It was a fundamental principle of the new institution that religion in any form should be neither a requirement for entry nor a subject for teaching. As a corollary it was decided that no minister of religion should sit on the Council. The Revd Dr Cox served therefore as Honorary Secretary of that body until he became UCL's Librarian in 1827.

From the outset the promoters sought incorporation. Brougham's soundings towards a Royal Charter in 1825 were rebuffed by the Tory government of the day, and his subsequent efforts to achieve an Act of Parliament were defeated by the influence of Oxford and Cambridge (Fig. 1.10). Parliamentary assistance was provided by Joseph Hume, one of the members of the original Council. A leading radical, Hume was indefatigable in support of the College as well as of those other great progressive causes of the age, Catholic emancipation and parliamentary reform. After 1832 he was joined in the House of Commons by another member of the original Council, William Tooke, a prominent solicitor who became the first Treasurer of the College and of the Hospital.

The strength of the combined opposition of Oxbridge and of the London medical profession to legal recognition of the College as a 'University' could not

Fig. 1.10 George Cruikshank's cartoon of 1825 portrays Brougham hawking shares in the projected University around Lincoln's Inn.

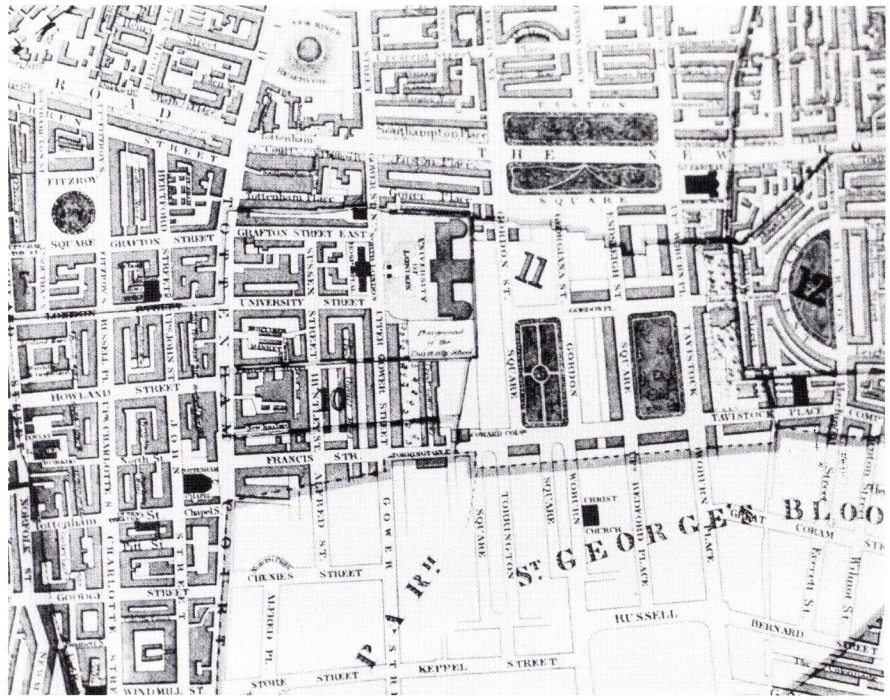

Fig. 1.11 The College and its environs, mapped to show the new parliamentary borough of St Marylebone after the 1832 Reform Act. The site was on the fringe of the expanding metropolis, with Euston Station (opened in 1837) not yet built.

easily be overcome in Parliament, despite the additional efforts of Brougham in the House of Lords, where he had gone in 1830 as Lord Chancellor. When UCL did eventually get its first charter in 1836, it took an unexpected form.

A base in Bloomsbury

One of the first acquisitions for the new University, even before it was officially constituted, was a building site. Nearly eight acres in Bloomsbury were bought in August 1825 for £30,000 by three of the richest promoters, Goldsmid, John Smith and Benjamin Shaw, and held by them until it could be transferred to the new University (Fig. 1.11). Previously the site had served variously as a drilling ground, a place for duelling and a rubbish dump. It had been intended to develop it as Carmarthen Square, a projected addition to the yet unfinished Bloomsbury. By the

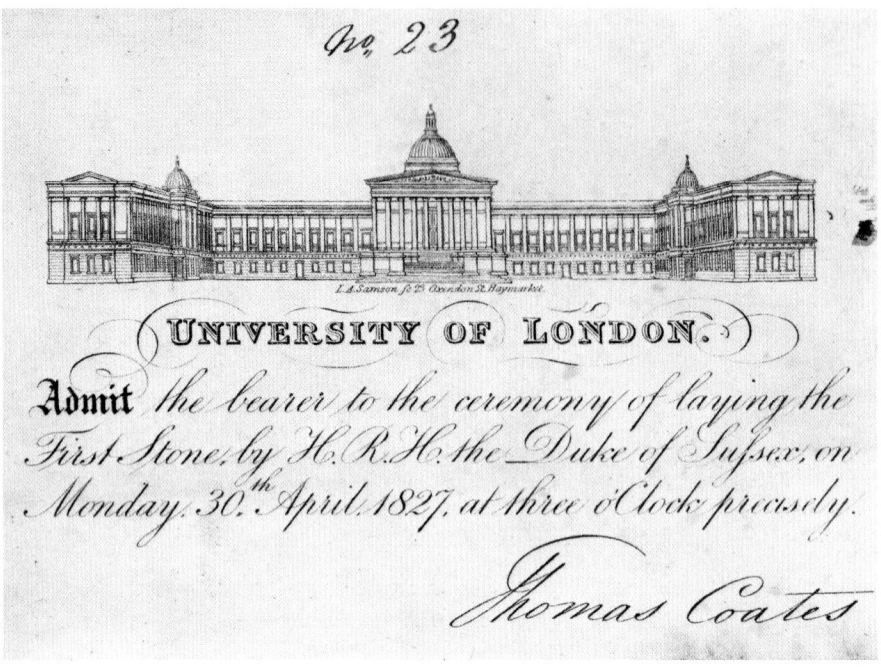

Fig. 1.12 An invitation to the foundation ceremony for the College on 30 April 1827.

time of the holding of the first meeting of the proprietors at the end of October 1826, 1,300 shares in the University had been sold, 200 fewer than the minimum believed necessary. Plans for the building were nevertheless being pressed ahead, and the digging of foundations was already underway. Despite the bad weather of the winter of 1826–27, work was sufficiently advanced by 30 April 1827 for the ceremony of laying the foundation stone (Fig. 1.12).

This was undertaken with full masonic rights by the Duke of Sussex; a brother of George IV and the only member of the royal family with any intellectual pretensions, he was well known for his liberal sympathies. A copper plate with an inscription duly read out by Cox was placed in a cavity in the stone together with the traditional coins. Afterwards some 500 people gathered for a dinner at the Freemasons' Tavern at which many speeches were made and £8,000 was raised. Henry Brougham made a memorably sarcastic oration attacking the opponents of the University, but annoyed Thomas Campbell's friends by appearing to accept credit for founding the University single-handed. Campbell was absent from the foundation ceremony, being occupied as Lord Rector of the University of Glasgow, and he did not serve on the Council beyond the first year. Squeezed out by Brougham, Campbell's connection with the University he had proposed ended as it was coming into being.

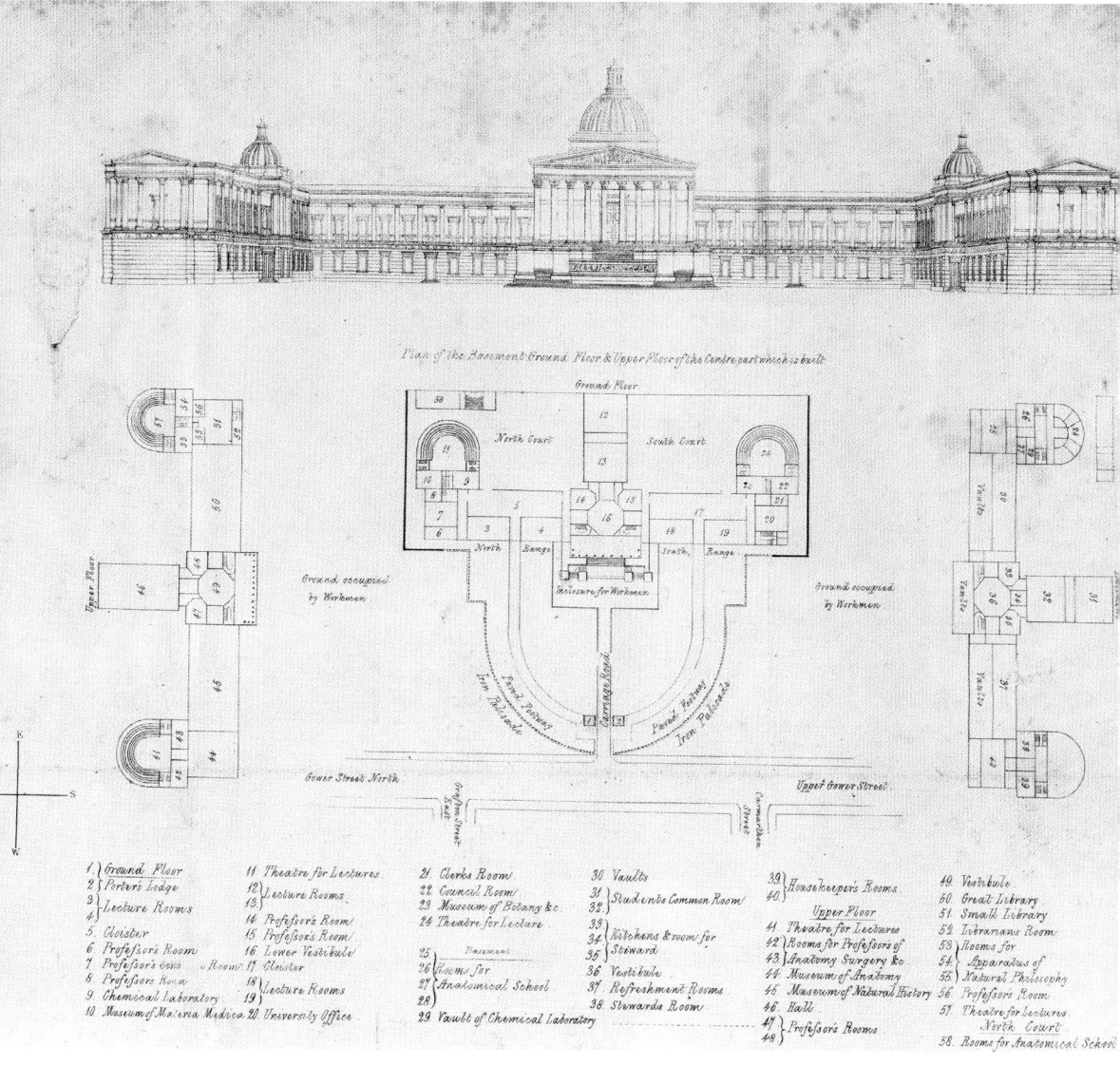

Fig. 1.13 The original plan for the College, designed by William Wilkins in 1825.

The architect chosen for the College was William Wilkins, whose fashionable, neo-Grecian design submitted in response to public advertisement in August 1825 was found exceedingly fine. Wilkins had previously designed new college buildings for Downing and King's College at Cambridge, as well as Haileybury, the East India Company's college in Hertfordshire. UCL is widely acknowledged to be Wilkins' greatest work, far more distinguished than the National Gallery he built in Trafalgar

Square a few years later. The main entrance was to be at the top of a wide staircase under a ten-column Corinthian portico topped by an elegant dome. A chapel was conspicuous by its absence, the main entrance being intended to give on to the three principal rooms: the Museum of Natural History to the left, the Library to the right and the Great Hall directly ahead. Lecture theatres of various sizes led off generous cloisters running to the impressive wings that contained further suites of rooms. In the event, shortage of money meant that Wilkins' splendid design was only partially carried out (Fig. 1.13).

Fig. 1.14 This engraving of the College buildings received a great deal of publicity in the late 1820s. The design shows the wings together with supplementary wings that were never actually built.

The lowest tender received from a builder for the construction of Wilkins' building was £110,000 – almost as much as the College had raised in total by autumn 1826. It was confidently declared that: 'the wish of the Council will appear to have been rather to select a great design suited to the wants, the wealth, and the magnitude of the population for whom the Institution is intended, than one commensurate with its present means.' To this heroic decision the College owes the iconic centrepiece to its present rambling and in many ways unimpressive premises; the Portico has long formed part of UCL's branding. It was decided to build the central range of the building with the Portico and Dome as envisaged by Wilkins, but to delay the addition of the two wings until the financial position improved. Together with the stone ornamentation, various fittings and the two front lodges, the cost was not to exceed £86,000 (Fig.1.14). Financial stringency also involved postponement of the Great Hall and strict curtailment of expenditure on the Museum and Library. The steps under the Portico thus became something of a lavish white elephant; 'the grandest entrance in London', it has been called, 'with nothing behind it' (Fig. 1.15, overleaf).

Augustus Pugin regarded the architecture of the College as pagan, adding acidly that it was 'in character with the intentions and principles of the institution'. The College had to put up with a good many such snide remarks and attacks, especially in the crucial years between Campbell's letter in *The Times* in 1825 and the opening in 1828 (Fig. 1.16). Verses and cartoons ridiculing what was quickly dubbed 'the

Fig. 1.16 A cartoon lampooning the College, published at the time of UCL's foundation in February 1826. Henry Brougham is shown hammering at the iron bar of philosophy on the anvil of public support.

Cockney College' or 'the radical infidel College' were published in the ultra-Tory *John Bull* and other papers:

> Come bustle, my neighbours, give over your labours,
> Leave digging and delving, and churning:
> New lights are preparing to set you a staring,
> And fill all your noddles with learning.
> Each dustman shall speak, both in Latin and Greek,
> And tinkers beat bishops in knowledge –
> If the opulent tribe will consent to subscribe
> To build up a new Cockney College.
>
> 'The Cockney College' in *John Bull*, July 1825

The opposition was provoked partly by the apparent pretension of a joint-stock company masquerading as a university in a period of financial speculation and partly by the College's appeal to social groups excluded from the two old universities – an appeal intolerable to the Establishment. Above all it was provoked by the rejection of all religious teaching and of compulsory religious conformity.

Despite the financial setbacks, the great hopes held by many for the new institution continued. Before the building had begun, the College was treated to the publication of what the historian Thomas Babington Macaulay called its 'horoscope' in the pages of the *Edinburgh Review*. 'We predict', he wrote, 'that the clamour by which it has been assailed will die away, that it is destined to a long, a glorious, and a beneficent existence, that, while the spirit of its system remains unchanged, the details will vary with the varying necessities and facilities of every age, that it will be the model of many future establishments, that even those haughty foundations which now treat it with contempt, will in some degree feel its salutary influence.' A very bold prediction at the time, Macaulay's words turned out to be remarkably percipient.

Fig. 1.15 UCL as it actually appeared at the time of opening in 1828 and for nearly 50 years afterwards.

CHAPTER 2

The University of London

1828–36

UNIVERSITY OF LONDON.

The MEDICAL CLASSES *will open on* Wednesday *the 1st of October.*

ANATOMY AND OPERATIVE SURGERY—GRANVILLE S. PATTISON, Esq. Daily (except Saturday), from Two to Half-past Three. Fee, First Course £4; Second Course £3.

PHYSIOLOGY—CHARLES BELL, Esq. F.R.S. Three times a week, from Eleven to Twelve. Fee, First Course £3; Second Course £2.

NATURE AND TREATMENT OF DISEASES—JOHN CONOLLY, M.D. Daily (except Saturday), from Nine to Ten. Fee, First Course £3; Second Course £3.

MIDWIFERY AND DISEASES OF WOMEN AND CHILDREN—DAVID D. DAVIS, M.D. Four times a week, from Ten to Eleven. Fee, First Course £3; Second Course £3.

CLINICAL MEDICINE—THOMAS WATSON, M.D. Physician to the Middlesex Hospital. Twice a week, from Six to Seven P.M. Fee, £4.

SURGERY AND CLINICAL SURGERY—CHARLES BELL, Esq. Surgeon to the Middlesex Hospital. Three times a week, from Six to Seven P.M. Fee, £4.

MATERIA MEDICA AND PHARMACY—ANTHONY TODD THOMSON, M.D. Daily (except Saturday), from Eight to Nine A.M. Fee, First Course £3; Second Course £3.

CHEMISTRY—EDWARD TURNER, M.D. Daily, from Ten to Eleven, commencing on the 3rd of November. Fee, First Course £4; Second Course £3.

COMPARATIVE ANATOMY—ROBERT GRANT, M.D. Three times a week, from Three to Four. Fee, £5.

MEDICAL JURISPRUDENCE—JOHN GORDON SMITH, M.D. At the conclusion of the Winter and Spring Courses.

BOTANY—JOHN LINDLEY, Esq. F.R.S. At the conclusion of the Winter and Spring Courses. Fee, £4.

DISSECTIONS AND DEMONSTRATIONS—JAMES BENNETT, Esq. Daily. Fee, First Course £3; Second Course £2.

HOSPITAL PRACTICE—Middlesex Hospital, daily, from Half-past Twelve to Half-past One. Fee for the Academical Session £12 12s.

DISPENSARY PRACTICE—University Dispensary, daily, from Half-past Twelve to Half-past One. Fee for the Academical Session £5.

The Introductory Lectures of the Medical Professors will be delivered in the following order:

    Three o'clock P.M. Wednesday, 1st of October—CHARLES BELL, Esq.
    ——————   Thursday, 2nd of October—DR. CONOLLY.
    ——————   Friday,   3rd of October—DR. DAVIS.
    ——————   Saturday, 4th of October—GRANVILLE S. PATTISON, Esq.
    ——————   Monday,   6th of October—DR. A. T. THOMSON.
    ——————   Tuesday,   7th of October—DR. WATSON.

The Medical Classes will close in May, but each Professor will give a Winter and Spring Course.

When all the Introductory Lectures of the several Medical Classes shall have been delivered, the Professors will commence their Courses at the hours above stated.

The Certificates of the Medical Professors will be received at the College of Surgeons, and at Apothecaries' Hall. The Lectures will be open to students who may not desire certificates, or who wish merely to attend single Courses.

The names of Students are entered at the University Chambers, 29, Percy Street, Bedford Square. All other particulars respecting the Medical School may be obtained by application to the Professors, or to Mr. Coates at the Chambers.

(By Order of the Council.)

THOMAS COATES, *Clerk.*

N.B. The Fee for the First Courses will be required to be paid at whatever period of the Session the Pupil may enter.

Printed by RICHARD TAYLOR, Red Lion Court, Fleet Street.

> My last account of the university . . . was full of gloomy forebodings. I cannot say that, looking at the institution at large and for any permanent futurity, these are much removed. It is the opinion of many, I almost fear of most, that it contains within itself the seeds of dissolution. The expenditure has been lavish, the plans are ill-digested, and vibrating, like all things in which the Whigs have a hand, between the desire of being popular and the fear of being unfashionable, so as of course to satisfy neither class whom they seek to conciliate by cowardly half-measures. The Council are not united, and the professors as a body are openly at war with the Council.

Sarah Austin, writing to her sister, April 1830

Although the building of the Portico and the Dome was not completed until the following year, the 'University of London' began its first academic session in October 1828 (Fig. 2.1). Selina Macaulay, daughter of Zachary, visited in the middle of the first term and the College impressed her as 'externally and internally a noble building'. She found 'the theatres extremely spacious and so arranged that it is much easier both to see and hear the lecturer than in any other building of the same size'. 'It seems so short a time', Macaulay concluded in her diary, 'since the whole scheme has been planned and executed that it reminds me of Aladdin's enchanted palace which sprung up in a single night.'

The first Professors

The most striking characteristic of the 24 Professors who constituted the teaching body of the College when it opened in 1828 was their relative youth. All but three were aged under 40, and six were 30 or under. The second striking fact is the number of posts in subjects not previously taught in English universities – nor, more significantly still, in British universities, nor even in European ones. The Chairs in the Modern Foreign Languages and in English Language and Literature were all especially notable innovations.

Fig. 2.1 The full programme of medical classes offered by the College in 1828–29, its first year of operation.

UCL's opening inaugural lectures were well attended by the public and were pronounced a great success. The first was delivered on 1 October 1828 by Charles Bell, the Professor of Surgery and the most famous member of the distinguished Medical Faculty that had been assembled (Fig. 2.2). He had been educated at Edinburgh and joined the Speculative Society there – a notable group which, brought together in the 1790s, was to provide the London University with no fewer than five members of its original Council and three of its first Professors. Bell conducted important research on the working of the nervous system and became a surgeon of repute at the Middlesex Hospital. John Conolly also studied medicine at Edinburgh; he graduated in 1821 and subsequently practised medicine at Stratford-on-Avon, twice becoming mayor of the town.

Neither Bell nor Conolly were to stay long at the College, however, owing to the unfortunate quarrels that soon engulfed the Medical Faculty. Bell resigned in 1830, going on to build up the medical school at the Middlesex and then returning to Edinburgh University. Conolly resigned in 1831, later taking charge of the Hanwell Lunatic Asylum, where he introduced humane methods of treatment for the insane and pioneered revolutionary changes in this field. His pupil and son-in-law Henry Maudsley (who qualified at UCL in 1856 and became Professor of Medical Jurisprudence, 1869–80) was to be commemorated by the Maudsley Hospital. Another contemporary of Bell's at Edinburgh, Anthony Todd Thomson, became Professor of Materia Medica. He too had come to London in the first decade of the nineteenth century to make his mark in the medical profession, and also in the literary world. He conducted original research into the composition of alkaloids and iodides, and published a good deal. David D. Davis, a Glasgow graduate of Welsh origin, became Professor of Midwifery and Diseases of Women and Children. He had established himself as a successful London obstetrician, becoming a leading private teacher of the subject and pioneering many advanced methods, especially associated with obstetric forceps. Davis achieved some prominence by delivering the future Queen Victoria at Kensington Palace in 1819.

Robert E. Grant was appointed Professor of Comparative Anatomy at the time of the opening; he remained in this post until his death in 1874, 46 years later, as the longest survivor of the original Professoriate (Fig. 2.3). Throughout this period he gave five lectures a week and was believed never to have missed one. Imposing if eccentric in appearance, he invariably wore full evening dress. Yet another Edinburgh graduate, Grant had done important research there prior to coming to the College, especially on sponges, a genus of which is named after him. Among his Edinburgh pupils was Charles Darwin, who was arguably deeply influenced by his ideas and lived next door to UCL in the early 1840s. A friend of French naturalist Georges Cuvier as well as of Darwin, Grant remained on the

Fig. 2.2 Sir Charles Bell, FRS, Professor of Physiology and Surgery, who gave the first inaugural lecture in October 1828.

Fig. 2.3 Robert E. Grant, FRS. He served as Professor of Comparative Anatomy (to which Zoology was later added) from the opening of the College until his death in 1874.

Fig. 2.4a The encyclopaedic Revd Dr Dionysius Lardner, FRS, Professor of Natural Philosophy and Astronomy, 1828–31, as pictured in *Fraser's Magazine* after his resignation.

fringes of his subject and new developments in its field. He gave his students breakfast in his house near Euston and took favoured ones on continental walking tours, but he did little further research. He left his valuable collection of early books on biology to the College.

The first holder of the Chair of Natural Philosophy was the Revd Dr Dionysius Lardner – an extraordinary man who has been described as making up in contemporary notoriety what he lacked in more lasting fame (Fig. 2.4a). He moved in the most fashionable literary and political circles, and was very successful as a popular lecturer and writer of great zest. His best-known work is the *Cabinet Cyclopaedia*, which he edited in 133 volumes between 1829 and 1849. His early lectures at the College attracted a good deal of attention (Fig. 2.4b), but Lardner, his apparatus, his courses and his salary caused more trouble for the Council than any other topic in the opening years. He resigned in 1831 to make more money from writing and giving lectures in the US. He subsequently eloped with the wife of a cavalry officer, becoming involved in very expensive lawsuits and having

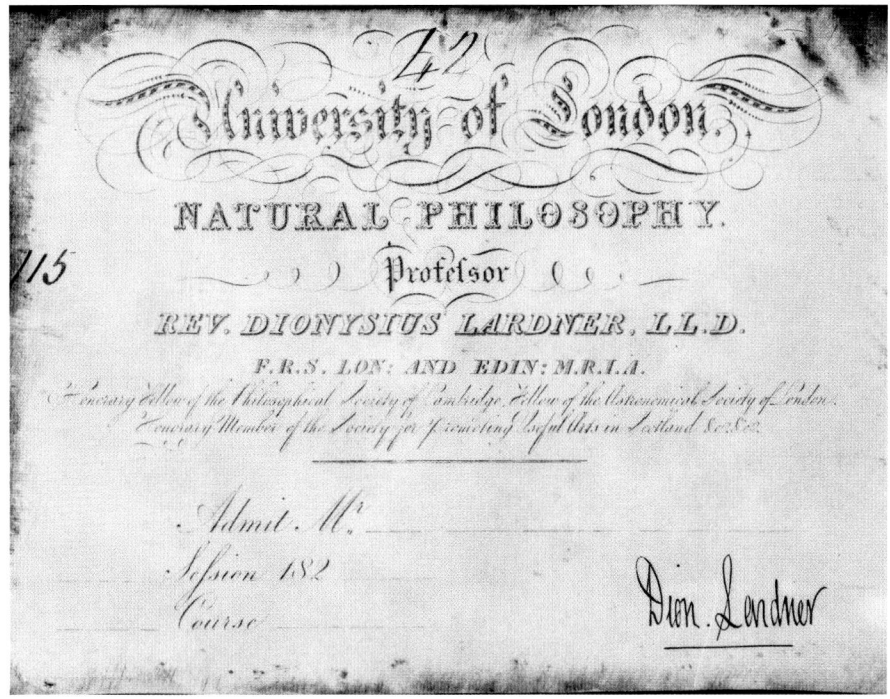

Fig. 2.4b A registration card for Lardner's Natural Philosophy class in UCL's first session. His early lectures were well attended and attracted much attention.

to settle in Paris. He cut rather more of a dash in life than many of his academic successors.

Only 21 and just down from Cambridge, Augustus De Morgan was the youngest of the original Professors when he was appointed to the Chair of Mathematics. He was to distinguish himself by resigning from this position on a matter of principle not once, but twice. For many, however, he was the outstanding figure in the first generation of the life of the College (Fig. 2.5). Sir Henry Roscoe, the chemist who was a student at the College in the 1840s, called him 'one of the profoundest and subtlest thinkers of the nineteenth century'. De Morgan taught logic and mathematics with a deft brilliance and penetration that his students found inescapably fascinating, and he exerted a captivating influence on many of them, including W. S. Jevons and Walter Bagehot. A prolific writer who made a key contribution to the development of modern symbolic logic, he was also a leading member of the Astronomical Society and the first President of the London Mathematical Society. He was also a great wit. When, as Chancellor of the Exchequer in the 1850s, Sir George Cornewall Lewis rejected a proposal for the decimalisation of the coinage on the grounds of the complexity of various schemes, De Morgan scornfully drew up a variety of proposals in which ten farthings would make a what's-its-name, ten what's-its-names a how-d'ye-call-it and ten how-d'ye-call-its a thingeme-bob, or ten farthings a George, ten Georges a Cornewall and ten Cornewalls a Lewis.

Fig. 2.5 Augustus De Morgan, as drawn by a student. A brilliant and charismatic personality, he was UCL's original Professor of Mathematics, 1828–31, when he resigned over the Pattison affair, and then again from 1836–67.

De Morgan resigned in 1831 over the sacking of Granville Sharp Pattison, the Professor of Anatomy (p.47). After the early death of his successor in 1836, he returned to the Chair, holding it for 30 years until his second resignation in 1867. The Council's rejection of the appointment of James Martineau as Professor of Mental Philosophy and Logic on the grounds that he was a Unitarian minister was, he argued, itself an ironic but fundamental desertion of the principles on which the College had been founded. He felt this so strongly that he refused to allow a bust or portrait of himself to be placed in the College to which he had brought such distinction.

Distinguished appointments were also made in Chemistry and in Botany. Yet a further Edinburgh medical graduate, Edward Turner, was appointed as the first Professor of Chemistry. He was rapidly to attain a European reputation in this subject. During his tenure of the Chair he was occupied in analytical work on the determination of atomic weights and in the writing of two textbooks, one of which, *The Elements of Chemistry*, became the standard work for many years. It was translated into German, and later edited by the great German chemist Liebig. Turner was also active in the Geological Society and began the teaching of Geology in the College. He died at the early age of 39 in 1837.

John Lindley was the first Professor of Botany, a subject originally conceived as an adjunct to the teaching of medicine. Lindley, the son of a Norfolk horticulturalist, was not himself a graduate. Employed originally by a seed merchant, he became librarian to Sir Joseph Banks, the noted naturalist and President of the Royal Society from 1822. Lindley's greatest contribution to the subject derived from the success of his efforts to preserve the Royal Botanic Gardens in Kew in the late 1830s. His *Vegetable Kingdom* and *Introduction to Botany* both enjoyed a long period as standard works. In 1839 the *Naturalist* noted the contrast between Lindley's own appearance, fresh, ruddy and hale-looking, and that of his pallid students.

P. F. Merlet, the original teacher of French, was not given the title of Professor until 1834, but chairs in German, Italian, Spanish and English, as well as in Latin, Greek, Hebrew and Hindustani, were established in the College from the outset. The modern languages were taught by refugees from their respective countries. German was taught by Ludwig von Mühlenfels, a progressive and independent thinker; he was appointed while passing through London on his way to join a band of fellow exiles in Mexico, having escaped from a Prussian political prison. Italian was put in the hands of Antonio Panizzi, who had escaped from a death sentence in Italy. Besides his post in the College, Panizzi took that of Assistant Librarian at the British Museum in 1831, becoming Keeper of Printed Books there in 1837 and eventually Principal Librarian in 1856. After giving up his Chair, he achieved permanent fame as virtual creator of both the library catalogue and the Reading

Fig. 2.6 Antonio Alcalá Galiano, Professor of Spanish, 1828–30.

Fig. 2.7 Sarah Austin, wife of the first Professor of Jurisprudence at UCL. An editor and translator from German to English, her publications were an important source of income for the couple.

Room at the British Museum. Spanish was handled by Antonio Alcalá Galiano – a marked man in Spain after 1832, when he moved a resolution against Ferdinand VII in the Spanish parliament and as a result was sentenced to death (Fig. 2.6). A leading figure in Spanish Romantic literature, Alcalá resigned in 1830 to go to Paris, hoping to take part in the July Revolution. In 1831 von Mühlenfels also left, hoping for an improved political climate in Germany. His successors in the Chair of German were of little or no consequence for many years, while Spanish was not taught again after 1830 until the establishment of the present Department in 1964.

Thomas Dale, the first Professor of English, took his holy orders very seriously and evangelically. 'I shall invariably aim', he announced in his inaugural lecture, 'to impart moral as well as intellectual instruction . . . I shall esteem it my duty . . . to inculcate lessons of virtue.' After two years of grappling with this task, he departed to devote himself to the ministry, becoming vicar of St Bride's, Fleet Street and later of St Pancras. Between 1836 and 1839 Dale was also to find what was doubtless a more receptive audience for his inculcation of lessons of virtue as the first Professor of English at King's College, London.

George Long, the original Professor of Greek, was a more significant figure. He had been recruited from Trinity College, Cambridge to be the founding Professor of Ancient Languages at the University of Virginia. He returned to England to take the Chair of Greek, but then resigned in 1831, along with several of his colleagues, over the sacking of Pattison. He went on to work full-time for the Society for the Diffusion of Useful Knowledge, first as editor of the *Quarterly Journal of Education* and then of the famous 29-volume *Penny Cyclopaedia*. Long was to return to UCL as Professor of Latin for four years in the 1840s, but left again to combine schoolteaching in Brighton with his literary and scholarly work.

The study of the workings of society was naturally not to be ignored in a College so influenced by utilitarian thought. Distinguished appointments in both Law and Economics were made at the outset. Law was taken to be an important subject of study from the very beginning, and UCL can fairly claim to have inaugurated the systematic university study of law. John Austin was appointed to the Chair of Jurisprudence in July 1827; he then spent a year in Bonn preparing his lectures while mixing with the great German scholars and jurists there. Austin was recognised as a powerful intellect, and his deep learning and original thought duly impressed the students, including John Stuart Mill. But he completed very little in his lifetime – not even managing the preparation of his lectures for publication, a task his wife Sarah had to finish after his death in 1859 (Fig. 2.7). Despite a promising start, UCL faced fierce competition after both the Law Society and the Inner Temple began to provide lectures in 1833, resulting in a sharply falling enrolment and leading Austin to resign. He became first a member of the Criminal Law Commission and later conducted an inquiry into the state of Malta, subsequently living in Germany and France. The other Law Professor, Andrew Amos, also held very popular and well-attended classes for the first few sessions, but he too left after student numbers collapsed. A successful barrister, Amos had earlier been the poet Percy Bysshe Shelley's only friend at Eton; he was later a county court judge and a Professor at Cambridge. His son, Sheldon Amos, was Professor of Jurisprudence at the College, 1869–78, while his grandson, Sir Maurice Sheldon Amos, was Quain Professor of Comparative Law, 1932–37.

In Economics the same story is repeated of high hopes unrealised despite an outstanding appointment. J. R. McCulloch was the first professional economist, in the sense of one who made his living from the subject as journalist, author and teacher (Fig. 2.8). An Edinburgh man, he was appointed to the Chair of Political Economy after coming to London to give the lectures established as an independent memorial to the economist David Ricardo. McCulloch soon embarked on a prolonged dispute about his salary, eventually refusing to lecture after 1835 unless the Council agreed to guarantee it at a higher level than the fees from the small number of students who attended. In 1837 his Chair was declared vacant.

Notable among the original appointments was that of a young German, F. A. Rosen. He brought the best of his country's scholarship to the College, introducing

notions basic to comparative philology. Professor of Oriental Literature at 22, Rosen was later Professor of Sanskrit for the two years before his early death in 1837. Teaching of various Oriental languages continued at the College until 1917, when they were transferred to the new institution that became the School of Oriental and African Studies (SOAS).

The three years of hopeful expectation prior to the opening gave way after 1828 to three years fraught with many problems and wasteful quarrels. The only sources of finance were firstly what could be raised through shares or donations as capital and secondly whatever the fees of the students brought in as income. The capital was splendidly but unwisely consumed by the cost of the site and the buildings (Fig. 2.9), and criticism was swift to follow. 'The expenditure has been lavish,' wrote Sarah Austin in 1830; she dismissed the plans as 'ill-digested'. Professorial dependence on a proportion of the fees meant that, when fewer students than expected enrolled, their incomes were unacceptably low: the Council's guarantees of at least £300 a year were hard to meet. The grievances of the teachers were compounded not only by their having no formal status as a body, nor any say in the running of the College, but also by the attitude of the Warden.

Fig. 2.8 J. R. McCulloch, Professor of Political Economy, 1828–37, painted respectfully clasping a copy of Adam Smith's *Wealth of Nations*.

Fig. 2.9 The most idyllic of the early prints of the College, again showing the wings as Wilkins planned them, but as they never appeared.

Fig. 2.10 The focus of many of the early quarrels: Leonard Horner, FRS (1785–1864), the first and only Warden, 1827–31.

The first appointment made by the Council had been that of Leonard Horner as Warden in May 1827 (Fig. 2.10). Horner came, like so many of the others, from Edinburgh, where he was regarded as 'one of the most useful citizens that Edinburgh ever possessed'. He was the founder of the School of Arts there in 1821, now Heriot-Watt University, and was an energetic Secretary of the Geological Society in London from 1810. From the start, however, Horner took a high-handed view of his new office. The generous salary of £1,200 a year, on which he had himself insisted, was itself a source of irritation to the Professors, and the Warden's continual petty interference in their work proved increasingly objectionable.

Matters came to a head in 1830–31 over the complicated issues raised by the criticisms against Granville Sharp Pattison, the Professor of Anatomy. The medical students were provoked by what they saw as Pattison's incompetence both as an anatomist and as a teacher (when he did turn up to lecture, he did so in hunting pink), and their opinions were supported by Charles Bell. However, Horner's clumsy attempts to sack Pattison led to the case being taken up by other aggrieved Professors as a stick with which to beat Horner.

The issue gathered many bitter subtleties, as such disputes do. It led to the first student demonstration, in 1830, eventually causing the resignations not only of Bell and Conolly from the Medical Faculty, but also, following the dismissal of Pattison, of De Morgan, Long and Rosen as well. In the end Horner himself was forced to resign and the office of Warden was abolished, being replaced by a Secretary on a salary of £200. Horner went on to enjoy a distinguished later career as the first Factory Inspector. The Pattison affair had many consequences. One was that the Professors were organised into a Senate and into Faculties, another was that the College managed without a full-time head for the rest of the century.

Challenges for UCL

Lying behind the financial difficulties of the early years was the problem of student numbers. There had been talk of providing for 2,000 students and at least 1,100 were deemed necessary in order to balance the books in the first year. In reality 641 materialised in 1828–29, and only about 630 in the following year (Fig. 2.11). Thereafter numbers fluctuated rather, and did not begin to increase substantially until the 1870s. It took over 80 years to reach the projected 2,000. Although UCL was open to men only, in 1829 the Council allowed some 'ladies' to attend a course of public lectures given by the Professor of Italian, Antonio Panizzi, and in 1832 the names of two women appear in the Register of Students as attending a course on the fashionable subject of electricity. One of these was Mrs J. P. Potter, whose husband and 14-year-old son were already students of the College.

If imitation implies success, however, the College achieved it before the doors were opened. An Establishment rival in the form of King's College began at a meeting in June 1828, chaired by the Duke of Wellington and attended by no less than three archbishops, seven bishops and 'the principal nobility'. The prime founder was the Revd Dr George D'Oyly, the Rector of Lambeth, who had been much disturbed by the exclusion of religious teaching from the curriculum of a University of London. D'Oyly believed that the Church of England 'presents Christianity in its most pure and perfect form', and that the interests of the Church and the State combined to demand a new institution with different principles to those adopted in Gower Street (Fig. 2.12). With the backing he naturally received, there was no difficulty in obtaining a charter in 1829. A new wing was built to Somerset House in the Strand and by October 1831 a second institution of higher education was opened in London. A healthy rivalry has been maintained between the two colleges ever since.

The system of education established at UCL was based upon instruction by means of lectures and upon written examinations. Modelled on the practices of Scotland and Germany, this was a deliberate departure from the method of the older English universities. The early years saw an enormous amount of lecturing taking place (Fig. 2.13). The naturalist and Registrar of the University, W. B. Carpenter,

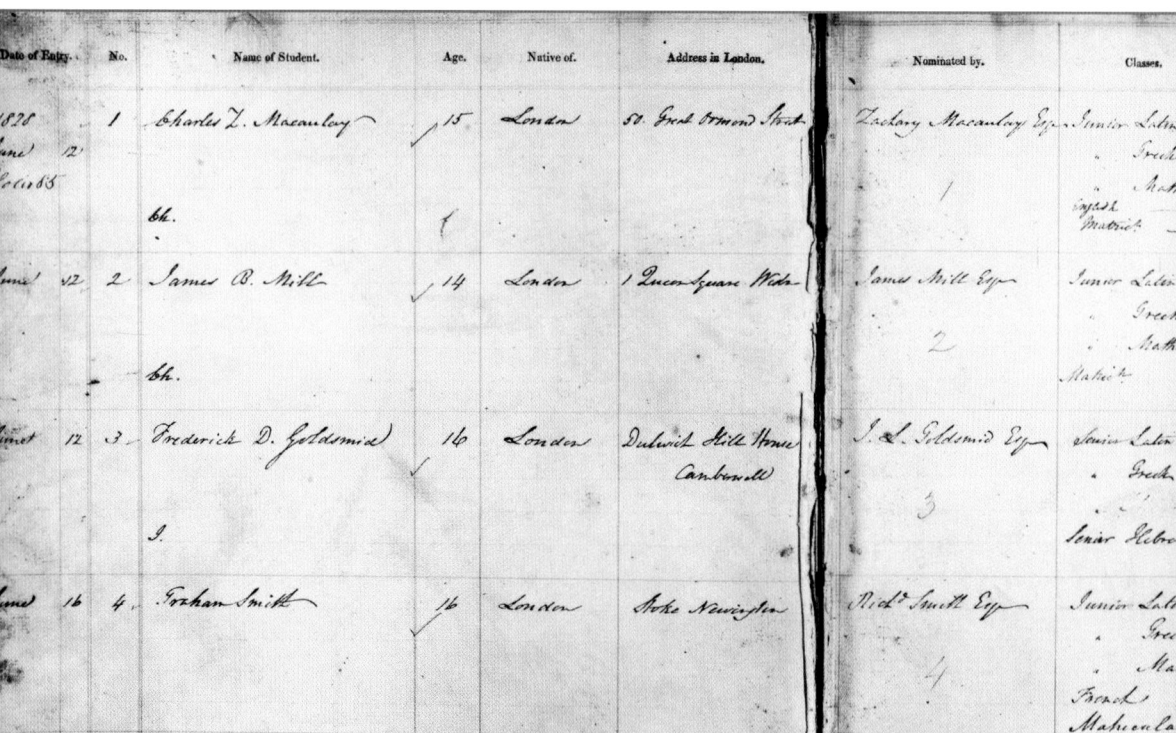

Fig. 2.11 The first entries in the register of students for the opening session in 1828. Among them are the sons of some of the College's founders, such as Charles Macaulay, James B. Mill and Frederick Goldsmid.

Fig. 2.12 A cartoon portraying the initial antagonism between UCL and the rival King's College, founded in 1828.

attended no less than 35 lectures a week as a student in the early 1830s. There was some bleak justification for Coleridge's contemptuous reference to the College as a 'lecture-bazaar'. Initially no degrees were offered. There was in 1830 a proposal to award the cumbersome degree of M. Med et Chir. U. L., but the absence of a Royal Charter was generally held to deny degree-giving powers to a body with no outside authority for calling itself a university. Instead Certificates of Honours were presented in connection with each course (Fig. 2.14), and a General Certificate was obtainable after three years of following an agreed programme of study. Fees were payable for each separate course of lectures. The average cost for a student nominated by a proprietor (such students were admitted at a lower rate) was approximately £22 7s. 6d. per annum – a sum that would have taken a coachman, for example, a year to earn. The College was thus well beyond the means of the working class.

Fig. 2.13 A later nineteenth-century photograph of the Botanical Theatre. It was one of four main lecture theatres in the semi-circular projections at the rear of the College.

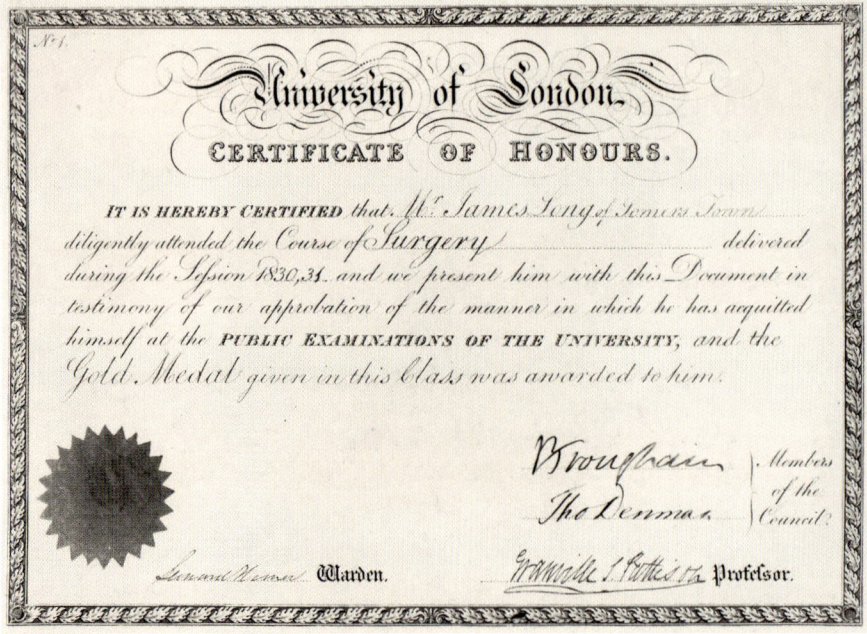

Fig. 2.14 A Certificate of Honours awarded in the early years of UCL's existence.

Fig. 2.15 (overleaf) The playground of University College School, drawn in 1833.

Fig. 2.16 Thomas Hewitt Key, FRS, Professor of Latin, 1828–42, and of Comparative Grammar, 1842–75, in a portrait by Langlois. Key was Headmaster of University College School from 1831–75.

A boys' school was established in connection with the College in 1830. From the start it prospered, at a time when the College was not otherwise growing. Opened in a Gower Street house with 80 boys in the first term, a year later the School had acquired 249 boys, and accommodation had to be found within the main building. After 1832 in an unforeseen way the School came to take up a good deal of space in the College, particularly in the area originally intended for the Great Hall and the rooms below it (Fig. 2.15). Thomas Hewitt Key and Henry Malden, Professors of Latin and Greek, were put in joint charge of the School once its success was evident.

Key, very versatile in his interests, had been the first Professor of Mathematics at the University of Virginia. In 1842 he gave up the Chair of Latin at UCL for that of Comparative Grammar – the first such chair in England, though his scholarship in this field was not beyond question. Key combined this post with that of Headmaster until the day of his death in 1875, proving a great and vigorous teacher (Fig. 2.16). Malden, meanwhile, was the more careful and urbane scholar; he gave up the joint headship in 1842, but continued to teach the sixth form until 1868. Other Professors also taught at the School, which quickly built up a considerable reputation for religious tolerance, a broad curriculum and a sympathetic relationship between teacher and pupil. It was one of the earliest schools to attempt to dissociate education and flogging.

The Library

The first Librarian of the College was the Revd Dr F. A. Cox, the original Secretary of the Council. By the beginning of 1829 he had judiciously built up a collection of some 6,500 volumes; a year later the number had increased to 9,027. 'The Council would gladly have announced a larger addition', recorded the *Annual Report* for 1830, 'but prudential considerations have limited the purchases.' The books were housed in what was called the Small Library at the southern end of the building, since

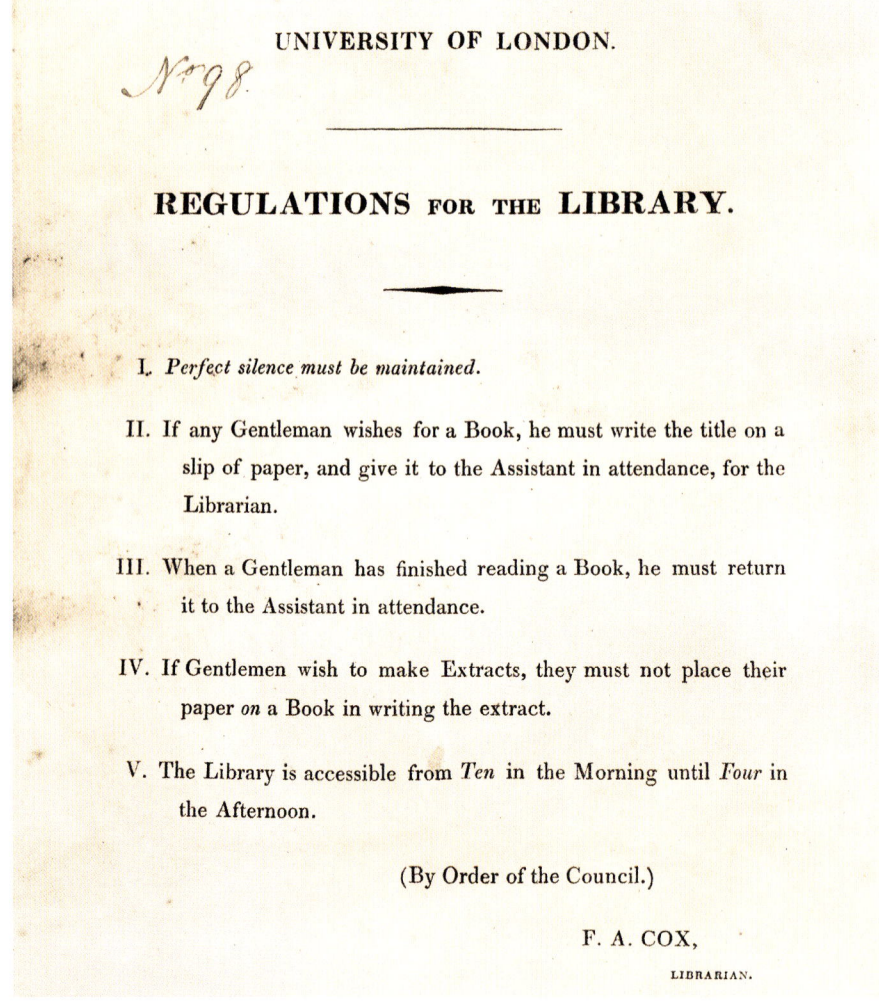

Fig. 2.17 The earliest Library Regulations, issued soon after the opening of the College's Library in 1829.

funds were inadequate for the proposed Great Library (Fig. 2.17). A further economy in 1831 was to dispense with the services of the Librarian: there was to be no proper successor until 1871, the Library being left in the charge of an assistant and sometimes simply of a Beadle, UCL's traditional uniformed porter-cum-lawkeeper. Less than £50 altogether was spent on books in the poverty-stricken four years 1832–35, while the average annual expenditure for the 43 years from 1832 to 1875 was a mere £51.

In this period, growth was therefore heavily dependent on donations and bequests. Some 4,000 books came from Jeremy Bentham in 1833, and Joseph Hume's large collection of tracts followed in 1855. An impressive number of collections were left by Professors of the College, the earliest really notable one being that bequeathed by J. T. Graves in 1870. Despite being Professor of Jurisprudence and later a Poor Law Inspector, Graves had formed a valuable library of over 14,000 items, chiefly devoted to early mathematics. His sister married Leopold von Ranke, the founder of modern historical method, and he was a forebear of Robert Graves. He once compiled a list of 2,862 anagrams on the name of Augustus De Morgan in English, Latin, French and German.

The 1830s saw retrenchment on other fronts besides that of the Library. No initial appointment had been made in History and the Chair was not filled until 1830 – and then only briefly and inadequately by a retired headmaster. There was no regular History teaching until after 1834. One of the few developments of the period, other than the School and the Hospital, was in Geography, though as it turned out even this was abortive. In 1833 Alexander Maconochie, Secretary of the newly-founded Royal Geographical Society, was made the first Professor of Geography at UCL – and the first in Britain. A retired naval captain, Maconochie left UCL in 1836 to go to Van Diemen's Land (Tasmania) as private secretary to its new lieutenant-governor and to investigate penal conditions. No successor was appointed, and Geography was not revived at the College until 1903.

Medical education

William Sharpey's active tenure of his Chair for nearly 40 years earned him the title of 'the father of modern physiology' in Britain (Fig. 2.18). Before being appointed in 1836, he had been trained at Edinburgh, studying at French and German universities where physiology was much more highly developed than it then was in Britain. Sharpey was a thorough and inspiring teacher. He hardly ever showed an experiment or piece of apparatus in classes, but he was one of the first to introduce

Fig. 2.18 William Sharpey, FRS, Professor of Anatomy and Physiology, 1836–74, photographed soon after his retirement.

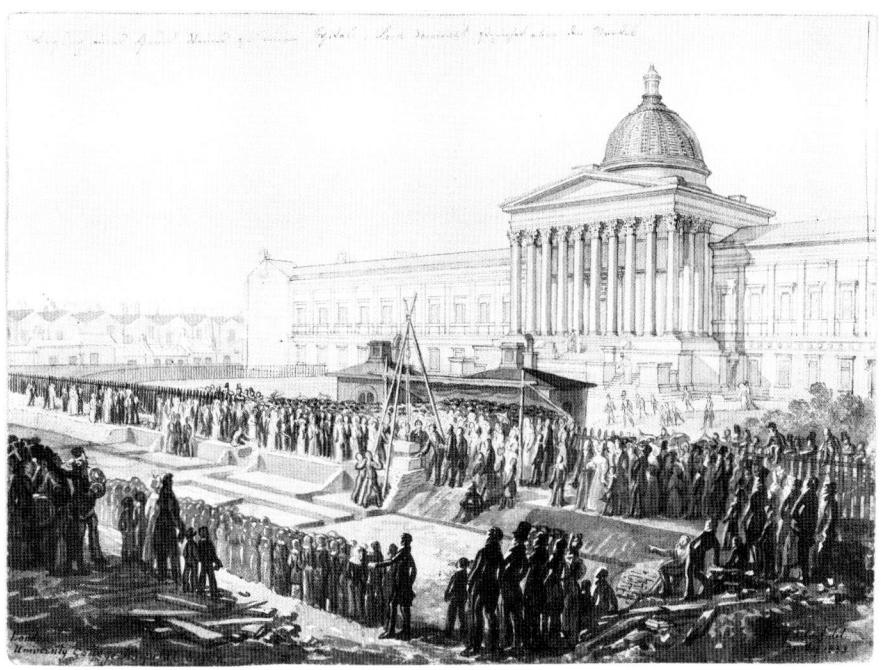

Fig. 2.19 A sketch by George Scharf recording the laying of the foundation stone for the College's new Hospital in May 1833. The new facilities, for which the Medical Faculty had long pressed, were located on Gower Street, developing an unused part of the UCL site.

the microscope for practical illustration of his teaching, having a table especially constructed for this purpose. He exerted a considerable influence through his students, who came to dominate the subject, and through being for 20 years after 1853 a powerful and effective Secretary of the Royal Society.

Sharpey's Chair was nominally in Anatomy as well as Physiology, but Anatomy was primarily in other hands. After Charles Bell's resignation the subject was taught by two brothers – Jones Quain, Sharpey's predecessor as Professor of Anatomy and Physiology, and Richard Quain, Demonstrator, 1831–32, then Professor of Anatomy, 1831–50, and subsequently surgeon at the Hospital, Professor of Clinical Surgery, 1850–66, and President of the Royal College of Surgeons. Richard Quain is remembered as the benefactor who left his fortune to UCL in 1887, the bequest establishing the Quain chairs and studentships, and for presenting the law library of his half-brother, Sir John Richard Quain – a judge and himself a former student of the College. Many of Bell's preserved anatomical and pathological specimens were acquired by the College as the beginnings of the Anatomy Museum, much later the Grant Museum.

Fig. 2.20 John Elliotson, FRS, the advanced but controversial Professor of Medicine, 1831–39.

A hospital had been regarded by the Medical Faculty from the beginning as an essential part of the College, but for some years they had to put up with the limited facilities offered by the University Dispensary in Upper Gower Street. Plans for the building of the 'North London Hospital' on the unused part of the College site on the other side of Gower Street were accepted in 1832, and the foundation stone was laid in May 1833 (Fig. 2.19). The first stage of the Hospital was opened in November 1834 with beds for 130 patients. It was built for less than £7,600, much more cheaply than the College itself: 'all architectural decorations', it was plainly stated, 'have for the sake of economy been studiously excluded'. The building was financed entirely through public appeals at a time when the College itself was seriously in debt. However, its intimate connection with the College was recognised in 1837 when its name was changed to 'University College Hospital'. A southern extension was added in 1841 and a northern one in 1846.

Much of the early success of the new Hospital was due to John Elliotson, Conolly's successor in 1831 with the title of Professor of the Theory and Practice of Medicine (Fig. 2.20). Exceedingly popular as a teacher, Elliotson was also a practitioner of great energy and originality. He was a pioneer of the stethoscope and he introduced the use of quinine for malaria. With the best of scientific intentions, however, Elliotson got involved in an early scandal arising from the Victorian craze for mesmerism. As part of a course of treatment for the epilepsy of two young sisters, Elizabeth and Jane Okey, he put the girls into mesmeric trances before a number of large and fashionable audiences. The sessions attracted much attention, including that of Charles Dickens, but the College found it all rather embarrassing, even before the *Lancet* exposed the sisters as fakes. Like some of his eminent predecessors at the College, Elliotson had to make an untimely resignation in 1838.

After a decade of existence, UCL had pioneered the university teaching of a range of new subjects and recruited an impressive body of instructors; it had also expanded its premises (Fig. 2.21). However, the College faced ongoing difficulties in securing and retaining the appropriate number of students, and was constantly plagued by financial difficulties as a result. It faced the rivalry of Establishment-backed King's College and had survived near ruin – brought on by, in Hale Bellot's words, the combination of 'a defective constitution' and 'a tactless Warden' with 'an autocratic, peremptory and parsimonious Council'. Nonetheless, UCL's enduring commitment to civil and religious liberties earned it the support of many. This was evidenced in 1836, when the first endowment for scholarships was made by an 80-year-old Roman Catholic lady known as Miss Flaherty.

Fig. 2.21 (overleaf) A watercolour showing the College from Old Gower Street Mews in 1835, painted by George Sidney Shepherd. Behind the Dome can be seen the uncompleted Great Hall, later destroyed by fire. The picture was acquired by UCL in 1988.

CHAPTER 3

University College

1836–78

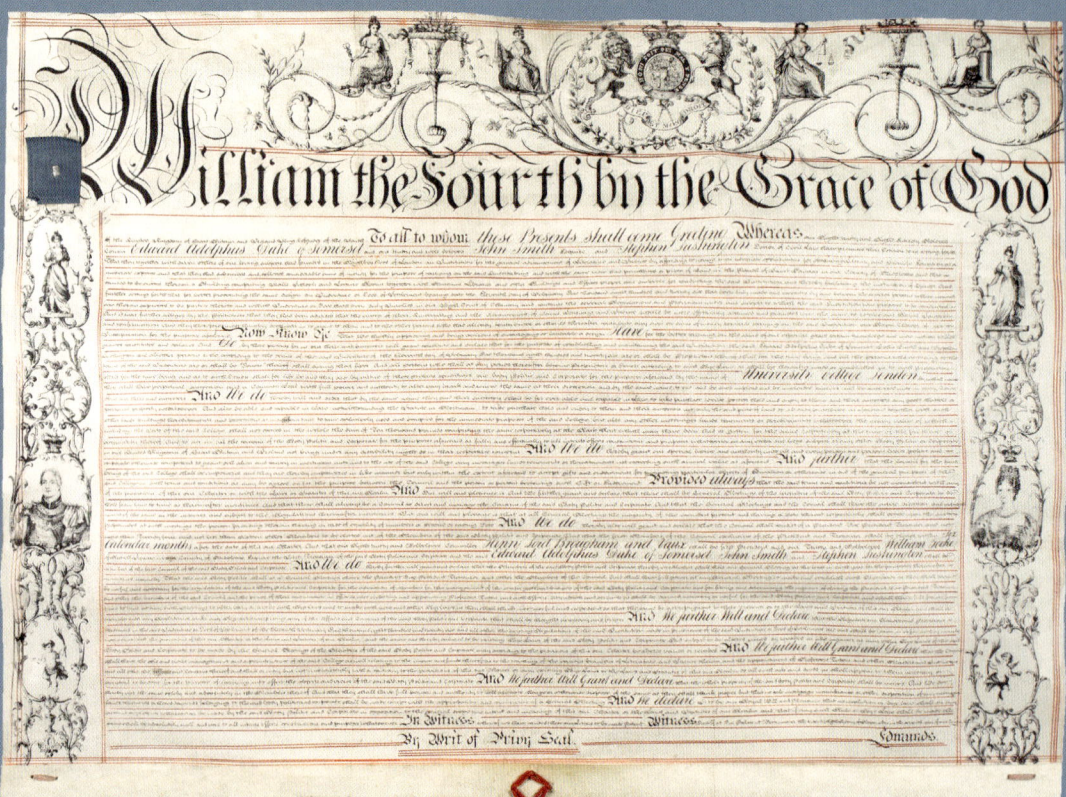

> Had some ices; danced; had supper at ½ past 1; danced a country dance etc.; took a cab to Walshe's [where he lived] at ½ past 3; read, etc., went to bed. Got up at 20m to 8; had breakfast; attended Prof. De Morgan's lecture on Mathematics till 20m past 10; wrote in my Sermon book for an hour; put some plants into my book of Botanical Specimens; attended Prof. Malden's lecture on Greek till 20m to 2; arranged my plants; had dinner; Tom Graham called and chatted until 3; dressed; . . . attended Prof. Potter's lecture on Natural Philosophy till 5, and Dr. Lindley's examination on Botany till quarter to 6; had a parcel from home, unpacked it; . . . dried plants until 8; Dr. Scratchley came to tea; finished dressing; took a cab at 20m past 9 to Mr. Grahame's; had some coffee, had ices; quadrilled and waltzed; had supper: Fine day.
>
> *F. J. Furnivall's diary for 13 May 1842, recording 24 hours from midnight to midnight in the life of an early UCL student*

On 28 November 1836 a Royal Charter was at length granted by the Whig government which included, in Lord Lansdowne and Lord John Russell, two of the members of the College's founding Council (Fig. 3.1). The strong opposition of Oxford and Cambridge to the award of degrees to non-members of the established Church was overcome; so too was that of the various hospital medical schools in London to the 'upstart' University College securing the power of awarding medical degrees which they themselves did not possess. These problems, and that of the existence of King's College, were solved by establishing an entirely new body as the 'University of London' (Fig. 3.2). The College gave up this, its original title, and took that of University College – a style first suggested in the medical press in 1833, though possibly a misleading one in that it suggested an Oxbridge model rather than a European or a Scottish one. Later the same day another Charter was granted to the new University of London, empowering it to award degrees in Arts, Laws and Medicine to students of both UCL and King's, besides such other institutions as might be approved later on. It was a sensible compromise, but the separation of teaching and examining stored up great difficulties for the future.

Fig. 3.1 The Royal Charter granted to the College in 1836.

Fig. 3.2 The examination in July 1842 for matriculation in the new, degree-giving University of London.

Engineering was one of the first victims of the College's financial insecurity. John Millington had been announced as Professor of the subject in 1827, but he resigned before the opening after the Council refused to guarantee him an adequate income. Not until 1841 was a Chair of Civil Engineering established, the first of its kind in the country. The period of intensive railway building had started and the first Professor, C. B. Vignoles, was a leading railway engineer and inventor of the 'Vignoles rail' (Fig. 3.3). He came to UCL having lost £80,000 in shares while Chief Engineer on the Sheffield and Manchester Railway. Vignoles was later responsible for the construction of railways in many parts of the world, especially in Russia. Here he built the Dnieper suspension bridge at Kiev, the largest of its kind in the world.

Two distinguished figures in other fields of engineering were appointed to new chairs in 1847. Both came from near Manchester, where they had sat at the feet of John Dalton and the inquiring scientific community there, but neither proved a successful teacher. Eaton Hodgkinson, who had started out as a pawnbroker in Salford, became the first Professor of Mechanical Engineering. He invented an important new type of cast-iron girder, the forerunner of the modern I-beam, and worked with Robert Stephenson on the Menai bridge between Anglesey and the mainland of Wales.

Fig. 3.3 Charles Blacker Vignoles, FRS, the first Professor of Civil Engineering, 1841–45.

Fig. 3.4 Thomas Graham, FRS, Professor of Chemistry, 1836–55, and later Maser of the Mint, where he was responsible for the change from copper to bronze coinage.

Bennet Woodcroft worked originally in his family textile firm, but made a range of ingenious inventions and became a consulting engineer. His great work was the creation of the modern Patent Office, to which he devoted himself after resigning the Chair of Machinery in 1851. The valuable collection of mechanical models, donated by the Society of Arts in order to form a Machinery Museum in the College, found their way, without apparent authority, to the Patent Office Museum and later to the Science Museum.

In 1846 Lord Brougham was obliged to say that his anticipations of success for the College 20 years previously had not been realised. Yet while the impoverished 1830s had seen major developments in the School and the Hospital, the barely better endowed 1840s saw the first new buildings for the College itself in the shape of the new General Library and the new Chemistry Laboratory. The latter, the first purpose-built teaching laboratory for chemistry in the country, was a particularly important innovation.

Turner's successor as Professor of Chemistry in 1836 was Thomas Graham, a chemist of real distinction (Fig. 3.4). 'If along the great highroad of Chemistry', one of his own successors stated later, 'temples were erected to the memory of the master minds who moulded and guided the science forward into the unknown future, one of

Fig. 3.5 The Birkbeck Laboratory, the College's first teaching laboratory for Chemistry, illustrated in the *Illustrated London News* soon after its opening in 1846. It was demolished in 1968.

the greatest of these would be to the memory of Thomas Graham.' Educated at both Glasgow and Edinburgh, he worked on the fundamental problems of the ultimate particles of matter and the diffusion of gases, formulating the earliest modern understanding of these questions. Graham was one of the founders and the first President of the Chemical Society in 1841. He also started the teaching of chemistry through the practical system of personal experiment by the student. Liebig's pioneering laboratory at Giessen was earlier (it was opened in 1826), but Graham introduced the modern method in this country. It led in 1845 to the founding of a Chair in Practical Chemistry and to the building of the Birkbeck Laboratory (Fig. 3.5).

Opened in January 1846, the new Laboratory was partly financed by money raised to commemorate George Birkbeck's services to the widening provision of education. With bench accommodation for 24 students, each place with gas and water laid on, it was pronounced 'the most perfect of its class in the kingdom' by the *Illustrated London News*. George Fownes, the newly appointed Professor of Practical Chemistry, had studied under Liebig in Germany and had a number of advanced features incorporated in the design. Fownes published some papers on fermentation and a *Manual of Chemistry* that was to go through 11 editions,

Fig. 3.6 A photograph of Thomas L. Donaldson, the College's first Professor of Architecture, 1841–65. He was also the founder of RIBA.

but he died young in 1849. The beginnings of Practical Chemistry were developed by Alexander Williamson, his more famous successor. When Fownes died, the *Lancet* wrote regretfully that the College 'could ill afford to lose so good a man', and declared that his death 'seems to second the efforts which intrigue had so successfully commenced for the destruction of this once flourishing institution'. It was to prove a premature judgement.

Along with Engineering and Practical Chemistry, Architecture also features as one of the most significant developments of the 1840s. The Chair of Architecture, the first to be founded in a university, was held by Thomas Leverton Donaldson from 1841 to 1865. Donaldson was an established architect of repute, as well as an outstanding draughtsman and lecturer (Fig. 3.6). He played a leading part in the foundation of the Royal Institute of British Architects (RIBA), becoming known as the father of the architectural profession in Britain. At UCL he designed the Birkbeck Laboratory and the General Library (Fig. 3.7), built in 1849 on the site of the unfinished original Great Hall, destroyed by fire in 1836.

An important addition to the life of the College in 1849 was the opening of University Hall in Gordon Square as UCL's first hall of residence (Fig. 3.8). The Hall

Fig. 3.7 The General Library was designed by Donaldson and is now named after him. It was built in 1849 on the site of the unfinished Great Hall, with the aid of a bequest from Jonathan Brundrett.

was built by the Unitarians in commemoration of the Dissenters' Chapels Act of 1844, 'the first recognition by the legislature', as an inscription on an interior wall originally proclaimed, 'of the principle of unlimited religious liberty'. It was also to be a place where theology, excluded from the College, could be taught. The first Principal was the highly eccentric F. W. Newman, the brother of Cardinal Newman and Long's successor in the Chair of Latin. He resigned before the opening, however, and was succeeded by the poet Arthur Hugh Clough, who for three years held the Chair of English. Clough had resigned his Oxford fellowship out of religious scruple, but found himself unhappy both at the College and at the Hall, and he too soon resigned. Subsequent distinguished principals included E. S. Beesly and Henry Morley.

At University College Hospital in 1846 Robert Liston performed the first operation under anaesthetic conducted in Europe – an event that marked one of the most striking advances in the history of surgery (Fig. 3.9). Present as a student

Fig. 3.8 University Hall (the present Dr William's Library), also designed by Thomas L. Donaldson. This was the first hall of residence for the College when it opened in 1848.

on that occasion was Joseph Lister, later to revolutionise surgery through his work on infection and antisepsis. Both developments made an enormous contribution to the reduction of human suffering. Liston was brought from the Royal Infirmary at Edinburgh to be one of the first surgeons at the Hospital when it opened in 1834, as well as Professor of Clinical Surgery at the College. He was remarkable for his dexterity while operating, at a time when speed was the only relief that could be afforded to the patient. It was said the gleam of his knife was followed so instantaneously by the sound of sawing as to make the two actions appear simultaneous. He could amputate a leg in 20 seconds. Liston began the era of anaesthetics for major surgery in Britain, after hearing of the first use of ether by a dentist in the Massachusetts General Hospital in October 1846.

On 19 December 1846 ether had been used successfully by James Robinson, a dentist operating in Gower Street and later attached to the Royal Free Hospital. After hurried consultations over the weekend, Liston used the new technique

Fig. 3.9 Robert Liston, Professor of Clinical Surgery, 1835–47. In December 1846 at University College Hospital he became the first surgeon in Britain to perform an operation under anaesthetic.

for an amputation on 21 December. The glass for administering the ether during the leg amputation had been devised by William Squire, a 21-year-old medical student. After the experience of the Okey mesmerism fiasco, any new attempt at avoiding pain at UCL was regarded with suspicion, but news of the success spread speedily and the innovation was rapidly adopted. 'This Yankee dodge', Liston had announced to the watching students, 'beats mesmerism hollow.'

Joseph Lister was appointed a house surgeon in 1851 – after he had taken his BA at the College, but before he had graduated in medicine. In 1853 he left for Scotland, serving as a surgeon in the Infirmaries of Edinburgh and Glasgow and as a Professor in both those universities in turn, thus beginning to repay a little of the College's considerable northern debt. It was at Glasgow that he made his revolutionary discovery of the startling effect of the antiseptic treatment of wounds, reported to the British Medical Association in 1867. Lister was inexcusably passed over for a chair at UCL, but he later returned to London to bring distinction to King's College. In 1897 he became one of the first academics to be raised to the peerage. Despite these clear signs of potential in the Faculty of Medicine, domestic quarrels continued to characterise the place, a particularly memorable one being that over Liston's successor in 1848. James Syme was so horrified at the 'spirit of dispeace in the College' that he packed up after a tenure of only five months and went back to Edinburgh.

The first students

To record the deeds of the Professors in the first decades of the College's existence is easier than to portray the lives of the students. Their dominant feature was that they were too few to start with, and that they got fewer. The 630 of 1829–30 was just exceeded in the peak of the late 1830s after the building of the Hospital, but then went no higher; by 1864–65 numbers fell below 400. This was despite the age limit being set as low as 15 (though some of the earliest students were even younger) and despite there being no entrance requirements whatsoever. The first University of London degrees were initially examined for in 1839, following a two-year course (Fig. 3.10).

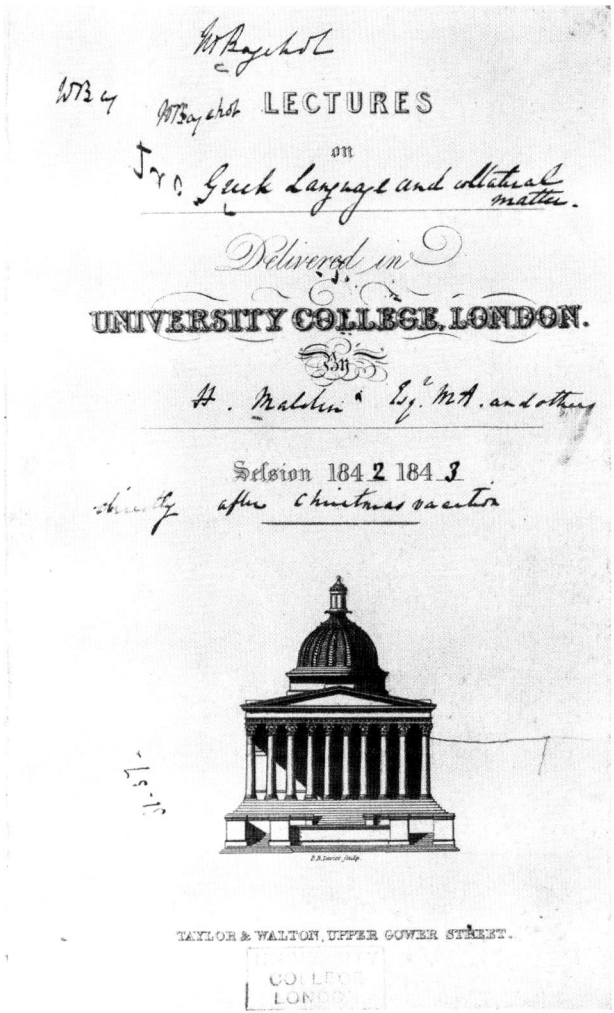

Fig. 3.10 Title page of a college notebook kept by Walter Bagehot as a student. He was later to write the classic *English Constitution* and become editor of the *Economist*.

These first students had access to a common room, and a number of societies were formed as early as 1828. They catered for both students and staff, as was common in nineteenth-century universities. The Medical Society, the Literary & Philosophical Society and the Law Society were among the earliest societies (Fig. 3.11), while there were a number of early experiments in student journalism. The handwritten *London University Examiner*, produced by the brothers Collet Dobson Collet and Edward Dobson in 1833, was one of a number of College publications; it contained reports of society meetings alongside radical articles on topics such as Ireland and the rights of women. The brothers reluctantly gave up editing the journal after four months in order to pursue their studies 'with more diligence than heretofore'. In 1837 *Punch* drew attention to the medical students who were reported as having assumed the wearing of gowns: 'This strange association of the garb of learning with the habits of the medical students as they live, produces a curious effect' (Fig. 3.12). In 1846 *Punch* commented again that 'as far as vulgarity goes, the concern in Gower Street may vie with the older establishments of the Cam and the Isis'. J. J. Sylvester was one of the first students to be expelled (for threatening another student with a refectory knife), but he returned as a Professor

Fig. 3.11 (opposite) Medical students in 1865, one of the earliest photographs of a College group.

Fig. 3.12 A be-gowned but dissipated student, as portrayed in a *Punch* cartoon of 1847.

CURIOSITIES OF COSTUME.

A SORT of academical epidemic has broken out among the medical students at the northern end of the town; and the youths at the University in Gower Street have not only trenched upon the collegiate trenchers, but have assumed the gown, which ill assorts with the paletot of private life. This strange association of the garb of learning with the habits of the medical students as they live, produces a curious effect; and the neighbourhood of Gower Street has been accordingly startled by the appearance that the combination presents.

We have not heard by what authority the assumption of the toga has taken place among the youths of Gower Street; and indeed it requires no less a person than old GOWER himself to come forth and explain the mystery.

in 1837. In the meantime he had been placed as Second Wrangler at Cambridge, though as a Jew he could not take his degree there. One of the great mathematicians of the century, Sylvester became an inspiring but baffling teacher. After four years he left for the University of Virginia, beginning to balance the College's account with that university. However, he did not stay long in Virginia either, returning instead to England to follow the profession of actuary. He ended up as a Professor at Oxford.

'Persons respectably dressed', noted a London guidebook in 1834, 'are allowed to see the interior of the University every day.' There would have been little to be seen, however, apart from the dignity of Wilkins' building itself, though after 1837 there was also Westmacott's statue of Locke. But from 1851 there was the large collection of casts and reliefs by the distinguished sculptor and artist John Flaxman. Flaxman, who died in 1826, had no connection with the College himself. The Gallery was the work of Henry Crabb Robinson, an extraordinary figure who lived to be 91 in 1867, the friend of Goethe, Schiller, Herder, Hegel, Charles Lamb, Wordsworth, Coleridge and Blake, and of a good many students at UCL for some 30 years (Fig. 3.13). Having studied at the university of Jena in Germany and been a correspondent for *The Times* in the Napoleonic Wars, Crabb Robinson worked as a barrister before retiring in 1828. In that year he bought a share in the College 'as a sort of debt to the cause of civil and religious liberty', and in his absence was elected to the Council in 1835. 'Old Crabb' devoted much thought and effort to the problems of the College throughout the rest of his life; as a Unitarian, he was particularly associated with

Fig. 3.13 Henry Crabb Robinson, the long-lived diarist and conversationalist who devoted himself to UCL for over 30 years after his retirement.

University Hall, of which he was a leading founder. His breakfast parties became an institution. 'There was little to gratify the unintellectual part of man', recalled Bagehot. 'Your host, just as you were sitting down to breakfast, found he had forgotten to make the tea, then he could not find his keys, then he rang the bell to have them searched for; but long before the servant came he had gone off into "Schiller-Goethe" and could not in the least remember what he wanted. The more astute of his guests used to breakfast before they came.'

Crabb Robinson regarded as his most memorable act the creation of the Flaxman Gallery, constructed between the Portico and the new General Library (Fig. 3.14). Into the Gallery were put the works of Flaxman presented by Maria Denman, Flaxman's sister-in-law and adopted daughter, who had been in financial difficulties until Crabb Robinson came to her aid. When the Gallery was redecorated in 1922, Tonks produced the large painting that included Crabb Robinson as well as Bentham among the 'founders' of the College. This painting was originally placed high above the casts under the Dome, then conspicuously hung in the North

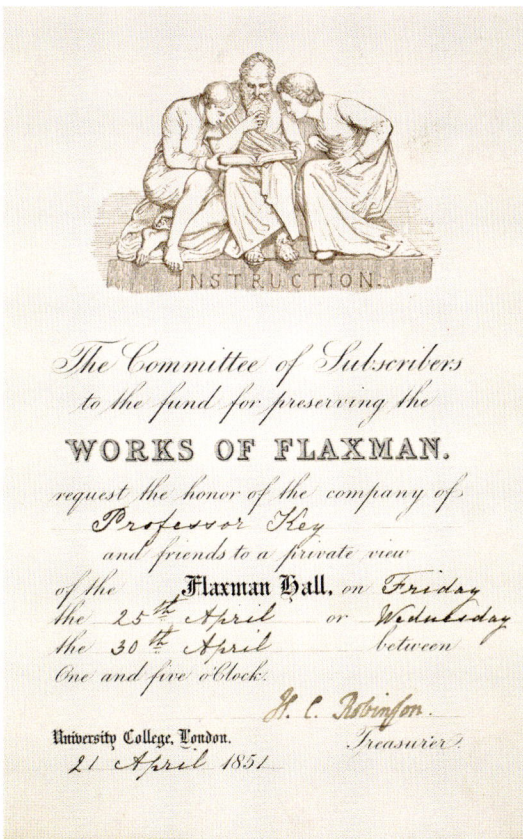

Fig. 3.14 An invitation to the opening of the Flaxman Gallery in 1851.

Cloisters for some years after the Second World War. In 1986, simultaneously with a restoration of the casts, it was put back in its original place in the Flaxman Gallery.

In September 1994 the plaster model for the sculpture of St Michael overcoming Satan, on loan to the Victoria and Albert Museum since 1973, was restored to its original position in the centre of the Flaxman Gallery, where it stands today (Fig. 3.15). The decision to revert to the original Victorian scheme for the whole gallery was not without controversy: one of the most elegant features of Albert Richardson's restoration after the wartime bombing had been an opening through which those in the Gallery could look down on passers-by in the Octagon below, while those in the Octagon could look up into the Gallery and the Dome above. Successive librarians, however, were convinced that those in the Gallery not only looked down, but also threw down the Library's books. Closing the gap thus became a major security objective.

In 1861–62 another experiment in lecturing to ladies took place, when 113 women attended a special, all-female course of Saturday lectures on the subject of animal physiology delivered by John Marshall. This course was instituted in

Fig. 3.15 The Flaxman Gallery, opened in 1851 and photographed here in 2017. Recent restoration has seen a return to the original Victorian design.

Fig. 3.16 Harriet Grote (1792–1878), wife of George Grote and a successful biographer, diarist and political hostess.

partnership with the Ladies Sanitary Association and was mostly attended by women involved in district visiting, education and charitable work.

Richard Potter marked a low point in the teaching of science. Although he did conduct experiments, it was in the terms of eighteenth-century optical theory; as a teacher he was notoriously weak. 'The apparatus', one student later recalled, 'was as worn out as the Professor. It never did what it was expected to do. Magnetic force, for example, would be demonstrated experimentally by holding a needle to what might once have been a magnet, but had ceased to attract, while the Professor said, "You see it wants a little helping, gentlemen".'

A Chair in Geology had been planned from the very beginning of the College, but no appointment was made; Professors of other subjects offered the teaching until 1841. Thomas Webster then accepted the Chair, but, though very distinguished, he had done his best work far earlier. A. C. Ramsey, who succeeded him in 1847, was a survey officer with the Geological Survey and a far more successful Professor, but after four years he resigned, owing to pressure of other work. And so John Morris, who stayed from 1853 until 1877, was the first to build any tradition in the subject. He it was who started field work and saw the Geological Museum founded as a result of gifts in 1855. The Chair itself was partly endowed under the will of

Morris's friend James Yates, who also left a collection of specimens to the museum.

At 33 George Grote had been the youngest member of the original Council, though his connection with the College had been severed abruptly over the appointment of a minister of religion, J. Hoppus, to the Chair of Philosophy in 1830. It was only resumed in 1849, when he was re-elected to the Council. In the meantime the young banker and MP had published the early volumes of his *History of Greece* and so become one of the most famous liberal scholars in Europe – far more distinguished than most of the Professors. Grote now played a leading role in the reform both of the University (of which he was Vice-Chancellor from 1862 to 1871) and of the College, where he became Treasurer in 1860 and then President on the death of Brougham in 1868. Mrs Grote was one of the 'formidable women' connected with the College during its early years (Fig. 3.16).

The University of London's reform of 1858 was far from popular with many of UCL's Professors. It opened University examinations to all comers, thus reducing still further the control of the teachers over the examinations; it also left the University with no teaching functions, a situation which was to lead to progressively more rigorous protest as the century went on. However, the same reform brought a major step forward, through the introduction of degrees specifically in Science; Science courses had previously simply been part of the Faculty of Arts. The College's own constitution was in turn reformed by Act of Parliament in 1869. The main purpose of the Act was the abolition of the system of proprietors and shareholders, which had become disused and discredited over the years. The proprietors were replaced by Governors, who had the right of nominating their successors, and Life Governors, who were appointed by the Council.

George Grote's final act of generosity to the College, on his death in 1871, was the endowment of the Chair of Philosophy of Mind and Logic. The conditions of the bequest were characteristic of his principles: 'If therefore any such Minister [of religion] should at any time or times be appointed by the Council to the Professorship of Mind and Logic … I direct that no payment should be made to him out of the present endowment.' It was the same issue over which he had resigned as a member of the Council in 1830, over 40 years before.

The revival

There can be no doubt that the late 1860s and early 1870s gave clear signs of new-found energy at UCL, whether or not Grote was responsible for the revival. New benefactors were attracted and new building undertaken. So far only the central

Fig. 3.17 University College School's device. Its Latin motto, *Paulatim*, means 'Little by little'.

Fig. 3.18 A drawing of the College showing Hayter Lewis's new South Wing shortly after its completion in 1876.

block had been built and Wilkins' grand plans for North and South Wings had not been realised. University College School, which had from the beginning proved one of the enterprise's more successful elements (Fig. 3.17), was occupying a considerable part of the building. The Council reported in 1866 that every room was in constant use and that the School could not be confined within the area allocated to it. In particular, the College needed the space for science teaching, while the School itself was looking for better facilities for its own physics and chemistry classes.

Fig. 3.19 A photograph of the South Wing housing University College School.

The answer came from Samuel Sharpe, a notable and wealthy Egyptologist and Unitarian translator of the Bible, who became a member of the Council in 1866. He proposed that the South Wing should be built as soon as possible and gave £1,000 to open the building fund, followed later by another £5,000. The new wing, designed to harmonise with Wilkins' building, was the work of Hayter Lewis, the successor to Donaldson in the Chair of Architecture. It was opened in three stages in 1869, 1873 and 1876 (Fig. 3.18). The School gradually moved into its new premises and the vacated space was re-allocated for College use (Fig. 3.19). The Library took over more of the first floor, sharing the new space with Arts, which moved upstairs from the ground floor. This in turn created room for a new Hygiene Laboratory following the creation of the Department of Hygiene and Public Health in 1869.

Fig. 3.20 The North Wing housing the Slade and other faculties, photographed in the early 1980s after the extensive stone cleaning of the Quad. Note the difference in appearance with Fig. 3.19.

The next development again began with a gift. Felix Slade was a famous London collector, especially of Venetian glass; his collections form a distinguished part of the British Museum. He died in 1868, leaving endowments for three professorships in Fine Art at Oxford, Cambridge and London. John Ruskin was appointed in Oxford and Digby Wyatt in Cambridge; but at UCL it was decided to take the opportunity to raise further funds and establish a new School of Fine Art for the teaching of professional artists. Further Slade money helped with the project, and also set up Slade Exhibitions and Scholarships for proficient students. These benefactions were received in 1870; another building fund was opened and Hayter Lewis again prepared plans, this time for the North Wing. The first section was completed very promptly and the new department opened in October 1871 (Fig. 3.20).

The Slade was an immediate success and had 220 students by 1875, but its expansion then had to be checked for lack of space. The first Professor was Edward Poynter, who had some experience of the French schools and set out in his opening address the principles the Slade was to follow: 'The superiority of foreign artists ... is undoubtedly due to a habit in the schools of thoroughly following out a course of study from the living model.' It was therefore Poynter who established the Slade

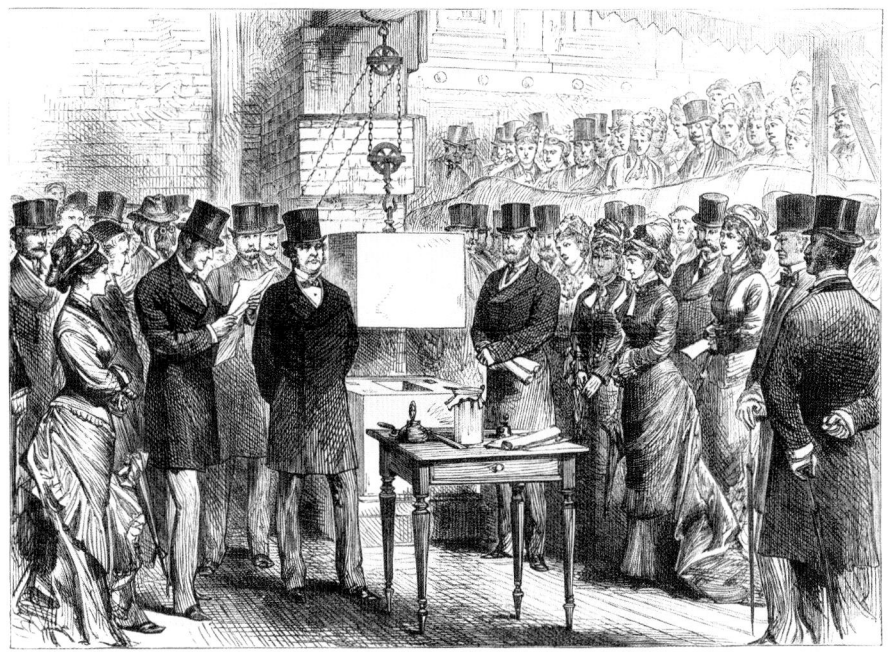

Fig. 3.21 Earl Granville, Chancellor of the UCL, lays the foundation of the North Wing on the occasion of the Jubilee Festival in 1878.

tradition of working from living models, though his own very academic work was totally remote from later developments.

The completion of the North Wing needed another appeal in 1878. It was launched in conjunction with the celebration of the College's Jubilee, at which the foundation stone of the extension was laid and an ambitious statement of the College's requirements issued (Fig. 3.21). Completed by 1881, the Slade occupied the first floor and some of the ground floor, Physiology the top floor and Chemistry the basement, while Zoology moved into the first stage of the building that the Slade had just vacated. The 12 years between 1869 and 1881 had seen both the North and South Wings added to the college, but neither were fully paid for. The College thus had to borrow money and its debts became progressively greater.

The 1860s to 1870s were marked by significant growth and development (Fig. 3.22), but also marked a break with the past: these years saw the departure of the last of the early Professors, as well as the deaths of the surviving founders. UCL had earned a hard-won a place for itself in the British academic world and was increasingly being recognised beyond the bounds of the UK.

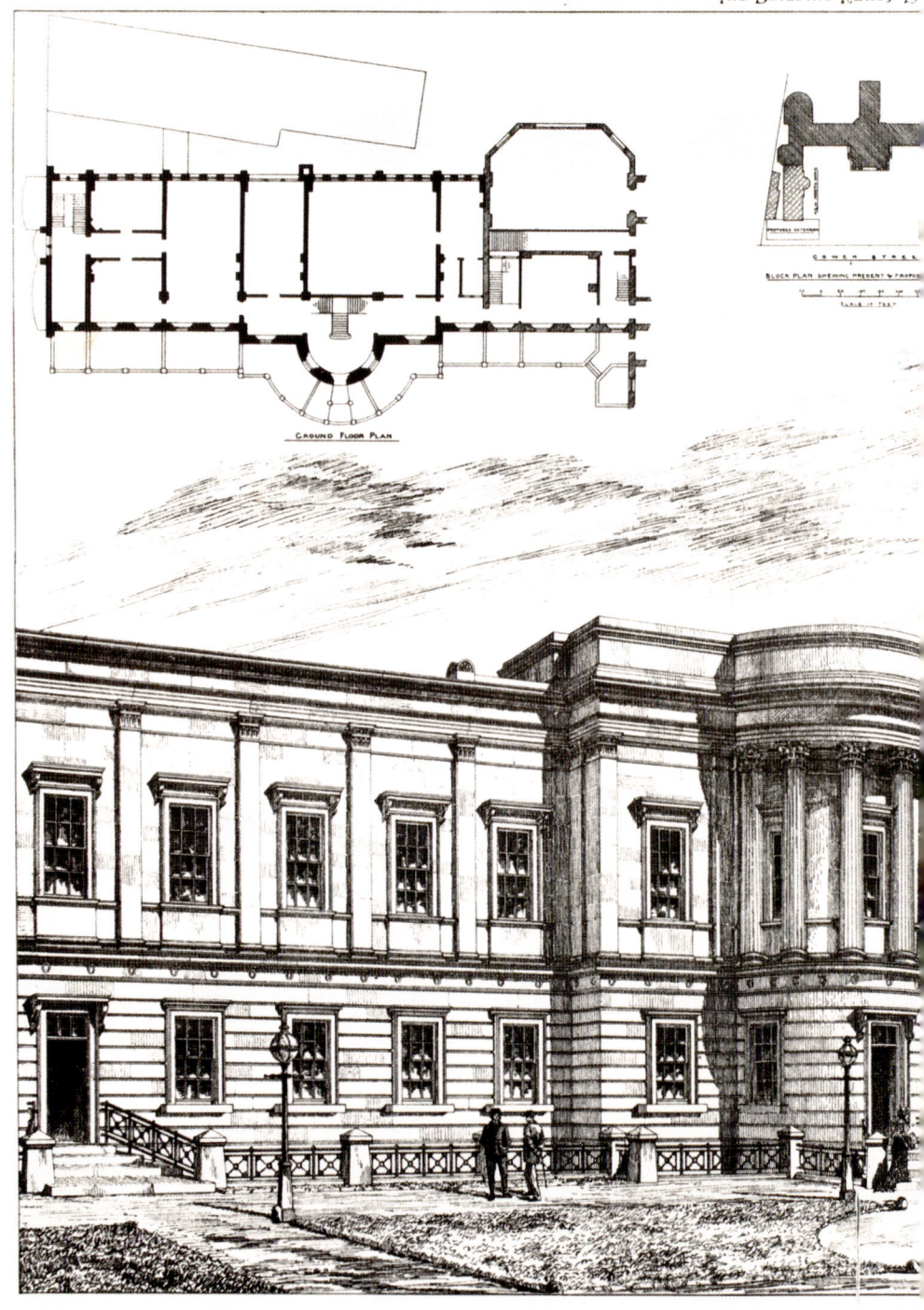

Fig. 3.22 An illustration of the North Wing shortly before its completion, as depicted in *Building News* in 1880.

CHAPTER 4

The Admission of Women

1878–1904

> I need not say how strongly I feel that it is the business of U.C. to be boldly first in recognising fully any new and real want of the time.

Henry Morley, writing to the Secretary of the College about the admission of women, 14 June 1872

The admission of women

The movement for admitting women to UCL began with the creation of the London Ladies' Educational Association in 1868. This was an independent body which organised classes for women and to which UCL Professors lectured, the first to do so being Henry Morley and Carey Foster. These first classes in English Literature and Physics, attended by 150 students, were very successful, and the curriculum was extended the following year to include Geometry, Chemistry, French and Latin. It may have been the intention from the beginning that this should lead to the opening of regular classes to women students, but the process was very gradual. Initially the women's classes took place off the College's premises; from 1871–72 all the classes moved into College, but the Association, not the College, was the responsible agent. Finally it became too much trouble to hold classes separately, and the Professor of Political Economy, John Elliott Cairnes, became the first to lecture to a mixed class. Edward Poynter, the first Slade Professor, had maintained from the time of his appointment that women could and should be taught in the same classes as the men – 'except of course those for the nude model' – and the Slade went on to play a key part in the introduction of women to College life. As early as 1872 the *Annual Report* noted with satisfaction that 'Professor Poynter and his Assistants report that not the slightest inconvenience has arisen from having classes composed of ladies and gentlemen, and the officers of the College are not aware that objections have ever been made by any of the students to this combined instruction'.

By October 1878 all the classes in the College, except those in the Faculty of Medicine, were open to both men and women, although many were still taught in separate groups. From 1878 women were able to study for University of London degrees, and the London Ladies' Educational Association, deemed to have served its purpose, was wound up. In an article on its achievements, 'The London Ladies' Educational Association and the Admission of Women to University College

Fig. 4.1 Photograph of an art student's bedroom in the original College Hall, the first hall of residence for women students, which was opened in Byng Place in 1882.

London', G. C. Foster commended the pioneering students' diligence and enterprise: 'The lists of prizes and honours which women have taken in University College [since 1878] is ample proof of their readiness to take advantage of the opportunities offered to them and of the success which they have attained.' The admission of women, described by Hale Bellot in his 1929 history as the most revolutionary development in the history of the College, had proved a considerable success. However, women students were not admitted on exactly the same footing as men. From 1883 to 1919 the so-called 'passing in rule' stipulated that all prospective women students needed to present an 'introduction or reference' acceptable to the Lady Superintendent of Women Students; men students required no such character reference. Women were not admitted to study Medicine until 1917.

In 1882 a hall of residence known as College Hall was opened in a house in Byng Place, catering for women studying either at UCL or at the School of Medicine for Women (Fig. 4.1). It was founded by sisters Annie Leigh Browne and Thomazine Mary Browne, with the support and help of UCL academics Carey Foster and Henry Morley. When they heard of this new venture two strong supporters of women's higher education, Eleanor Grove and her close friend Rosa Morison (Fig. 4.2), both of whom had taught at Queen's College, Harley Street, offered their services free for the first year. Grove became the first Principal of College Hall and was assisted as Honorary Vice-Principal by Morison until they both retired in 1900.

Morison was a strong supporter of women's suffrage and a firm believer in co-education. In 1883 she was appointed the first Lady Superintendent of Women Students at UCL, a post she held until her death in 1912. Her successor Winifred Smith took the title of 'Tutor to Women Students', the students' suggestion of creating the post of 'Vice Provost' having been rejected. Despite these developments, no women were appointed to the academic staff until the late 1890s. Women students were also denied access to the male students' clubs and societies, so they started their own. In 1883 Morison persuaded the College to provide a Reading Room for women students, and a Reading Room Society soon followed. The Women's Union Society (WUS) was formed in 1897, with Morison serving as its President until 1908.

Henry Morley was another of the most energetic and sympathetic College figures of this period (Fig. 4.3). He had come to UCL from King's as Professor of English in 1865, with a reputation already established by his *English Writers*, a massive survey of English language and literature. Apart from up to 20 hours a week of teaching in College, he lectured generously for Ladies' Educational Associations all over the country, for schools and for the Royal Institution. In 1882 Morley became Principal of University Hall, and was the founder in 1884 of the University College Society – the forerunner of both the Union and the Old Students' Association. As editor of *Morley's Universal Library*, he also pioneered cheap reprints of the classics.

Fig. 4.2 Rosa Morison, Lady Superintendent of Women Students at UCL for nearly 30 years (standing). She is photographed with her close friend and companion Eleanor Grove (seated), Principal of College Hall.

Fig. 4.3 Henry Morley, the indefatigable Professor of English, 1865–89, was one of the leading figures in all the developments of UCL in the late nineteenth century.

His nickname, Professor More-and-Morley, was hard-earned. There is no denying the success of his classes nor the devotion he inspired in his pupils, but it has to be remembered how isolated his success was in the Faculty of Arts in these years. The greatest advances in the late nineteenth century were almost all to be in the fields of Science and Engineering.

Science and Engineering at UCL

The dominant figure in science at UCL in the mid-nineteenth century was Alexander Williamson (Fig. 4.4). He succeeded Fownes in the Chair of Practical Chemistry in 1849, and united both chairs in the subject (Practical Chemistry and Chemistry) from 1855 until 1887. He suffered severe physical disabilities, being paralysed in one arm, blind in his right eye and myopic in his left. When Williamson came to UCL he was already in touch with the leading continental centres of research and theory; he was a professed follower of Auguste Comte, and had studied with

Fig. 4.4 Alexander Williamson, FRS, Professor of Chemistry, 1849–87.

Fig. 4.5 The five Japanese students who first came to London in 1863, four of whom stayed to study at UCL. They are (left to right) Bunta Inoue, Endo Kinsuke, Nomura Yakichi, Yozo Yamao and Ito Hirobume.

Liebig at Giessen. The impact of such connections was swiftly felt. The accepted theory of etherification at the time was that ether was formed from alcohol by the loss of water. Williamson was able to show that the relationship had to be one of substitution rather than of the addition or loss of water; he postulated a process of continuous atomic exchange, in which atoms and molecules were conceived of as being in motion rather than static. It was a masterly piece of research and made Williamson's reputation when presented to the British Association in 1850.

Williamson's period of productive research then came to an end. He became instead a considerable College figure, largely responsible for the introduction of separate science degrees in the University and for the creation of UCL's Faculty of Science in 1870. He also built up his foreign connections and was for many years Foreign Secretary of the Royal Society. In his later years Williamson acted as host to some of the earliest Japanese students ever to reach the West, in the period before foreign travel from Japan was legalised (Fig. 4.5). The very first of the five students arrived in London in July 1863; he then stayed in Williamson's house as well as registering for his classes. All five later played important parts in the development of the new Japan after the Meiji restoration of 1868; one of them, Ito Hirobume, eventually rose to be Prime Minister. He and Bunta Inoue (who seems never to have registered for courses) returned after a year, but the three others stayed longer. They were still studying at the College in 1865 when a second group of 13 students arrived from Kagoshima, at the southwestern tip of Japan's four main islands, where the importance of their visit is still recognised in the form of a monument.

The flow of students from Japan continued throughout the nineteenth century and into the twentieth. One of the most influential was Joji Sakurai, who studied with Williamson from 1876 to 1881 and later became the originator of scientific research in Japanese universities. His achievements were recognised by the College in 1937, when he became its first foreign Fellow.

Not so recognised by the College was another student of the period, Ernest Satow. A student at University College from 1859–61, he became the first Englishman to speak and write Japanese and played an essential role in establishing contacts between Japan and the West. Only in 1989 was Satow's importance belatedly acknowledged by the creation of a Satow Chair in Japanese Law. In fact, all these numerous early connections between UCL and the opening up of Japan to Western culture were largely forgotten after the 1940s. However, since the 1980s many visits have been exchanged to mark the importance of UCL's role in shaping Japan's relationship with the West.

Richard Potter retired in 1865 from his Chair in Natural Philosophy, and his work in the subject was shared between T. A. Hirst and G. Carey Foster as Professors of Mathematical and Experimental Physics respectively. In 1867 Hirst succeeded De Morgan in Mathematics and Carey Foster became Professor of what was now called Physics. Foster's great achievement was the introduction of the systematic teaching of Experimental Physics to students (Fig. 4.6). The original 'Physical Laboratory' was created by clearing out the level space at the top of the seating in one of the semicircular lecture theatres. Before this the Professor certainly had some equipment, but actual teaching had been by means of lectures and demonstrations. Now for the first time experimental teaching, as in Chemistry, was offered to the individual student. Here again the College had become a pioneer of new methods in England – an example followed in many of UCL's other science and engineering subjects in subsequent years. Despite this early start, the facilities for Physics remained very restricted until 1893 when new laboratories, named after Carey Foster, were opened at the back of the main block. These remained in use until destroyed by bombing in 1940.

Carey Foster himself was remembered as a modest man, who published relatively little. He is now chiefly remembered for the 'Carey Foster Bridge', a very much more accurate variation of the Wheatstone Bridge. But he wielded great influence as a teacher and organiser who laid the foundations on which subsequent

Fig. 4.6 G. Carey Foster, FRS, was the effective creator of the Department of Physics as Professor between 1865 and 1898. He subsequently became the first Principal of the College, 1900–04.

achievements in physics have been built. His last service to UCL was to be its first Principal, an office created in 1900 and held by him for four demanding years after his retirement as Professor.

Physics at UCL was a pioneer in adopting modern teaching methods, but it was really only Physiology that rivalled the distinction of Chemistry in its contribution to nineteenth-century scientific knowledge. Pupils of William Sharpey dominated the subject as they began to colonise other universities and found new departments. At UCL Michael Foster became Professor of Practical Physiology, while Sharpey still held his Chair of Anatomy and Physiology in 1869. In that same year Foster and T. H. Huxley gave the first practical courses ever offered in Biology. In 1870 Foster went to establish physiology as a subject in Cambridge, and was succeeded at UCL by J. S. Burdon Sanderson. After Sharpey retired in 1874 Burdon Sanderson combined both Chairs until he in turn left to establish physiology, this time at Oxford, in 1883. The third of Sharpey's pupils then took over the Chair – E. A. Schäfer, later Sir Edward Sharpey-Schafer, a name he somewhat confusingly took in honour of his teacher. These men virtually created physiology as a research subject in the UK.

Burdon Sanderson's years at UCL saw a transformation of the whole position.

Fig. 4.7 The *Spy* cartoon of Sir John Burdon Sanderson, Chair of Physiology.

Physiology – with some pressure from T. H. Huxley as external examiner – became in 1871 a compulsory subject for all medical students, and laboratory facilities had to be expanded to deal with the extra numbers. In 1873 the Chair received its own endowment from T. J. Phillips Jodrell, a wealthy eccentric, so that Burdon Sanderson became the first Jodrell Professor (Fig. 4.7).

A landmark was the creation of the Physiological Society. Its first meeting was held in Burdon Sanderson's house and it retained close connections with the College. Originally brought into existence by way of self-defence against the active anti-vivisectionist movement of the 1870s, it subsequently became both a link between physiologists working in different parts of the country and a clearing-house for ideas and research. Burdon Sanderson's own research was on problems of cardiac function – in particular the contraction of the heart and all

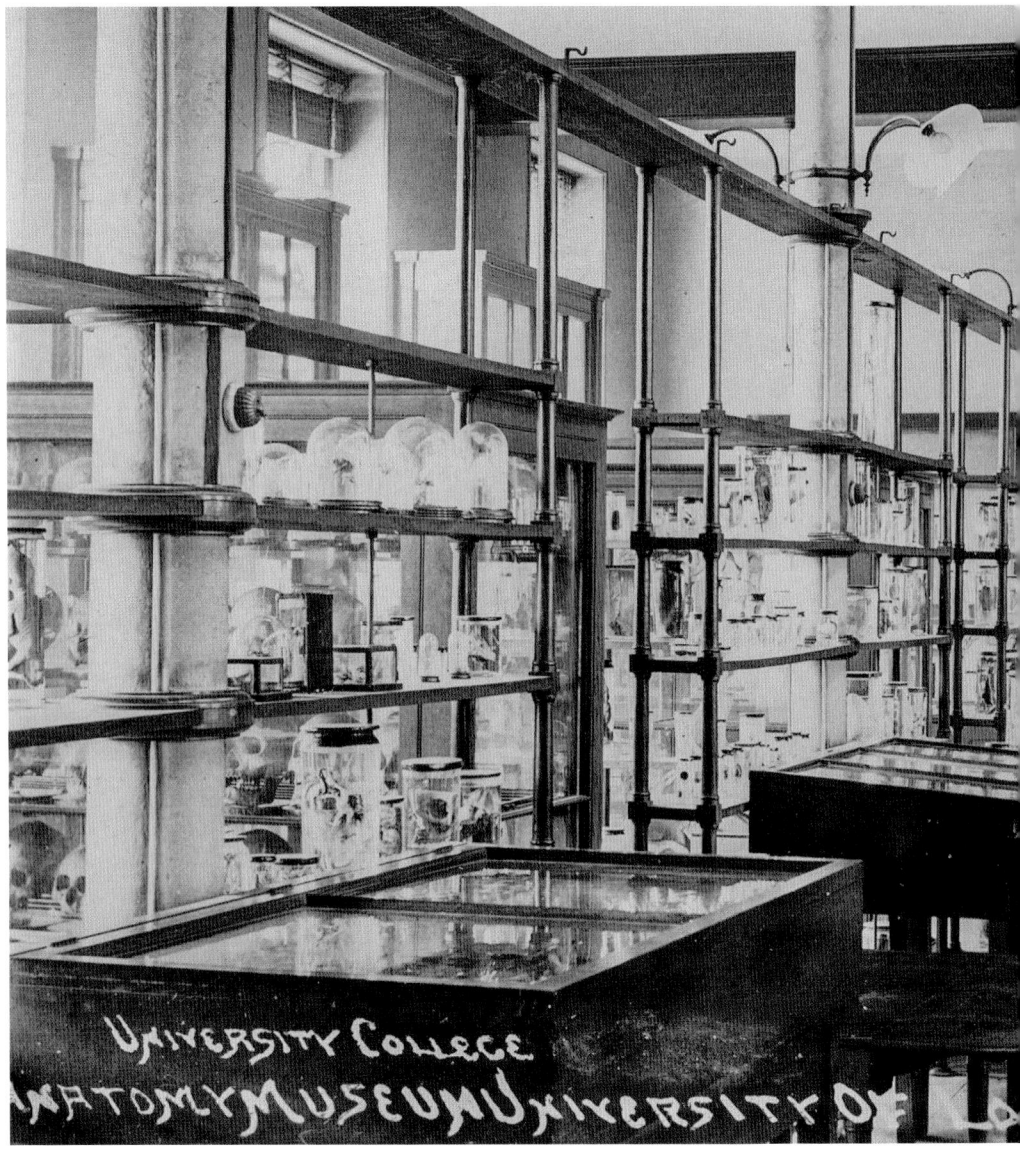

Fig. 4.8 A late nineteenth-century view of the Anatomy Museum, an important part of the teaching of Medicine at the time.

the accompanying phenomena – and this was to be a major research area in the Department for many years (Fig. 4.8). But perhaps his most significant contribution lay in the introduction of experiment as a central part of a student's education, and in the development of the laboratory facilities which this approach required.

By the time Burdon Sanderson left, the new accommodation for Physiology at the top of the North Wing was open. His actual teaching was less distinguished, as he was notoriously absent-minded and far from lucid as a lecturer. A pupil looking back in 1905 recalled that his eccentricities 'invested what he did with something of the same charm that the conjuror arouses in juvenile spectators ... we were in a state of suppressed excitement based on the uncertainty as to what Dr Burdon Sanderson might do next'. Zoology too found a major research scholar

as its Professor in 1874. It also received an endowment from Jodrell, though sadly the donor became insane before he could complete the making of the gift, requiring the Masters in Lunacy, the body that helped to oversee the welfare of mentally ill people, to act on his behalf in a complex legal situation. E. Ray Lankester was only 27 when he took the Chair, having previously been a Fellow of Exeter College, Oxford. He was a large man with a massive frame, a mobile, expressive face, a booming voice and an impetuous temperament – 'a veritable swashbuckler amongst Professors' (Fig. 4.9). Lankster was a dominating figure in his subject, editing the major zoological journal of the period for 50 years and placing his pupils in many of the Chairs in the subject at home and across the Empire. He wrote prolifically on a wide range of subjects including fossil fishes, molluscs and arthropods, and in his later years on prehistory and early human history.

Soon after his appointment Lankester introduced practical work into the Zoology courses. With the exception of Huxley's experimental courses, this was another innovation for a British university. Laboratory experience was increasingly becoming an integral part of a science undergraduate's course, and in this case

Fig. 4.9 Sir Ray Lankester, Professor of Zoology and Comparative Anatomy, 1874–91. He is depicted in this *Spy* cartoon in genial discourse with a hornbill, overheard by a fossil fish *cephalaspis*.

Fig. 4.10 Students attending one of Lankester's courses in 1887.

Fig. 4.11 The Zoology Museum in the 1880s. Many of its exhibits have remained at UCL, and are now part of the Grant Museum.

the practical classes proved so successful (Fig. 4.10) that a laboratory assistant, H. Jessop, was appointed in 1879 to prepare experiments. His work was pioneering in the running of a zoological laboratory, and Jessop became a notable College figure for many years. In 1891 Lankester returned to Oxford and was succeeded by W. F. R. Weldon – who again succeeded him at Oxford ten years later following Lankester's appointment as Director of the Natural History Museum. Weldon was one of the first men to introduce quantitative methods into zoology, together with Francis Galton. He went on to create a new branch of the subject known as biometrics, the statistical study of animals. Weldon's own research, especially on shrimps, was designed to test the theory of natural selection through carefully devised statistical analyses of inherited characteristics (Fig. 4.11).

Three Professors of Botany spanned the whole first century of the College's existence. Daniel Oliver succeeded Lindley, one of the original Professors, in 1860, and in 1888 he was in turn succeeded by Francis Oliver, his son, first as lecturer for two probationary years (aged 24), and then as Professor for 39 years until 1929. Both Olivers made notable contributions to their subject and advances in its teaching. Daniel Oliver worked for 30 years primarily as Keeper of the Herbarium at Kew Gardens, then the world's botanical Mecca, where he helped to form an

Fig. 4.12 A photograph of soil investigations undertaken at Bouche d'Erquy in 1904. In the foreground is the young Marie Stopes, who took a First Class degree in Botany after only two years' study at UCL.

incomparable systematic collection of the plants of all continents. Oliver lived at Kew, and for 28 years gave his lectures in College every morning during the summer terms at 8 o'clock – which meant being woken by the Gardens night-constable rapping on his window at 5 am. He regularly brought with him six different specimens for each of the students to examine.

The subject took a major step forward in 1880 with the establishment of its first Laboratory in the narrow former Microscope Room in the North Cloisters. Botany was no longer a subsidiary subject for medical students, one in which they could often see little point: it had gained the status of a scientific discipline in its own right. Soon after the young Oliver succeeded his father, he put a plan requiring further accommodation to Sir John Erichsen, then President of the College. However, it is recorded that Erichsen opened the interview and closed the matter with the admonition: 'Mr Oliver, you are a very young man and not the only professor in the College.'

In 1903 Francis Oliver began taking small groups of students to study marshland and the vegetation of maritime habitats around the Norfolk Broads and the nearby coast. Over the next few years he extended these expeditions, taking larger groups to Bouche d'Erquy on the French coast (Fig. 4.12) and then to

Blakeney Point in Norfolk. After 1910 these field courses found a settled home at Blakeney Point, offering perhaps the finest stretch of marshland coast in Britain. Oliver was instrumental in having the area preserved by the National Trust from 1912, enabling students to 'come face to face with the operations of Nature in its most dynamic form'. A series of Blakeney Point publications followed, and Oliver's approach to the changing relations of habitat and vegetation had a very significant effect on the development of the subject in the UK.

Ecology has remained an important interest of the botanists of the College. The UCL outpost at Blakeney Point – known since 2015 as the Francis Wall Oliver Research Centre – is still regularly used in field trips by undergraduate and postgraduate students (Fig. 4.13). Since 1960 there has been a postgraduate Diploma in Conservation (later an MSc course), originally set up as a result of a joint initiative with the statutory Nature Conservancy. Ecology and conservation were thus matters of concern at UCL long before they became fashionable words in the 1970s and beyond. The Centre for Biodiversity and Environment Research (CBER) is the latest manifestation of UCL's involvement in, and commitment to, greater environmental understanding.

As head of the Botany Department Francis Oliver was also an important champion of academic women at UCL. In 1889 he appointed a Quain studentship – the prestigious prize established as part of the bequest of Richard Quain – to a woman, and later created a number of non-professorial positions which were filled by women. Among them were Ethel Thomas, Winifred Smith (later Tutor

Fig. 4.13 Francis Oliver pioneered Botany field trips to Blakeney Point in Norfolk, making a base at an old lifeboat house. The buildings are still used for field trips, and in 2015 were renamed the UCL Francis Wall Oliver Research Centre.

Fig. 4.14 Sir Alexander Kennedy, FRS, Professor of Mechanical Engineering, 1874–89, as drawn by one of his students.

to Women Students) and Marie Stopes, who in 1910 was elected a Fellow of the College and in 1911 became a lecturer in Palaeobotany. Stopes had taken a First in Botany in 1902 after studying for only two years at UCL, followed by a DSc; she then received her PhD from Munich after a further two years of study. Stopes made major contributions to knowledge of the construction of coal, but was increasingly drawn into writing on the subject of birth control and sexuality, publishing the bestseller *Married Love* in 1918 and a short pamphlet, *A Letter to Working Mothers*, in 1919. In 1920 she resigned from her post at UCL, going on to open a birth control clinic in 1921.

Like Lankester, Alexander Kennedy came to University College in 1874 when he was 27 (Fig. 4.14). He stayed 15 years, during which time his achievements give him a fair claim to be considered the creator of modern engineering education. At the time of his arrival, Engineering at the College was in some trouble, both his predecessors having departed for better paid posts after only short stays. The *Annual Report* of 1874 acrimoniously commented on the resignation of Kennedy's predecessor to go to one of the new provincial university colleges, noting that it 'furnishes an additional illustration of the unequal competition with state-aided institutions to which this wholly self-supporting college is exposed, and which from time to time robs it of able teachers, to the detriment of its usefulness and prosperity'. Despite the low salary (less than £200), Kennedy's immediate contribution was to provide new teaching methods and approaches by providing translations of up-to-date foreign research.

Fig. 4.15 The Drawing Office on the top floor of the Engineering Building long desired by Kennedy, soon after its eventual construction in 1893.

More significantly, Kennedy followed the lead of Carey Foster in establishing laboratory work as a fundamental part of a science undergraduate's education. By the time of the Jubilee in 1878, the College had firmly adopted his line and the formation of a new Engineering Laboratory – the term itself being new – was one of the objectives of the Appeal. Space was provided in the main building and here, with a small grant and much improvisation, the pioneering laboratory

which was to serve until 1893 was established (Fig. 4.15). Kennedy was versatile and restless: he left the College in 1889 to start a new career, founding Kennedy and Donkin, a highly successful firm of electrical consultants. In his later years he wrote on topics as diverse as mountaineering and on archaeology; he was knighted and much honoured. It is a measure of Kennedy's impact on UCL that he left three Chairs where he had found one: in 1883 a separate appointment was made to the Chair of Civil Engineering, with Kennedy limitiing himself to Mechanical Technology. In 1885 came a completely new and very important departure – Electrical Technology.

Fig. 4.16 Sir Ambrose Fleming, FRS, Professor of Electrical Engineering for 45 years from 1885, in a portrait by Sir William Orpen.

Fig. 4.17 The thermionic valve invented by Ambrose Fleming at UCL, one of the most important inventions of the twentieth century.

Ambrose Fleming was the first Professor of Electrical Engineering, holding the post between 1885 and 1926. He was born in Lancaster in 1849, but educated at University College School and UCL, where he studied Physics under Carey Foster and Mathematics under De Morgan. He had taught science in schools and at University College, Nottingham before being offered the new Chair established by Kennedy (Fig. 4.16). Fleming was to hold the position until he retired at 77; he lived on to be 95. It is clear that his teaching duties were not over-onerous – for many years he gave one lecture a week on Fridays at 11 am. This gave him plenty of time for wide public lecturing and for profitable service as scientific consultant to Marconi, a connection that led to Fleming's most celebrated achievements. The plans for the world's first long-distance wireless station at Poldhu in Cornwall were, he later claimed, drawn on the lecture table of the Electrical Engineering Department. His key discovery, made in 1904, was the thermionic valve (Fig. 4.17). This revolutionary new technique for receiving high-frequency electromagnetic waves made radio possible and marked the birth of modern electronics. Fleming realised that use could be made of an effect noted by Edison: that if a metal plate is introduced into an ordinary evacuated carbon filament electric lamp, current will flow in only one direction. From this clue Fleming developed a bulb capable of acting in relation to electric current as a valve acts in a water pipe. The system was improved later by others, but Fleming had made the fundamental breakthrough.

The equipment Fleming found when he took his Chair was 'a blackboard and a piece of chalk'. The situation improved slowly, but in 1891 yet another appeal initiated a new building to accommodate the developments in both Mechanical and Electrical Engineering; facing onto Gower Street at right angles to the South Wing, it began the enclosure of the Front Quadrangle. Only a part of the upper storeys could be built due to lack of resources, so some of the ground floor was left with a temporary roof.

Nothing worried the Victorians more than their drains, and here, as in other respects, the College was responsive to society's needs. Hygiene was at first taught as part of medical jurisprudence, though its most famous teacher Edmund Parkes – 'the father of hygienic science' – was in fact Professor of Clinical Medicine from 1848 to 1860, before leaving to become Professor of Hygiene at the Army Medical School. In 1869 the Council decided to appoint a Professor of Hygiene and Public Health, since 'the subject has become so extensive in its developments and applications'. W. H. Corfield, one of the leading authorities in the field, held the Chair for 34 years, simultaneously holding posts as a Medical Officer of Health and running a large consulting practice. In 1875 Corfield opened the first laboratory in London for the practical teaching of Hygiene. It was located on the ground floor of the main building, where it remained until 1908.

When Sir Edwin Chadwick died at the age of 90, he left a large sum in trust 'for the improvement of sanitation'. Chadwick had been Jeremy Bentham's secretary in his last years and, as a leading disciple, played a combative, if not truculent, part in the struggle to achieve satisfactory public health and sanitary conditions. A large collection of his papers is kept in the Library. The combination of the Benthamite connection with the presence of the teaching of Hygiene in the College meant that Chadwick's trustees chose UCL as the home of a new course of instruction for young men likely to become municipal engineers. Both the new Chair of Municipal Engineering and the existing one of Hygiene became Chadwick Chairs.

By a somewhat curious arrangement, the new Chair was first occupied by Chadwick's son Osbert. As chairman of the trustees he drew no salary and performed his duties vicariously, though he did organise the syllabus and the courses, with admirable skill. The Department of Hygiene was moved to the top floor of the South Wing when the School moved out, but in 1929 Medical Hygiene left the College entirely, becoming a major part of the new School of Hygiene and Tropical Medicine. Municipal Hygiene, however, was retained in Engineering at UCL. Major research activity in the Department dates from the opening of a new Chadwick Laboratory in 1930, thanks to the continued support of the Chadwick

Trust. Municipal Engineering and Hygiene remained as a separate Department until 1947, when it was merged with Civil Engineering.

William Ramsay came to University College in 1887 from University College, Bristol, where he had been both Professor of Chemistry and Principal. He had already completed distinguished research, travelling widely and making personal contact with most leading contemporary scientists. However, the research that

Fig. 4.18 Sir William Ramsay, Professor of Chemistry, 1887–1913.

Fig. 4.19 This cartoon by Henry Tonks shows William Ramsay receiving the news that he has been awarded the 1904 Nobel Prize for Chemistry for his discovery of the inert gases. The drawing was originally given by Tonks to Gregory Foster, and later by Foster to College Secretary C. O. G. Douie as a wedding present.

was to make him famous was undertaken at UCL (Fig. 4.18). The physicist Lord Rayleigh had discovered that the density of the element nitrogen obtained from the atmosphere was always greater than that of nitrogen produced from its chemical compounds. With Rayleigh's consent, Ramsay set out to provide an explanation. Using the fact that nitrogen is taken up by heated magnesium, he established that the progressive removal of nitrogen from air concentrated in the residue an unknown gas, heavier than nitrogen.

The result was the discovery of a chemically inert gas which Ramsay called argon (the Greek for 'idle'). Furthermore, he realised that if one inert gas existed then there should in fact be a whole group of such gases, filling a gap in the periodic table of the elements. Between 1895 and 1900 Ramsay established in rapid succession the existence of terrestrial helium (the presence of helium had already been detected in the sun's chromosphere during the eclipse of 1868), as well as of neon, xenon and krypton. His successes brought swift recognition; he was knighted in 1902 and received the Nobel Prize together with Rayleigh in 1904 (Fig. 4.19).

Ramsay's great discoveries were made in the North Wing basement laboratories that had been built for Williamson in 1881. Williamson had evidently inspired little activity in his last years, and a good deal of the space then allocated had not in fact been used. Ramsay's staff at first consisted of two assistants, both of whom had to be paid out of the Professor's fees. Later he was able to appoint a student

Fig. 4.20 The Department of Chemistry in 1899, one of the earliest surviving departmental photographs. William Ramsay is standing in the centre.

demonstrator. No money was available for research expenses, and indeed Ramsay paid for his own scientific work very largely out of his own consultancies. The Department of Chemistry expanded rapidly from this slender foundation.

In the early 1890s the whole laboratory was fitted with working benches and extra space in the basement cleared out. In 1902 a second Chair, this time in Organic Chemistry, was established; it was filled by J. Norman Collie, one of the two assistants when Ramsay first came to London. Student numbers increased year by year; Ramsay was closely involved with their instruction and toured the laboratory twice a day, at least in the early years (Fig. 4.20). He and his wife also established personal relations with students, inviting groups of them to dinner regularly through the winter. He was also a notable public figure. Before coming to UCL he had been a leader of the movement to obtain government support for higher education, a campaign which led to the first Treasury grant in 1889; an initial £15,000 was to be shared between all the universities and university colleges in England. Ramsay worked for some years in connection with the Royal Commission on the Disposal of Sewage and was a leading advocate of the reform of the University of London. He was honoured throughout the world.

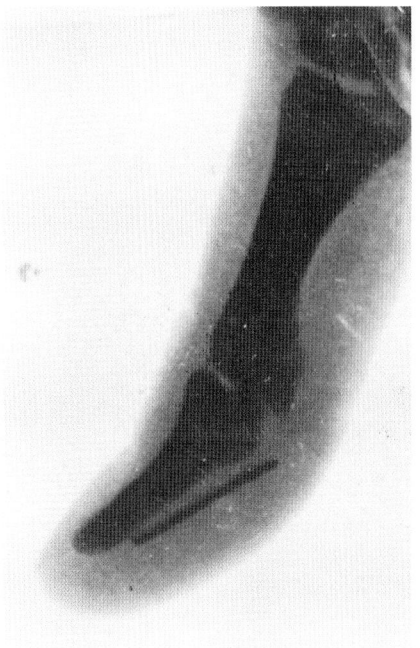 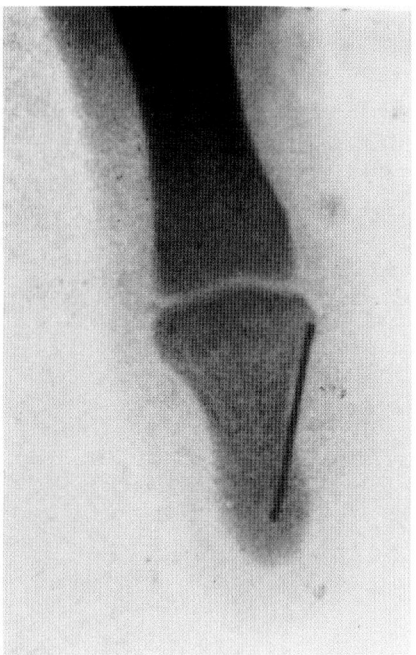

Figs **4.21a** and **4.21b** The first X-ray photographs used in Britain for clinical purposes, taken by Collie in 1896. They show a broken needle in the thumb of a patient at University College Hospital.

Norman Collie, Ramsay's professorial colleague, was involved in his younger days as an assistant with the development of X-ray photography. In 1882 he had gone to Würzburg in Germany to do his PhD (a degree not yet introduced into Britain), and happened to be there again in 1895 when Röntgen accidentally discovered the remarkable properties of what he called X-rays. Two months later, in February 1896, Collie had returned to London, where he was responsible for taking the first X-ray photograph used for clinical purposes in Britain (Figs 4.21a and 4.21b). The subject was a patient at University College Hospital who had a broken needle in her thumb. The use of X-rays for medical diagnosis and treatment was rapidly taken up after this signal example of co-operation between scientific research and medicine in the College. Within a few years the Hospital had acquired an expanding radiography department.

Collie went on to work with Ramsay on the inert gases. He later co-operated in pioneering work on the 'emanations' of radium, later known as 'radon', and the decomposition of this into helium. Here the men were unquestionably working on the fringes of current understanding of atomic structure, although the most dramatic discoveries were to be made in Cambridge some years later and through different techniques.

A 'new science': Eugenics and UCL

Karl Pearson was one of the dominating figures in the academic history of the College, with interests and enthusiasms ranging across politics, literature, law and science (Fig. 4.22). Of the beginnings of his long and productive association with UCL, he characteristically said: 'Professor Beesly, just because I had lectured to revolutionary clubs, Professor Croom Robertson, just because I had written on Maimonides in his journal *Mind*, Professor Alexander Williamson, just because I had published a memoir on atoms, and Professor Henry Morley, just because I had attended and criticised lectures of his on the Lake Poets, pressed me to be a candidate for the Chair of Mathematics!' It was Alexander Kennedy who finally persuaded him to forsake the law and take the Chair of Applied Mathematics in 1884.

In the 1890s Pearson became more and more interested in applied statistics and the correlation of biological and sociological data. He was captivated by Francis Galton's *Natural Inheritance* (1889) and the beginnings of eugenics (Galton coined the term in 1883), based on the conviction that the ideas of Charles Darwin, Galton's cousin, might be applied purposively to improve the human race. In 1901 Pearson, Galton and Weldon founded the journal *Biometrika*, and in 1903 the Drapers'

Fig. 4.22 Karl Pearson, FRS, Professor of Applied Mathematics and Mechanics, 1884–1911 and Galton Professor of Eugenics, 1911–33, photographed in 1910. On the desk is his beloved Brunsviga adding machine.

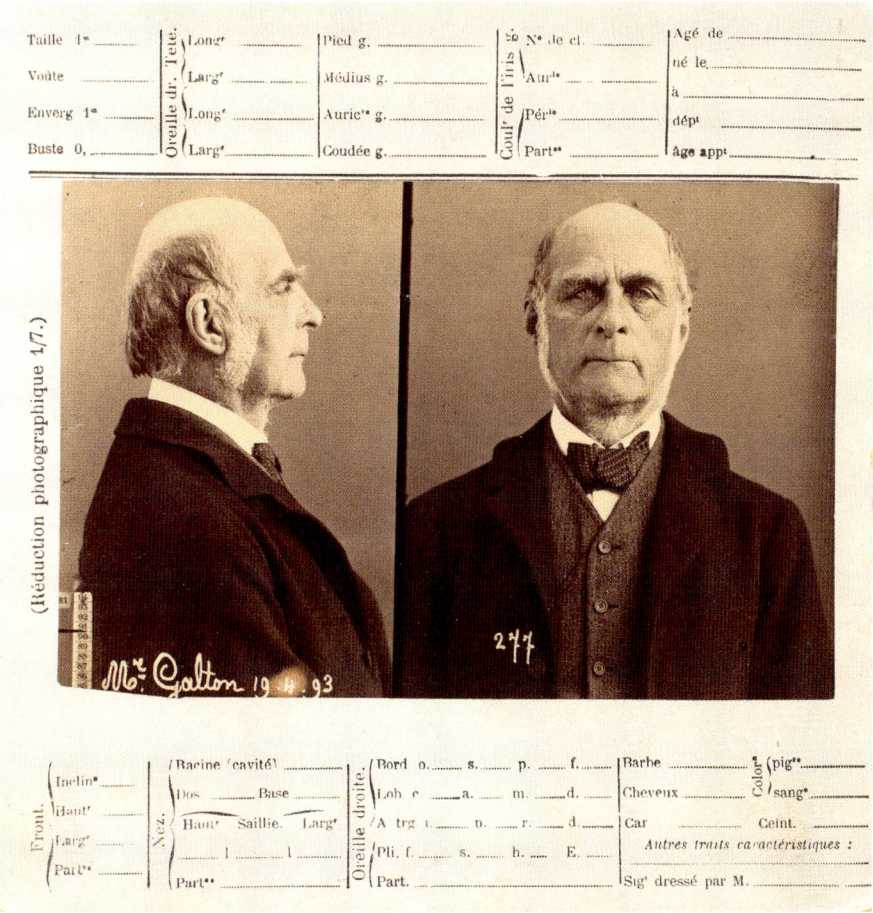

Fig. 4.23 Anthropometric record card of Francis Galton, including profile and full-face photos taken by Alphonse Bertillon in 1893, with spaces for key body measurements. The founder of the new science of eugenics, Galton considered the measurement of human features to be indicators of human ability and behaviour.

Company funded a new Biometrics Laboratory for Pearson. Soon afterwards Galton set up the Eugenics Record Office – later the 'Galton Laboratory' – in a Gower Street house (Fig. 4.23). After his death in 1911 Pearson came to have charge of both laboratories as Galton Professor.

The two laboratories conducted an enormous output of research on many aspects of intelligence, craniometry, heredity and Eugenics. Both offered new career opportunities to women scientists: in 1908 five out of a total of 14 researchers were women, including Alice Lee and Ethel Elderton. UCL was therefore instrumental in the establishment of the exciting new science of Eugenics, which, although almost completely discredited after the Second World War, was encouraged by much progressive opinion in the Edwardian and interwar periods. Supporters included the economist John Maynard Keynes, the scientist Julian Huxley and the birth control pioneer Marie Stopes (Fig. 4.24). After 1920 the work moved into the Bartlett Building from its former home, possibly in the South Wing. In 1980 it was renamed the Pearson Building, just before the death of Karl Pearson's son, Egon Pearson. The establishment of Eugenics at UCL was treated in typical tongue-in-cheek undergraduate fashion by a poem in the UCL *Union Magazine* of 1912:

> Here's a welcome to Eugenics, let each other science quake;
> The sum of human happiness is proved
> To depend upon the measurement a scientist shall take
> Of his forty-second cousin, once removed!

Francis Galton has long been a problematic figure for UCL because of his controversial research into issues of race and heredity. Lionel Penrose, successor to Pearson and R. A. Fisher as Galton Professor, 1945–65, disliked the term Eugenics; he led the department's shift of focus away from this discredited area of research towards a broader enquiry into the genetics of disease. In 1954 Penrose changed the title of the Galton Laboratory's journal from *Annals of Eugenics* to *Annals of Human Genetics*. In 1963 he also succeeded in having his Chair renamed as the 'Galton Professor of Human Genetics'. The term survived at UCL until 1965 when the Department of Eugenics, Biometry and Genetics, formed in 1944, was split into the Department of Human Genetics and Biometry and the Department of Animal Genetics.

UCL inherited a large collection of Galton's papers, books and artefacts, among them personal effects and custom-made anthropomorphic instruments (Fig. 4.25). In 1960 the papers were transferred to the Library, and in 1968 the objects moved to Wolfson House when the Galton Laboratory relocated there. The UCL Galton Collection was fully catalogued in the early 2000s and is now used extensively for teaching, research and public engagement on the history of science and the history of racism. The centenary of Galton's death in 2011 prompted a critical reassessment of his legacy at UCL through an exhibition and a series of events. More recently UCL students and staff have begun asking hard questions about the College's association with Galton and his racist views, in line with similar movements such as 'Rhodes Must Fall' at the University of Oxford.

The Revd T. G. Bonney succeeded Morris as Professor of Geology in 1877 and remained for almost 25 years. He came from St John's College, Cambridge, retaining his Fellowship there and originally continuing to teach and live in Cambridge while also commuting to London. Bonney was a vigorous and respected teacher, though

Fig. 4.24 Marie Stopes in academic robes. She was a lecturer in Palaeobotany at UCL from 1911 until after the publication of her groundbreaking text on sexuality and birth control, *Married Love*, in 1918.

Fig. 4.25 The UCL Galton Collection contains hundreds of artefacts used in Galton's research. This box of 16 glass eyes has shades ranging from light blue to dark brown.

the Department remained a small one; he published prolifically and authoritatively, specialising in the study of rocks and in the geology of the Alps. Throughout his years at UCL Bonney remained a part-time Professor; he was a very active Secretary of the British Association for five years and in the 1890s found lucrative employment writing for a London newspaper.

In his brief tenure of the Chair of Applied Mathematics W. K. Clifford left an enduring impression of quite exceptional abilities. A brilliant mathematician and an original thinker on the philosophy of mathematics, he was one of the pioneers of the conception of non-Euclidian space. His lectures were given with a minimum of preparation beforehand and from the briefest notes. 'The worst of these examinations', he once said, 'is that you have to think what to ask the fellows before you come in, whereas when you lecture you need not think at all.' His health soon deteriorated and he died of 'pulmonary disease' in 1879, aged only 33. T. H. Huxley regarded his death as one of the greatest losses to science in his time.

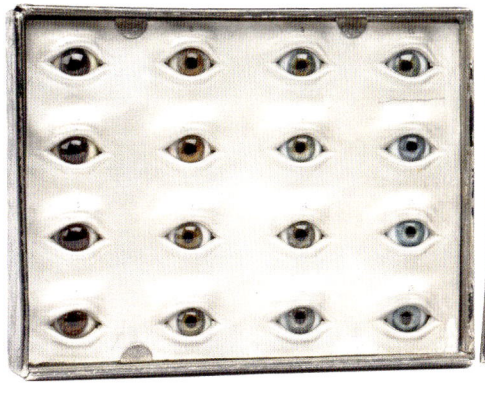
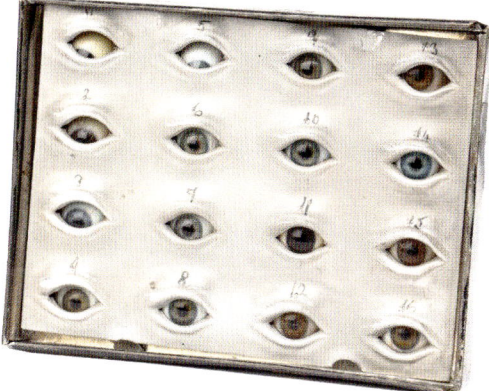

History, Law, Philosophy and Economics

It is paradoxical that the College's weakest subjects in the nineteenth century were those in which a Benthamite foundation might have been expected to be most creative – History, Law, Philosophy and Economics. The problem resulted from a shortage of students and money rather than of talented teachers. E. S. Beesly, for instance, Professor of History for over 30 years, was an important figure outside the College. A follower and translator of Comte, he was an active socialist and one of the first British academics to be in touch with the Labour movement, indeed with Marx and the First International. *Punch* honoured him with the nickname 'Professor Beastly'. Crabb Robinson lamented that 'Beesly is going to a meeting of bricklayers and says they conduct business better than scholars'; a serious attempt to sack him in 1867 was narrowly diverted by Grote. His commitment to his classes, however, was minimal; he used to 'come into his lecture room at 2 o'clock every Thursday, give us one lecture on Ancient History, one on Modern History, put on his comforter and hat; walk out; and that was all we saw of him till next week'.

Philosophy by contrast found a devoted and inspiring teacher in Croom Robertson, despite the bitterness which attended his original appointment. Intellectually active, and editor of *Mind* for its first 16 years, he was a trenchant critic of the existing degree examining system. In Political Economy too a distinguished Professor had little impact. W. Stanley Jevons was a former student of both University College School and UCL, where he had developed his scientific interests; they led him to his pioneering application of quantitative and statistical techniques to economics (Fig. 4.26). Jevons was the first to apply the modern concept of 'utility' in economics. But he found lecturing a great strain and, as his health deteriorated, gave the Chair up after six years. Neither he nor his successor H. S. Foxwell made any significant progress towards the creation of a school of economics at UCL and in 1895 the foundation of the London School of Economics (LSE) was a conscious reaction to the failure of the College to develop the social sciences.

An unmistakable failure even on his own view ('I could not help feeling I was scarcely a success') was the Revd A. J. Church, Professor of Latin, 1880–89. His cousin Sir John Seeley, Regius Professor of Modern History at Cambridge, who had himself held the Chair of Latin in the 1860s, tried to dissuade him from putting in for it since 'as a Christian' he would find his position uneasy at UCL. He certainly met with student protest. The first signatory of the petition against Church's classes was later to become the College's first Provost.

In this period payment to the Professors was still being made, with the exception of a few endowments, on the basis of the number of students who attended their classes. If the class was small, the Professor earned little. Apart from

Fig. 4.26 W. Stanley Jevons, Professor of Political Economy, 1875–81.

those who succeeded in attracting large classes and the famous scientists who could supplement their incomes by consultancies, UCL Professors were effectively part-timers who had to earn their living when not giving their lectures. One improvement was made in 1868, when a 'Retired Professors Fund' was created for the first time through the generosity of Samuel Sharpe; but the situation regarding salaries remained unsatisfactory. The difficulties of the Arts Faculty in this period are illuminated by a number of letters in in UCL records which draw attention to the rather perilous financial position of many Professors at the time.

In 1876 the Dante scholar H. C. Barlow died. He left the College his library, his papers relating to Dante and a fund for the endowment of public lectures on the *Divine Comedy*. The foundation played a significant part in the development of Dante studies in this country, and it also provided some small relief (the sum of £30) for the Professor of the day, Antonio Farinelli. He held the lectureship from 1880 to 1886 and was deeply offended when replaced by Edward Moore, the most distinguished Dante scholar of the day. Farinelli's protests were not quite unavailing, since the College was able to make him a small grant from the Quain fund in 1887. A. J. Butler, who took the Chair of Italian in 1898, became the first Englishman to hold it after a succession of Italians; a distinguished scholar, he took it strictly as a part-time job and with certain reservations.

The Slade

The Slade was one part of the Faculty of Arts which proved a great success; it went from strength to strength. Its second Professor, Alphonse Legros, came from the Parisian art world and the heart of the realist movement (Fig. 4.27). However, if he came as a new influence in 1876, Legros fairly soon lost touch with the latest developments in Paris. He became an increasingly isolated figure, speaking little English and teaching mostly by demonstration – but the School continued to prosper and expand in his years. Among his pupils were William Rothenstein and Frederick Brown (Fig. 4.28), who succeeded him in 1893 and admired him as a teacher. All the same, it is said that as Legros left UCL for the last time he muttered, 'Vingt ans perdus'. The College still possesses and prizes a splendid collection of Legros' etchings; it was not until many years after his death that he received wider acclaim as an artist.

The first really significant and influential period of the Slade's history occurred when Frederick Brown was Professor and Henry Tonks and Wilson Steer his assistants. It was Brown who discovered Steer's talent as an artist and he who persuaded Tonks (Fig. 4.29) to leave his job as a demonstrator in anatomy in a London hospital and join the Slade. The three men were friends and all members of the New English Art Club, the focal point of the most adventurous English artists in the 1890s. At first they introduced the ideas of the Impressionists and later developed their own reaction to them. At this stage the Slade was the mediator

Fig. 4.27 Alphonse Legros, Slade Professor of Fine Art, 1875–83.

Fig. 4.28 (opposite, above left) Frederick Brown, Slade Professor, 1892–1918.

Fig. 4.29 (opposite, above right) Henry Tonks, Assistant from 1893 and subsequently Slade Professor, 1918–30. He was the third of the great teachers at the Slade in one of its most influential periods.

Fig. 4.30 The assembled Slade School photographed in 1905. Women students at the Slade consistently consistently outnumbered men at this date.

THE ADMISSION OF WOMEN: 1878–1904

Fig. 4.31 A class of female students at the Slade in the early years of the twentieth century. Working as a professional artist was one of the few acceptable careers for ladies in Edwardian times.

Fig. 4.32 A watercolour group portrait in 1897 by Gwen John, featuring her brother Augustus John and a possible self-portrait in the reflection.

Fig. 4.33 Augustus John, OM, a Slade student from 1894 to 1898 and hence one of the earliest of Brown's successful pupils. His legendary talent and famously bohemian lifestyle exerted a strong influence over Slade students for several years.

Fig. 4.34 Percy Wyndham Lewis, a Slade student from 1898–1901 and later the leader of the extreme avant-garde in London.

of the new Parisian methods and ideas; students who passed through between 1894 and 1914 were to play a leading role in all the new currents in English art up to the 1930s. Women students consistently outnumbered men at the Slade, which produced many practising artists at a time when the number of respectable professions for women was very limited (Fig. 4.30). Among them were Edna Clarke Hall (née Waugh), Edith Elizabeth Downing, Dora Meeson Coates, Gwen John, Ida Nettleship, Mary Sargent Florence, Ursula Tyrwhitt and Ethel Walker (Fig. 4.31).

The greatest strength of the Slade tradition lay in the variety of talent and technique that it fostered (Fig. 4.32). Brown and Tonks stood for a sort of impressionism, putting great emphasis on the individuality of the natural object and the artist's response to it. However, not very consistently, they taught a strongly academic tradition, derived from the Old Masters and emphasising structure and proportion in drawing above all else. This core tradition influenced artists as diverse as Augustus John (Fig. 4.33), William Orpen, David Bomberg, Dora Carrington, Stanley Spencer and Wyndham Lewis. Brown and Tonks were soon left behind by events; they reacted with hostility to the whole postimpressionist invasion. Walter Sickert and the Fitzroy circle represented the antithesis of the Slade, but Slade-trained artists such as Percy Wyndham Lewis (Fig. 4.34) and Edward Wadsworth were in the forefront of new movements.

'What a brood I have raised up' was the austere Tonks' remark about his aberrant pupils. The memories of a contemporary student, Lilian Lancaster, give a vivid picture of one moment in this story of alienation. She and her friend had studied with Sickert and then joined the Slade's classes in 1908 – 'serving God and Mammon', said Sickert. Lancaster wrote: 'it is not surprising that this new way of painting caused something of a sensation among the Slade students … We used to peep through the crack of the door in the rests and saw a number of students crowding round our paintings examining them with great interest, and one day, when I came back to my work, I found "Stipple be damned" scrawled in charcoal in a corner of my canvas.' Miss Lancaster and her friend were discreetly asked to leave at the end of the session.

Archaeology and the Arts

The first Professor of Classical Archaeology was Charles Newton, a distinguished excavator and one of the founders of the Hellenic Society. He was also Keeper of Classical Antiquities at the British Museum, a post he combined with the professorship. Newton's appointment in 1880 coincided with the height of the aesthetic movement and of the vogue for Greek art, so the new Professor's opening lectures on this topic were a sensational success; the fashionable crowds in the Botanical Theatre were led by Oscar Wilde and Lily Langtry. 'But Newton,' remarked one of his successors, 'never lectured down to his audiences … and the attendance soon fell to a normal level.' Five years later the College received an endowment for the Chair. The benefactor was James Yates, an antiquarian and collector who had taken an interest in UCL from its foundation – and indeed even earlier, for he had written on the need for a new university in 1826, before he heard of the plans of Campbell and Brougham. When Yates died in 1871, his will left endowments for Geology and Archaeology, the money to be paid on the death of his wife. Yates's intention had been to regulate the behaviour of his new Professor by rules and regulations: 'Another prohibition on which I would insist is that the Professor should not smoke tobacco, nor distinguish himself by moustachios, beard or whiskers. He should be a gentleman in manners and appearances and set a good example to his pupils in this and all other things.'

Fortunately Yates never completed the drafting of these rules and regulations; but on these grounds his wife tried to dispute the bequests. There was prolonged litigation on the point, the College only eventually winning the case in the House of Lords. Newton's successor, R. S. Poole, was again a part-time Professor, holding a British Museum post as Keeper of Coins. It was E. A. Gardner, the Yates Professor

Fig. 4.35 Sir Flinders Petrie, the Egyptologist for whom a Chair was endowed in 1892. This photograph of 1921 shows him with exhibits from UCL's remarkable Egyptology collection.

from 1896 to 1929, who became the first to organise the Yates Archaeological Library and set up a working department. Another bequest started the Department of Egyptology. Miss Amelia Edwards, a novelist and explorer, founded a Chair in the subject specifically for W. M. Flinders Petrie (Fig. 4.35). It was her wish that the Professor should spend his winters excavating in Egypt; the Department stood at the centre of the British archaeological effort in Egypt from that date on. Petrie's great achievement was to establish the archaeological chronology of Egypt by collecting and analysing the whole material culture of Egypt; previous scholars had mostly devoted themselves to art or inscriptions (Fig. 4.36). His collections were eventually acquired by the College and, displayed in the Petrie Museum, illustrate the long history of Egypt in all its aspects.

Fig. 4.36 Henry Wallis's romantic painting of 1895 depicts Flinders Petrie excavating at Thebes.

Fig. 4.37 Margaret Murray, Petrie's assistant for many years. She taught Egyptian hieroglyphics and history to students for nearly 50 years.

Another notable member of the Department from 1894 was Margaret Murray (Fig. 4.37). She taught Egyptian Hieroglyphics and History at the College for the best part of 50 years before becoming in her old age a highly controversial figure in the historiography of witchcraft. With Petrie away in Egypt for a large part of every year, Murray kept the Department running, giving a theoretical grounding to generations of field archaeologists alongside lecturing and writing extensively for a general audience. In 1908 she became the first woman to lead a public mummy unwrapping before an audience of 500 at the Manchester Museum. Aged over 100, she published memoirs which included entertaining, though wildly inaccurate, memories of UCL in a chapter entitled 'Alma Mater, loved and splendid'. Also featured here was an account of her own part in the formation of the women's common room.

A revival in the Arts at UCL began with the appointment within a few years of three remarkable scholars: W. P. Ker in 1889, A. E. Housman in 1892 and Arthur Platt in 1894. All three played their full part in not only in the intellectual but also the social life of the College, and were much in demand as speakers in an age of debates and dinners. Ker, Henry Morley's successor, was to be Professor of English for over 30 years. He published little at first, but his later writings on medieval literature were to have a wide influence. His pupils found him an awe-inspiring figure, full of erudition and a disconcerting sour wit. Of the three men, Ker was the politician. He was one of the creators of the Honours School of English in the University and, at the end of his career, he initiated Scandinavian Studies in the College, acting as the first Director of what remained for a long time a unique Department. He was famous for his silences. After his *Dark Ages* was published, Mrs J. R. Green expressed her appreciation of it to him. Ker gazed at her, but said nothing and did not help the conversation till she stopped in some embarrassment. After a long pause, he said, 'Go on; I like it'.

Arthur Platt, the Professor of Greek, was very different. He was remembered as the creator of the common-room life of the academic staff, at first using his own private room as a meeting place after lunch. 'There he sat for more than a quarter of a century, instructing Chemists in the Humanities and teaching Zoologists wisdom,' wrote a colleague – an Arts colleague, of course. He inspired affection in all, including the animals at the Zoo; even the giraffe, a contemporary student recalled, would bend its long neck down and rub its head on Platt's bald pate.

The most famous of the three is, of course, Housman (Fig. 4.38). He had had a chequered early career, having obtained a First in Mods at Oxford, but then failed in Greats. For ten unhappy years he worked at the Patent Office, though during the latter five he also published a series of remarkable papers on classical literature. It is one of UCL's proud achievements to have brought him back into the

Fig. 4.38 A. E. Housman, Professor of Latin, 1892–1911 and author of *A Shropshire Lad*. This charcoal portrait was done in 1926.

Fig. 4.39 The medical staff of UCH in 1897. In the centre are Christopher Heath, the Surgeon and Professor of Clinical Surgery, 1875–1900, and his successor Sir Victor Horsley, FRS, 1900–07.

Fig. 4.40 (overleaf) The new Hospital at the time of its opening in 1906. The building was refurbished in the 2000s as the Cruciform Building.

university world; when he left after 17 years, it was to the Latin Chair at Cambridge. Housman's main work was limited in scope to the exposition and textual criticism of Latin poetry – he produced three editions of unsurpassed quality. He struck contemporaries in College as austere and reserved, though all his letters to Platt were destroyed by Mrs Platt after her husband's death as 'too Rabelaisian'. He must have seemed, then as now, a tissue of inconsistencies. There was kindliness beneath the cold exterior, especially towards young people; but he attacked other scholars with extraordinary ferocity. However, his treatment of women students is far from edifying. R. W. Chambers recalled that Housman would reduce female students to tears one week, then profess the following one not to remember them at all. He was a poet – *A Shropshire Lad* was published during his years at UCL – who would write nothing about the beauty of ancient poetry, and devoted 30 years to elucidating the text of a writer for whom he felt little sympathy.

The new Hospital

In the second half of the nineteenth century, the Faculty of Medicine was less rent by quarrels and its teaching came to be regarded as unequalled. It certainly had some outstanding Professors (Fig. 4.39). Three became baronets: Sir William Jenner, Physician to Queen Victoria and the undisputed leader of the profession, then at the height of his career; Sir John Erichsen, Danish by origin, Surgeon Extraordinary to the Queen, whose *Science and Art of Surgery* long shaped the teaching of the subject; and Sir Henry Thompson, Assistant Surgeon at UCL from 1856 and Professor of Clinical Surgery, 1865–75, a man of very wide interests, founder of the Cremation Society and of Golders Green Crematorium. Christopher Heath was the last of the great surgeons of the old style: he took to Listerian surgery only under protest, operating in an old frock-coat, turning green, which hung on a hook outside the theatre.

The Hospital itself was by no means as modern as it needed to be, and in 1896 Sir John Blundell Maple, the furnishing shop millionaire, offered £100,000 for its rebuilding. Alfred Waterhouse's design for the new Hospital was arresting; its redbrick and terracotta Renaissance style was not to everyone's taste, but its diagonal cruciform plan was practical from the point of view of ventilation and drainage (Fig. 4.40). In the end it cost £200,000, but Maple generously paid it all.

Student affairs

In 1893 the men's Union Society was formed to co-ordinate better the various student social, debating and athletic clubs (Fig. 4.41) that had grown up under the aegis of the University College Society and the separate Old Students' Association from 1890. These associations had to work under the 'unsympathetic and autocratic' College Office, which had the power to veto topics for debate that it did not consider 'suitable for the undergraduate mind' and to impose restrictions on common room opening hours. The Union's formation was preceded by radical agitation about the inadequacies of the sports grounds and bureaucratic obstructions by the College Office. A brief but spectacular contribution was made by *The Privateer*, a journal edited by E. V. Lucas which began and ended in 1892–93. Towards the end of 1892 a committee chaired by Edward Schäfer, the Professor of Physiology, put a proposal up to the Council for a 'combined athletic and social union'. By June of the following year the Council had not given its consent, but at a student meeting a constitution was adopted and a provisional committee set up. The Council then gave its retrospective blessing and from this point on the new Union seems to have received full support from the College. It was given control of three student common rooms and began its first session in October 1893, with Schäfer as its first – rather

Fig. 4.41 One of the earliest team photographs owned by the Union, showing the UCL Cricket Club First XI in 1906. On the ground to the right is E. N. da C. Andrade, later Professor of Physics at UCL.

Fig. 4.42 The innovative *University College Gazette* lasted until 1904, providing a valuable focus for students' issues and concerns. It was succeeded by the UCL *Union Magazine*, the cover of which is shown here.

Fig. 4.43 A photograph showing the commandeering of Phineas by UCL students and boys from the School, in celebrations marking the relief of Ladysmith in 1900.

reluctant – President. Not until 1903 was there a student President. An important early activity of the Union was in establishing the *University College Gazette* in 1895 (Fig. 4.42), inaugurating a long tradition of student dissatisfaction with College catering with a complaint against the management of the Refreshment Room.

For the seventieth anniversary of the College in 1897, the Union proposed a number of celebrations which became the first Foundation Week. Besides the sports, a concert in the Botanical Theatre and a Union dance in the Holborn Restaurant there was the first Oration: given by G. Vivian Poore, one of the Professors of Medicine, it was a lively and well received survey of the history of the College. Foundation Week remained a regular feature of the College for many years.

Another event significant in the College's history was the first commandeering of what was to become UCL's mascot, Phineas, during celebrations after the relief of Ladysmith in South Africa in March 1900 (Fig. 4.43). The *University College Gazette* reported it thus: 'The students then filed into Gower Street, and marched round the Hospital to the tune of nothing in particular admirably rendered by the bugles and penny whistles. … An exploring party in Tottenham Court Road seized the famous Highlander, and placed him in the post of honour on the Portico – he was soon joined by a representative of the Army, who had been carried to the College on the shoulders of an enthusiastic crowd.' There followed a procession to the West End in a large festooned cart lent by Sir Blundell Maple, a rendition of 'Rule Britannia' outside the War Office and finally a bonfire in the Front Quad.

The 'famous Highlander' was Phineas Maclino, a large wooden tobacconist's sign which stood outside Catesby's in Tottenham Court Road (Fig. 4.44). From this occasion onwards he was repeatedly commandeered for rags, riots and celebrations. In the course of time Phineas came to be a resident of UCL, if a somewhat erratic one, as the College mascot. He has frequently been the victim of raiding parties from other institutions, but is now in the Union's safe-keeping, sprucely re-painted by Slade students and displayed in the Phineas Bar on the third floor of the union building on Gordon Street.

University reform

The College's situation at the end of the nineteenth century was far from secure. Building developments had led to a debt of £30,000, a sum that the College had no means of paying off. The salaries of Professors were in general inadequate and they had no proper means at all of financing their research. Moreover the administration of the College had not succeeded in keeping pace with its expansion, though UCL was in fact on the verge of a great leap forward in terms of student numbers, buildings and research. Meanwhile University reform had been under discussion for many years, and this was to affect the College's development in a radical way.

From the 1880s there was a strong campaign to promote a 'Teaching University', examining still being the University of London's only function. The solution arrived at in 1898, after two Royal Commissions and innumerable setbacks, was that an organic connection should be established between the teaching College and the degree-giving body. The teachers were given representation on University committees and on Boards of Studies set up to control the various subject areas, while students were to be required to complete courses of study in the colleges if they were to take 'internal' degrees. However, UCL wanted to go further than this. It proposed that the College and all its assets should be vested in the University, and that all its activities should be carried out under the University's authority. Eventually, after the Drapers' Company paid off virtually all the College's debts, this plan was given effect by the University College (Transfer) Act of 1905.

Fig. 4.44 Phineas Maclino, appropriated as UCL's mascot following the events of Ladysmith night, 1900. Today he resides in the Phineas Bar in Gordon Street.

THE ADMISSION OF WOMEN: 1878–1904

CHAPTER 5

The Gregory Foster Years

1904–29

> Both before and after my time, University College lay under the strong hand of Sir Gregory Foster, provost. Foster was an imposing figure of a man, with a sultry countenance and a Socratic forehead that concealed little in the way of academic understanding but a great capacity for administrative push. His ambition was to make University College bigger and wealthier every day and in every way. Alas, he succeeded. He never paused to think that he was nailing down and forcibly feeding a perfectly good goose with the sole object of putting more and more fatted liver on the market. He never reflected that 'It is not growing like a tree in bulk doth make a man better be'. There were many things on which he did not reflect, for his was not a reflective nature.
>
> *Sir Mortimer Wheeler,* Still Digging *(1955)*

The first Provost of UCL was Sir Gregory Foster (Fig. 5.1). Since the ill-starred days of Leonard Horner as Warden, the College had only had the formal leadership of the President, who chaired the Council, while another member of the Council acted as chairman of the Senate. In 1900 it was decided that there should once more be a salaried head, with the title of Principal, who was to chair the Senate and act as the Professors' link with the Council. Carey Foster held the post for four years, during which some of the toughest problems were faced. He was then succeeded by the man who had been Secretary since 1900, Gregory Foster (no relation), while Walter Seton took over the Secretaryship (Fig. 5.2). These two men were to guide the College through a long period of substantial change and development. Gregory Foster had been a UCL student in the 1880s; he became a teacher at University College School and then an assistant in the English Department in the 1890s, and third President of the Union in 1896. His title was changed from Principal to Provost in 1906, evidently to avoid confusion with the Principal of the newly reconstituted University of London.

Walter Seton was an even younger man: he had come to UCL on his seventeenth birthday and was only 22 when he became Secretary. He too had strong academic interests, particularly in Scottish history and in Franciscan studies. Seton was a hardworking Scot, with a somewhat underdeveloped sense of humour, while Foster

Fig. 5.1 Sir William Orpen's portrait of Sir Gregory Foster who was the first Provost, 1906–29, having already been Secretary of the College, 1900–4 and Principal, 1904–6.

Fig. 5.2 Walter W. Seton in his office as Secretary of the College, 1904–27. Like Sir Gregory Foster, he devoted himself to the College in its period of transformation.

was a very popular figure, at least with the students. He insisted on interviewing all of them personally at the beginning of each session throughout his Provostship, an increasingly time-consuming exercise which repaid itself in terms of the regard in which he was held. Gregory Foster was very largely responsible for founding the twentieth-century College, as distinct from that of the nineteenth.

The decision to 'incorporate' the College fully into the University meant the separation of two elements of the College – the Advanced Medical School and the Boys' School. Both had therefore to be found new premises away from UCL. For this purpose the Faculty of Medicine had to be split, the College retaining the pre-clinical teaching and the new 'University College Hospital Medical School' taking over the advanced courses in surgery and medicine (Fig. 5.3). A site and a building were needed. The site was provided opposite the College on the corner of Huntley Street in 1903 through an anonymous gift. The building was presented wholly by Sir Donald Currie, founder of the Castle Steamship Company and one of the richest men in England, who gave well over £100,000 to the project (Figs 5.4a and 5.4b). He

Fig. 5.3 The new Medical School almost ready for opening in 1907.

had had no previous connection with the College or with the area, but his life had been saved by a doctor from UCH. The College, after thanking Sir Donald for his gift, passed a vote of thanks to Dr Batty Shaw 'for having so successfully interested Sir Donald Currie in the Scheme'.

University College School was to move a great deal further away – to the site in Frognal, Hampstead, which it still occupies today. Money was again raised by an appeal and the School was re-founded as an independent body. The leave-taking on 25 July 1907 was a solemn affair: 'the School, headed by the Cadet Corps, marched into the College quadrangle, formed three sides of a hollow square, facing the great steps and Portico, where a chair had been placed for the Provost, Dr T. Gregory Foster. The Head-Master, supported by Beadle and Sergeant, advanced into the Square, and when the Provost had taken his seat above, read the valedictory address before giving up formally the keys of the School building.' Moving speeches were made about the maintenance of intimate links between School and College – hopes which found little fulfilment in the succeeding years.

Fig. 5.4a Sir Donald Currie, the wealthy shipowner who financed the University College Hospital Medical School after his life was saved by a doctor from University College Hospital.

Fig. 5.4b The crest of the Medical School, with Currie symbolised by a ship.

The formal act of incorporation took effect on 1 January 1907. From now on the College was to be controlled by a Committee of the Senate of the University; the College Senate became the Professorial Board and the College itself ceased to have a separate legal existence from the University. It is ironic that it was exactly 70 years later, in 1977, that UCL completed the lengthy and expensive business of undoing the effects of incorporation. In 1907 it had been an act of faith in the new order, but only King's College followed the lead; instead the University became a federation of independent colleges, so that UCL and King's found themselves in an increasingly anomalous situation. In 1977 the College became once more an independent corporation, with a new Royal Charter. The short-term effects of the constitutional change of 1907, however, were unquestionably beneficial.

The departure of the School and of the Medical School enabled a major reorganisation of accommodation to take place. Geology took most of the first floor of the South Wing and began a considerable expansion under E. J. Garwood, who had succeeded Bonney in 1901 and who was the first full-time Professor. Extra space was provided for Electrical Engineering and Applied Mathematics while the Eugenics Laboratory was moved into College from 88 Gower Street. Philosophy was also housed in the South Wing, with the Psychological Laboratory adjoining it.

Research and enquiry

Perhaps the chief beneficiary was the Library, whose reorganisation is one of the great success stories of the period. When R. W. Chambers was appointed Librarian in 1901, he inherited a rich but disorganised domain, largely consisting of bequests and gifts (Fig. 5.5). Many of them were very valuable, and many had been the collections of the Professors themselves. But there had been intervening years of neglect. From 1831 to 1871 there was no proper Librarian. There was a printed catalogue, thanks to the generosity of Samuel Sharpe and the efforts of Adrian Wheeler as Librarian between 1871 and 1901, but there was no card index to facilitate the cataloguing of accessions, no space to store them and no administrative structure.

Chambers had been a pupil of Ker and was to succeed Gregory Foster as Assistant Professor in 1904; he later succeeded Ker himself as Quain Professor in 1922. He took over as Librarian to face great problems – not least a profound controversy between those who wished to see the Library develop a single, centralised organisation

Fig. 5.5 R. W. Chambers, FBA, Librarian 1901–22, the creator of the modern College Library who later succeeded Ker as Quain Professor of English Language and Literature, 1922–41.

and those who preferred subject libraries under the Professor's own control, and hence available for teaching use within the department. Chambers fought from the beginning for the integrity of the Library and the solution adopted conceded his main point: the books were to remain under the Library's control, but be kept in separate though linked rooms, as far as possible one for each main subject. With this plan in mind, the Library was able to use the 1907 reorganisation to the best effect: the area to the south of the Flaxman Gallery became a series of linked Arts libraries, while the area to the north – the old Anatomy Museum – became the College's first coherent Science Library.

A most distinguished accession in 1906 was the library of Frederick Mocatta, the wealthy collector and philanthropist, who left his collection of Jewish books and antiquities to the Jewish Historical Society. They arranged, as a memorial to him, that a library, a museum and a room for the meetings of the Society should be provided by the college: in return, UCL became the permanent home of one of the most important Jewish libraries in Britain (Fig. 5.6).

The years after incorporation saw significant steps towards the establishment of sustained research programmes of the type that was to become increasingly

Fig. 5.6 The old Mocatta Library, destroyed by bombing in 1940.

familiar in the twentieth century. Ernest Starling as Jodrell Professor of Physiology played a major role. A medic from Guy's, he had been working with William Bayliss (his brother-in-law) for some years before coming to UCL in 1899. Their collaboration was at first directed to the functioning of the heart and to the analysis of cardiac failure. Then in 1902 they turned to work on intestinal function and rapidly made startling discoveries, leading to the principle of hormonal control mechanisms; they were the first to establish that messages were conveyed by chemical agents, transported in the bloodstream, and Starling himself introduced the word 'hormone' in 1905.

Starling conceived and brought to fruition plans for a new medical complex at UCL involving Anatomy and Pharmacology as well as Physiology, intending to transform both medical education and research in London. The first stage, the Institute of Physiology – a title little to the taste of the Provost, who feared secession – was built in 1909 on what had been the school playground (Fig. 5.7). In 1912, through the generosity of Andrew Carnegie, the second stage was added for Pharmacology. Starling went on to evolve a general theory of the regulation of the heartbeat (Starling's law of the heart). His experiences in the First World War left him bitterly convinced of the sheer ignorance of the British ruling classes, and he campaigned vigorously for basic educational reforms with a scientific curriculum. He resigned the Jodrell Chair in 1923, but remained in UCL as a Royal Society Professor. He died, ironically of a heart attack, at sea off Jamaica in 1927.

The 'Brown Dog Affair'

A great sensation for several years in the first decade of the twentieth century was the 'Brown Dog Affair'. It all began in May 1903 when Stephen Coleridge (a leading anti-vivisectionist of the day) made a widely reported speech to the National Anti-Vivisection Society. In this he accused William Bayliss – Starling's collaborator and a teacher at UCL since 1888 – of having carried out cruel and illegal experiments on a dog without anaesthetic in the Physiology Laboratory at the College. Bayliss had in fact given a lecture showing an experiment involving a dog, which was already anaesthetised, for research on pancreatitis and diabetes being carried out by Ernest Starling, the Professor of Physiology. The lecture was attended by two Swedish women, active in the anti-vivisectionist cause, and their very garbled account was the basis of Coleridge's absurd charges against the College: 'into its dark portals there passes a never-ending procession of helpless dumb creatures … into a scene of nameless horror…' Both Sir Victor Horsley, the UCH Surgeon, and Starling himself

Fig. 5.7 The Institute of Physiology, built on the former University School playground, soon after its opening in 1909.

encouraged the wealthy Bayliss to bring a libel case which, amid much publicity, he won. It was clearly established that the dog had been humanely treated and that the experiments were necessary and legal; Bayliss won £2,000 damages which he at once donated to the College for the furtherance of physiological research.

The matter, already a *cause célèbre*, did not end there. The anti-vivisectionists arranged for a statue of the 'Brown Dog' – as the Press had named the creature – to be mounted on a drinking fountain in Battersea. This was erected in 1906 (Fig. 5.8). With its insulting inscription referring to the laboratories of UCL, it was naturally found offensive in a College proud of the various pioneering laboratories it had built up during the previous generation. The students especially rose to the provocation, and in 1907 an attempt to knock the statue down took place, resulting in ten medical students being fined. Marches, bonfires and other riotous demonstrations ensued, as well as a vigorous correspondence in *The Times* and the *British Medical Journal*. Eventually in 1910, while the College was still taking legal advice, Battersea Council had the statue removed, though the site was for some time afterwards guarded by the police. The outcome of the affair, so far as the anti-vivisectionists were concerned, was a loss of credibility while, according to Walter Seton, this was the first time that the students of different colleges of the reconstituted University had united in support of a common cause.

Fig. 5.8 The Brown Dog statue in Battersea Park.

Fig. 5.10 The programme of events at the three-day Bazaar and Fête of 1909.

Student life before 1914

Before 1897 the College had no playing fields of its own and teams had to rent pitches in Regent's Park or Primrose Hill, the area in which many of the students were accommodated. From 1897 to 1906 the Union Society rented a ground at Acton, but by 1905 this had proved too small and 15½ acres were bought at Perivale, which was to be the centre of athletic activities until after the Second World War. The Perivale ground was formally opened in June 1908. Like the Men's, the Women's Union Society was responsible among other things for athletic facilities, and so a ground for women also became a priority. The problem was solved by buying another 7½ acres adjacent to the men's ground at Perivale. The cost of the two together was £3,600; including equipment and drainage, the requirement of the two Unions by 1909 was £7,000. Fundraising activities therefore took up a good deal of student time in the following years. The great Bazaar and Fête of 1909 lasted for three days, occupying the Front Quadrangle and large parts of the College buildings as well (Fig. 5.9). The programme included a fair, dances, concerts, demonstrations, exhibitions and scenes from Shakespeare, as well as Indian and Homeric tableaux. The whole affair was a great success, raising more than one-third of the sum needed (Fig. 5.10).

Fig. 5.9 A view of the scene in the Front Quad during the Bazaar and Fête in July 1909.

Fig. 5.11a The Men's Union Lounge.

Fig. 5.11b The Women's Union Lounge.

Fig. 5.12 Stafford Cripps, the Union's President for 1910–11.

R. STAFFORD CRIPPS,
President 1910-11.

As early as 1912, there was talk of amalgamating the two Unions, a project which in fact had to wait over 40 years. The proposal was roundly denounced in the *Union Magazine* for June 1912, which expressed the hope that 'this futile chatter and the exaggeration with which it is embroidered will cease; as it may endanger the present cordial relation which exist between the two Union Societies'. By the early 1900s students were able to access their respective union rooms six days a week, and these were kept open until 8 or 8.30 pm on week days in term time (Figs 5.11a and 5.11b). Stafford Cripps, Men's Union President for 1910–11, oversaw the elegant but economic furnishing of the Union's rooms; later, as Sir Stafford, he served as the austerity Chancellor of the Exchequer in 1947–50 (Fig. 5.12).

These prewar years also saw a major development in the provision of accommodation for men students. This had been gravely deficient since 1889, when the old University Hall was acquired by the Trustees of Dr Williams's Library. A committee was set up, with Seton as its secretary and Sir William Ramsay as treasurer, to acquire land in Ealing – about a quarter of an hour's walk from the new athletic ground. University College Hall, Ealing was opened in 1908 with room for 50 students, and extended in the 1920s. Walter Seton continued to take a great interest in the new Hall and was its Warden from 1912 to 1922.

In the years before the First World War women sought a wider role in College life. They secured representation on the College Refreshment Room Committee, for example, and established a number of new clubs and societies. Between 1898 and 1912 about a dozen women were appointed to the academic staff, mainly in the departments of Botany, Chemistry, Geology and Applied Statistics. In 1913

Margaret Gilliand, Headmistress of Haberdasher's Aske's School, became the first women appointed to the College Committee; she was a former student who been made a Fellow of the College. Following the death of Rosa Morison in 1912, the Women's Union Society protested that the 'passing in' of new women students by the Lady Superintendent was a 'relic of bygone days' that should be done away with – although in fact the rule was not removed from the College Calendar until 1919.

Although both Morison and her successor Winifred Smith were well-known supporters of women's suffrage – as were several of the College's research and teaching staff, including Marie Stopes and Margaret Murray – the Women's Union remained officially neutral on this divisive topic before the First World War. The WUS minutes stated explicitly that it not include support for the suffrage movement in its programme, but it did follow the development of an Intercollegiate Suffrage Society in 1914 with interest. Many individual students, often connected with the Slade, were involved in suffrage activities, while alumnae such as Marion Wallace-Dunlop, who in 1909 became the first suffragette to go on hunger strike, were high-profile campaigners. Women educated at UCL made significant contributions to wider society at this period. For example, two of the first women reading for the Bar, following the 1919 Sex Disqualification (Removal) Act, were UCL students E. Lloyd and M. M. Geikie Cobb, who had served as the President of the Women's Union Society just before the war. Countess Markievicz (née Constance Gore-Booth), a former Slade student, was the first woman elected to the Houses of Commons in December 1918, though as a Sinn Féin candidate she did not take up her seat.

The years before the First World War saw a vigorous continuation of building activity assisted by benefactions. In 1911 Sir Herbert Bartlett, a building contractor, provided practical support to the proposal that the Departments of Architecture at King's and UCL should be merged by donating £30,000 for the necessary building. The benefaction was also intended to provide for the accommodation needed by Karl Pearson's department; the whole building would provide a north-west frontage onto Gower Street. Almost complete by the outbreak of war, the Bartlett Building was first used as a temporary wartime hospital under the management of UCH.

The other major benefaction on the eve of the First World War provided expanded accommodation for the work of the Department of Chemistry (Fig. 5.13). Sir William Ramsay's successor as Professor of Chemistry was F. G. Donnan – a distinguished physical chemist who had first come to UCL to work in Ramsay's laboratory in 1898, and subsequently held posts in Dublin and Liverpool before his return in 1913. He is now best remembered for the 'Donnan membrane equilibrium', concerned with the transport of ions and molecules across the living cell. By the time he took over the Department the building of the new laboratories, facing Gower Place and extending the College site northwards, was already well advanced.

Much of the money had been given in 1911 by Sir Ralph Forster, commemorated by a plaque in the entrance; a closing order was obtained for Little Gower Place in 1912 and the impressive building, designed by Simpson, was in use, though not finished, by 1915. The building was renamed the Kathleen Lonsdale Building, after UCL's first woman Professor, when the Chemistry Department moved out.

UCL and the Great War

The College's work continued during the First World War, though the number of students declined sharply and many clubs and societies suspended or reduced their activities. Over 2,600 members and former members of College served during the war (Fig. 5.14). Two hundred of these were younger men who had been students or

Fig. 5.14 The College Christmas and New Year card for 1915–16, sent jointly by the Provost and the President of the Union to all members of the College serving in the forces.

Fig. 5.13 The new Chemistry Laboratories facing onto Gower Place, first opened in 1915.

staff at the College in the decade preceding the outbreak of war. A high proportion never returned; no fewer than 301 members or former members were the College's contribution to 'the lost generation' (Fig. 5.15). Women students contributed to the war effort through UCL's Voluntary Aid Detachment (VAD), set up in 1914, which maintained an Ambulance Squad in St Pancras and sent students to nurse in military hospitals in France. Others worked on the land during vacations as part of a 600-strong group from the University of London; yet other women served as munition or canteen workers, or provided 'substitutes for men in innumerable capacities'.

Serving in the Royal Army Medical Corps, Henry Tonks made a series of important drawings of facial war wounds and surgical reconstruction. He was appointed an official war artist in 1918, and the realism of his paintings moved many at the Royal Academy's 'War Artists' exhibition in 1919. Tonks was appointed Slade Professor in 1918. Slade-trained Anna Airy became one of the first female war artists, employed in 1918 by the newly founded Imperial War Museum to paint typical scenes at munitions factories.

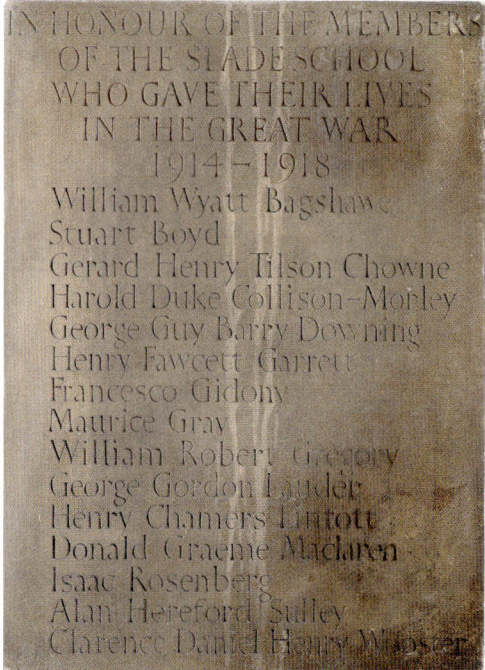

Fig. 5.15 The Slade war memorial tablet, featuring the name of the poet and artist Isaac Rosenberg, which was unveiled on 11 November 1921.

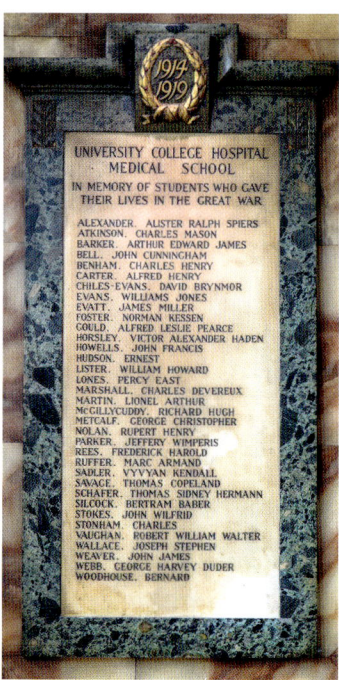

Fig. 5.16 One of six First World War memorials still visible on UCL's campus today. This tablet, dedicated to medical students, is in the entrance to Rockefeller Building.

Fig. 5.17 The South Cloisters in the early 1920s showing photographs of the College's war dead alongside the Roll of Honour, guarded by a Beadle.

A committee was set up in 1917 to develop plans for a joint war memorial for the College, Hospital and Medical School. In 1919 it announced a target of £30,000 to establish a Great Hall, endow University College Hall, Ealing and fund a commemorative album and memorial tablets. These tablets were displayed around the College, for example in the Slade and Medical School, and several are still in place today (Fig. 5.16). In the interwar years Armistice Day was commemorated by the reading of the Roll of Honour in front of the Portico, while the South Cloisters displayed hundreds of photographs of the fallen and the two handsome leather volumes of the memorial album (Fig. 5.17). After the war student numbers were boosted as hundreds of ex-service students enrolled or re-enrolled at UCL, many of them in receipt of new Board of Education grants for ex-service students. These students played an active role in College life through a new Ex-Service Students' Association and other societies.

Fig. 5.18 One of a series of elegant views of the College buildings drawn by J. D. M. Harvey in the years after the First World War.

Fig. 5.19 (overleaf) An aerial photograph of the College and its vicinity taken in about 1920, before motor traffic had begun to make much impact.

Building activities

Between the 1890s and the 1920s the expansion in the College's activities was matched by striking developments in the buildings (Fig. 5.18). First the Front Quadrangle was closed in by the new buildings added to the North and South Wings and fronting on to Gower Street – Engineering, Architecture and Statistics. Secondly Physics, Chemistry, Physiology, Pharmacology and Anatomy began the process whereby the larger science departments moved out of the original building into more generous quarters on the periphery, leaving the main building for the most part to the Library, administration and the Arts. After westward and northward moves up to the 1920s, further expansion was to be eastward and southward (Fig. 5.19).

In 1905–07 the two distinctive round observatories were built on the lawns of the Front Quad. These additions were partly the initiative of Karl Pearson and partly of M. T. M. Ormsby, later Professor of Municipal Engineering, whose interest was in their relevance to surveying courses as well as to astronomy. The Chadwick Trustees largely paid for one and the Drapers' Company largely for the other. They remained in use up to the Second World War, serving subsequently for the storing of garden tools, the teaching of Classics and as an office for the manager of the College branch of NatWest bank.

The third stage of Starling's plans for medical sciences achieved completion with the opening of the Anatomy Building in 1923. This was funded by the Rockefeller Foundation as an expression of American friendship towards the British Empire. The £370,000 given was the College's largest benefaction up to that time. The building adjoins a further extension to the Institute of Physiology and faces the Medical School across Gower Street. All these buildings are physically linked, with the intention of encouraging the correlation of their activities; even the Medical School is connected by a tunnel under Gower Street (Fig. 5.20).

Also in 1923, Anatomy was strengthened by the transfer of Histology and Embryology from Physiology. 'Paradoxical as it may appear', wrote Sir Grafton Elliot Smith, Thane's successor as Professor of Anatomy, 'the reforming zeal of Professor Sharpey at this College seventy years ago had as one of its ultimate results the crippling of anatomical effort in England…' Anatomy had become very largely a descriptive science; by restoring to it the study of the nervous system from development and growth to degeneration, Elliot Smith laid the foundation of a tradition of research on the brain and the lower nervous system at UCL that continues to produce striking experimental results. He is also remembered for his diffusionist anthropological theories on the development of culture – theories that, in their extreme form, led to the view that all culture was ultimately derived from ancient Egypt. Whatever the value of his theories, Elliot Smith made UCL a

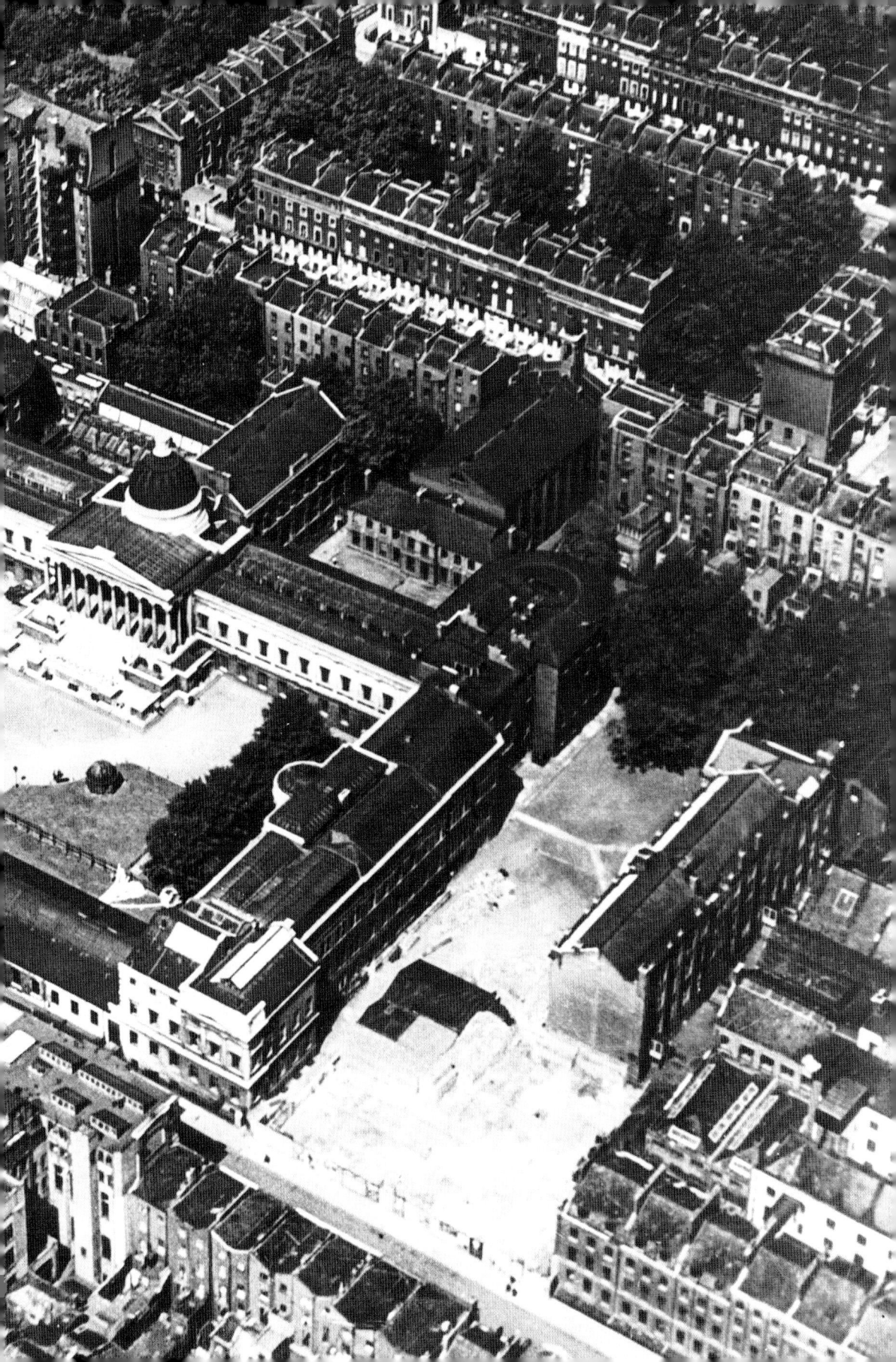

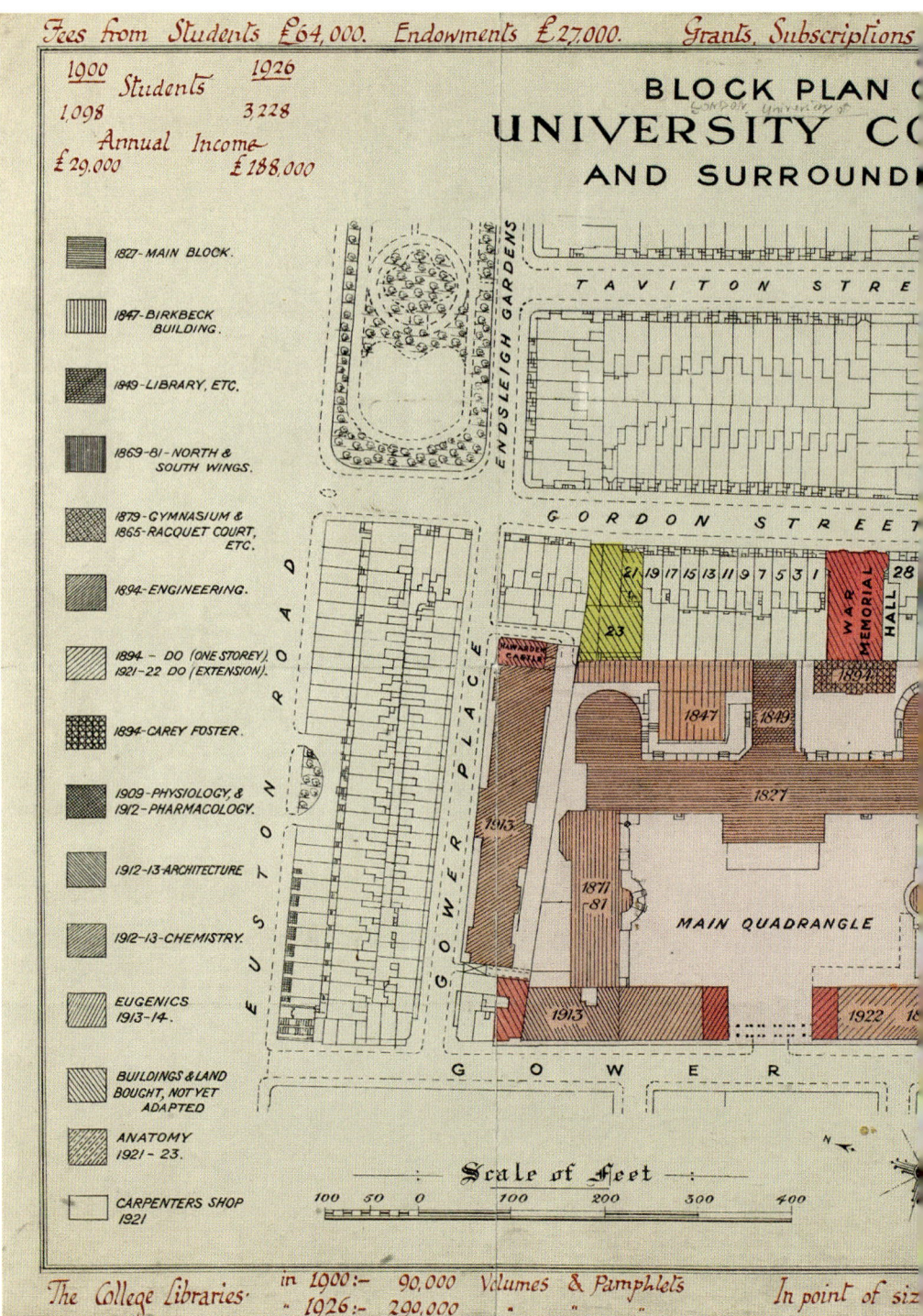

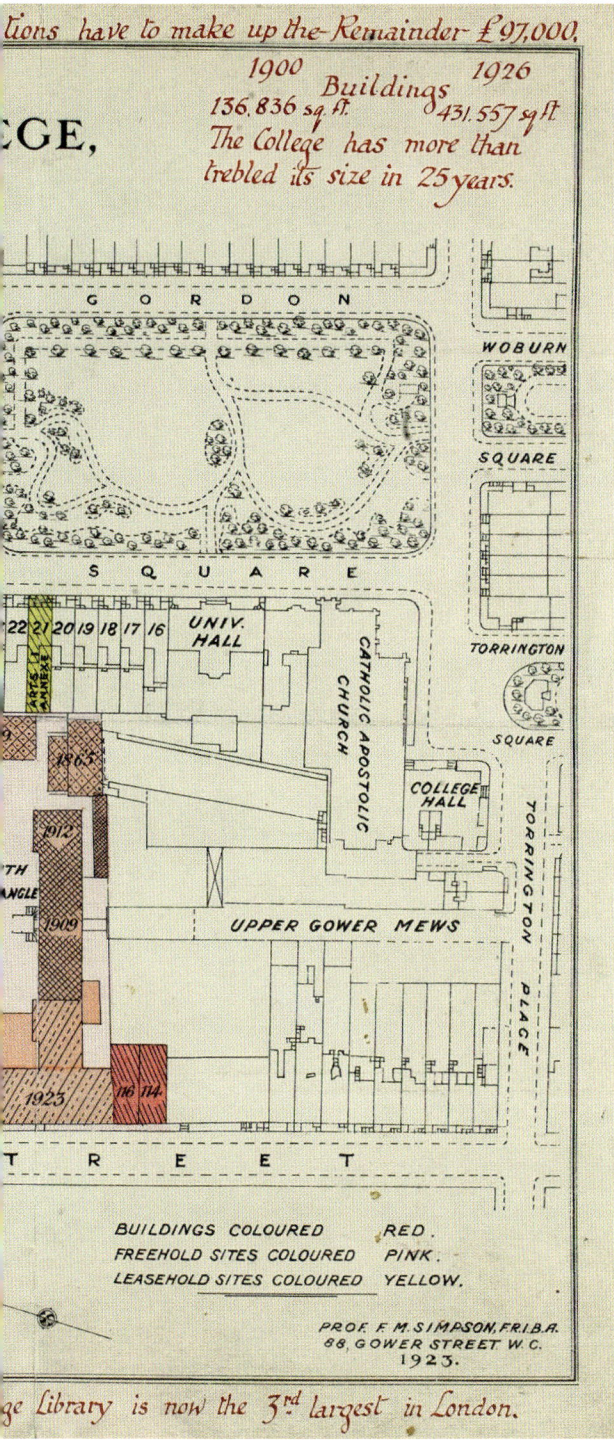

Fig. 5.20 A block plan of UCL prepared by F. M. Simpson in 1923, after his term as Professor of Architecture. It shows the distribution of the Departments shortly before the centenary, but is rather inconsistent in its dating of the various buildings.

Fig. 5.21 A. V. Hill, CH, FRS, Jodrell Professor of Physiology, on the occasion of his being awarded the Nobel Prize.

Fig. 5.22 Sir William Bragg, FRS, Professor of Physics, 1915–23, winner of the Nobel Prize for Physics in 1915.

centre for both physical and cultural anthropology, and the current Department of Anthropology descends from his work. Another branch of study that owes its origins to the growth of Anatomy in the 1920s is the History of Medicine – an active subject until 2013, when postgraduate degrees were withdrawn.

In Physiology, Starling's successor when he gave up the Jodrell Chair was A. V. Hill (Fig. 5.21). Soon after his arrival Hill received the Nobel Prize for his work on the energy cycle associated with the contraction of muscles. He held the Chair for only three years, but remained at UCL as a Royal Society Research Professor until his retirement in 1951. This relieved him of responsibility for teaching, and he developed a very influential research unit within Physiology; this unit worked on problems in the physics of muscle and nerve function and after his retirement became the Department of Biophysics. Hill was a public man, serving on many national and international bodies; he was also MP for the University of Cambridge during the war and President of the British Association in 1952. Charles Lovatt Evans succeeded Hill when he gave up the Jodrell Chair in 1926; he had for many years worked with Starling on the functioning of the heart and he continued the tradition of research in this area.

In the new Physiology building of 1909 there was already provision for 'chemical physiology', thanks to R. H. A. Plimmer, Assistant Professor and later Reader in what was then a new subject. He was succeeded in 1919 by J. C. Drummond, who became the first Professor of Biochemistry in 1922; predictably enough, the new Chair was funded by the Rockefeller Foundation. The Professor of Pharmacology, A. J. Clark, showed unprecedented generosity for a Head of Department in giving up some space to the new unit, and Pharmacology did not return to its 1912 boundaries until 1960, when Biochemistry moved on.

Drummond's interests lay in nutrition and especially in vitamins – in the analysis, identification and even naming of which he played a notable part. He always sustained a broad range of interests, which extended later to practical questions of nutrition policy and to the history of diet, on which subject he published *The Englishman's Food* in 1939. He was most successful in making his unit exercise an influence out of all proportion to its size. During the Second World War Drummond became Scientific Adviser to the Ministry of Food; after the war he resigned his Chair to become Director of Research for Boots. In 1952 he, his wife and daughter were murdered while camping in France, a sensational and unsolved crime.

Biochemistry was restored after the wartime chaos by Sir Frank Young, who created the independent Department in the subject. Between 1958 and 1961 it moved into its new quarters in the Biological Sciences building, by which time it was offering undergraduate as well as postgraduate courses.

A research school of Physics, in the sense in which it would be understood today, does not go back earlier than the twenties. It owes its origin to Sir William

Bragg (Fig. 5.22) and to his successors A. W. Porter, Professor of Physics, 1924–28, and Edward Neville da Costa Andrade. Bragg graduated from Cambridge in 1884 and soon afterwards went to Australia, where he held the Chair of Mathematics and Physics in Adelaide. He came back to Leeds in 1909 and moved to the Quain Chair at UCL in 1915. In the same year he received the Nobel Prize for Physics, jointly with his son, later Sir Lawrence Bragg. William Bragg had been quite unusual in starting serious research relatively late in his career. He was already in his forties when, in 1904, he began to be fascinated by the work then being done in the areas of radioactivity and X-rays. In particular, he and his son succeeded in establishing a technique for studying the arrangement of atoms in a crystal by the use of X-rays. This was basic work which helped to lay the foundations for the science of crystallography. Among Bragg's research students in this period at UCL was Kathleen Lonsdale. Andrade had studied physics at UCL in the 1900s and returned as Quain Professor of Physics 1928–50, where he worked with students on the viscosity of liquids and on the mechanical properties of metals. He was also a popular science writer and a regular on the BBC radio show *The Brain's Trust* during the 1940s.

Fig. 5.23 L. N. G. Filon, FRS, Professor of Applied Mathematics, 1912–37, Vice Chancellor of the University of London 1933–35, photographed in the Senior Common Room.

L. N. G. Filon was of French origin; he came to UCL as a student and became a faithful pupil of M. G. M. Hill and Karl Pearson. He became a Lecturer in Pure Mathematics in 1903, but worked on the theory of stresses (Fig. 5.23). After Pearson moved over to Eugenics, Filon succeeded him in the Chair of Applied Mathematics, which he held until 1937. He became progressively more of a figure in academic administration, acting as the first Director of the Mill Hill Observatory in 1929, becoming Vice-Chancellor of the University in 1933 and serving as Vice-President of the Royal Society in 1935–37. One of the most prolonged research projects the College had seen was the work pioneered by Filon, together with E. G. Coker (Fig. 5.24), on photo-elasticity between 1909 and 1934, and the resumed programme of research undertaken by their successors after the Second World War. In 1909 Coker was head of the Engineering Department at Finsbury Technical College and Filon still a lecturer in Pure Mathematics at UCL. Filon had worked on elasticity in connection with the bending of beams. He was much impressed by a paper jointly authored by Coker, which suggested that the use of xylonite models would allow the stresses in engineering components to be studied by optical techniques. Filon

Fig. 5.24 E. G. Coker, FRS, Professor of Civil and Mechanical Engineering, 1914–34, photographed with his photoelasticity students in 1919.

supplied the theory, Coker the practical application. In 1912 Filon, as Professor of Applied Mathematics, obtained his own laboratory; two years later Coker became a Professor at UCL and Head of the Department of Civil and Mechanical Engineering for 20 years (Fig. 5.25). He too set up a photo-elastic laboratory which worked in parallel – sometimes uneasily – with Filon's.

Their joint publication *Treatise on Photo-elasticity* (1931) was the most authoritative account of the subject possible at that date. Coker, however, failed to convince industry of the viability of his new methods. When he retired in 1934 his laboratory was virtually abandoned and, on the outbreak of war, completely dismantled. After the war new advances in the technique made in the USA, together with a new interest in British industry, caused the programme to be resumed. Coker's laboratory was reconstructed, and a new research group created under H. J. Jessop.

The Faculty of Arts

Two fundamental changes affected the Faculty of Arts in the years after incorporation into the University: the rise of the 'Honours' degree, which enabled students to specialise, and the proper funding of salaries, which enabled Professors to become full-time. The teaching of History especially was revolutionised. From 1896 the Honours degree in the subject was available, and from 1905 the 'internal' Honours degree in the reorganised University. The moving spirit in the ensuing transformation was not F. C. Montague, Beesly's successor in the Chair of History, 1893–1927, but the redoubtable Tudor historian A. F. Pollard (Fig. 5.26). In 1903 there was a vacancy in the Chair of Constitutional Law and History, and the two outstanding candidates were Pollard and W. S. (later Sir William) Holdsworth. The appointing committee hit on the idea of splitting the Chair into two and taking both men. 'Why not?' suggested the presiding genius. 'There is no stipend for either, and it will cost the College no more to have two chairs than one.'

Pollard had worked in the 1890s as Assistant Editor of the *Dictionary of National Biography*, and his involvement in that great exercise in co-operative scholarly organisation proved formative. It provided the model for his postgraduate seminar and the germ of the Institute of Historical Research, which he founded in 1921. Pollard was also the architect of two other important developments in the subject: he created the School of History and, at a meeting in UCL in 1906, he founded the Historical Association as a forum for the teachers of the expanding subject. Ten years later he became first editor of its journal, *History*. For many years from 1950,

Fig. 5.25 The assembled staff and students of the Engineering Department during the First World War.

Fig. 5.26 A. F. Pollard, FBA, Professor of Constitutional History, 1903–07, of English History 1907–27, and then, while Director of the Institute of Historical Research, again Professor of Constitutional History.

two years after his death, Pollard was commemorated, in a way that would have shocked him, in the *Pollardian* – an irreverent journal of the History students.

The study of German was placed on a firm academic footing by Robert Priebsch, the correct but kind Austrian who held the chair of German for 33 years from 1898. Priebsch was a medievalist with a consuming passion for manuscripts; his great published work was a catalogue of German manuscripts in England. In building up a notable Department of German, Priebsch was considerably aided by John G. Robertson, a modernist. Between 1903 and 1933 Robertson had held a chair of German shared with Bedford College; he also succeeded W. P. Ker at UCL as Director of Scandinavian Studies.

A conspicuous figure in Anglo-Italian life was Antonio Cippico, a writer and journalist who became a teacher of Italian before the First World War and Professor of Italian in 1918. A fervent and poetic Italian patriot, he was one of the earliest apostles of the fascist movement and founder of the Fascio of London; following Mussolini's march on Rome in 1922, he became a senator. For a few years Cippico combined his public duties in Rome with his teaching in London, but resigned in 1925 to become Italian delegate to the League of Nations.

Most of the teachers of Law, if distinguished, were transient figures in College, devoting themselves to their own professional careers. A more consistent presence, over the 42 years for which he was in post, was A. F. Murison, Professor of Roman Law from 1884 to 1925. A Scottish schoolmaster turned barrister, he worked tirelessly on the text of an early paraphrase of the Institutes of Justinian, written by a contemporary lawyer. A myth grew up around Murison, fostered by the *Dictionary of National Biography* article on him, but accepted elsewhere, including earlier editions of this book. He was supposed to have worked on the manuscripts of the Institutes themselves (he did not), learning every European language bar Turkish in the process and travelling everywhere, although Murison said himself he could not afford to do so. He claimed in fact that he was paid no more than £30 per annum during the first 30 years of his tenure of the Chair. Under the old system, phased out only in 1912, unendowed Professors were paid per student attending the course, at the rate of 5 shillings in the guinea from their fees. His successor, the far more successful H. F. Jolowicz, was guaranteed £800 per annum. This reform was to have profound effects on the nature and structure of academic life.

Fig. 5.27 The Front Quad in November 1927 during one of the greatest battles against the students of King's College.

'100 not out': UCL in the twenties

Student life in the interwar period was marked by much greater co-operation between men and women students. By the session 1925–26 women numbered 1,074 out of a total of 2,426 full-time students. An Inter-Union Standing Committee was set up in 1919 to take responsibility for joint activities such as producing the annual student handbook and College magazine, managing the Hard Tennis Court, running the Foundation Play and Dance and representing UCL at intercollegiate level through the University of London Union and the National Union of Students (NUS), formed in 1922. It also established a 'mixed lounge' for men and women students to socialise in, which by the late 1930s was caricatured as a sanctuary for 'Love Birds', who after about 5 pm could be found 'seated together in the welcome gloom'. Several College 'sing-songs' were held each year, and a College Song Book was first published in 1926.

The great age of rags spanned the period between the two world wars, although it was revived for a short period after the Second World War. It began before 1914, as can be seen from the jollifications involving the capture of Phineas (p.134). In the heyday of rags there were some great set-piece battles with King's. The target was Reggie, their lion mascot, while weapons included flour, sprays of water, mud, deception, furniture vans and debagging (Fig. 5.27). Annual bonfires and firework

displays on 5 November were a great institution too, until the Provost announced in 1952 that 'much to his regret he cannot sanction a bonfire in the Main Quadrangle this year'. The era of indulging in such escapades had begun to fade, and the original pressing need to raise money for hospitals in this way had passed.

The centenary of the College was celebrated in some style in June 1927 (Fig. 5.28). It was inaugurated by the visit of King George V and Queen Mary (Fig. 5.29) and included – inevitably – a new Appeal for funds, as well as the opening of the Great Hall, the receiving of delegates from universities throughout the world, a series of lectures, a variety of exhibitions and dinners, a centenary history of the College (Fig. 5.30) and a service of thanksgiving in Westminster Abbey. The Union Society quite reasonably objected to the sectarian nature of this last celebration, but the centenary as a whole was found an agreeable exercise in self-congratulation (Fig. 5.31). The king made an interesting and uncharacteristically controversial point in his speech, one that the press reported as producing cheers of an enthusiasm that broke royal protocol. 'The State', he said, 'now aids University Institutions

Fig. 5.28 The cover of the Rag Magazine produced on the occasion of the celebration of the College's centenary in 1927.

Fig. 5.29 (overleaf) George V and Queen Mary on their official visit in June 1927 to commemorate the centenary of the College.

Fig. 5.30 H. Hale Bellot, author of the definitive centenary history of the College. He was first Commonwealth Fund Professor of American History, 1930–55, and became Vice-Chancellor of the University of London, 1951–53.

on a scale which, to your founders, would have seemed impossible, but there are limits to public assistance. Moreover there is some danger to our national ideas of University freedom in too great reliance upon State grants'.

G. K. Chesterton, a former student, was in more characteristic mood for his lecture a few days later. 'It was at the Slade School', he claimed, 'that I discovered

Fig. 5.31 Enthusiastic undergraduates brandishing copies of the centenary Rag Magazine for sale.

Fig. 5.32 The dedication of the new Great Hall by Prince Arthur of Connaught in June 1927.

that I should never be an artist; it was at the lectures of Professor A. E. Housman that I discovered that I should never be a scholar; and it was at the lectures of Professor W. P. Ker that I discovered that I should never be a literary man. The warning, alas! fell on heedless ears, and I still attempted the practice of writing, which, let me tell you in the name of the whole Slade School, is very much easier than the practice of drawing and painting.' He went on, with perhaps a touch of exaggeration, to claim that the centenary was in fact that of the opening of the modern world.

The College had never had a Great Hall since the abandoning of the one originally planned by Wilkins. It was decided to remedy this by a suitable conversion of All Saints' Church, built by Donaldson in 1846 at the rear of the College. The building was in a dilapidated state when the College bought it in 1914. After the war it was agreed that it should also serve as a war memorial to those members of the College who had been killed. The reconstruction was finely undertaken by A. E. Richardson, the Professor of Architecture, and the opening constituted a major part of the centenary celebrations (Fig. 5.32). The Centenary Appeal was less successful. The aim was to raise £500,000, but such was the difficulty in deciding how it should be spent that the centenary had to be postponed from February 1926 to June 1927. As it turned out, the time chosen was one of deepening economic depression; by July 1930 less than half the expected total had been raised and the Appeal was closed.

One success that did result from the Appeal was the benefaction of Gustave Tuck, Treasurer and President of the Jewish Historical Society, for the rebuilding of the Mocatta Library and the provision of a new lecture theatre (Fig. 5.33). Much of the Mocatta Collection was destroyed in the Second World War, but the renewed library is now once again an important resource for the activities of the Department of Hebrew and Jewish Studies and for all students of Judaism.

In the week of the centenary celebrations, it was finally settled that the University of London should acquire a central headquarters site, to the south of UCL, after its years in Burlington House and in South Kensington. After complicated negotiations involving the Duke of Bedford, the government, William Beveridge and the Rockefeller Foundation, the scene was set for Senate House to rear its head in Bloomsbury.

Fig. 5.33 The Gustave Tuck Theatre as it then was, before its destruction in the Second World War.

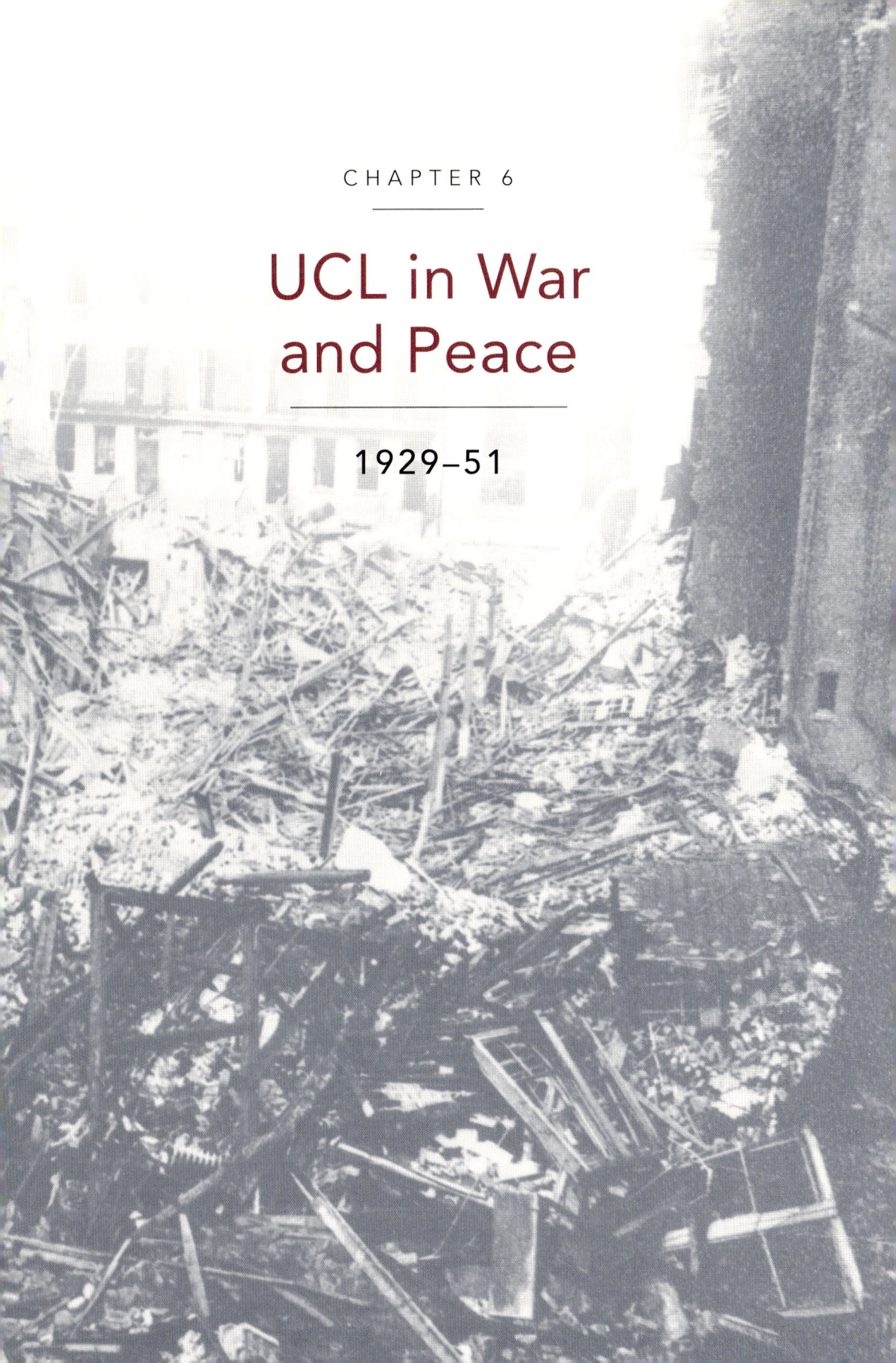

CHAPTER 6

UCL in War and Peace

1929–51

> The events of World War II threatened the survival of the College. Departments were scattered to ten different centres away from London. The historic buildings of the College were largely destroyed by enemy action, the extent of war damage being more severe than at all other university institutions in the country apart from medical schools. This is not the place to describe in detail the difficulties which resulted. Though much has been delayed, and though some departments have suffered frustrations and hard conditions, nothing in the spirit of the College or in its capacity to continue its major contributions in advanced studies has been destroyed.

Sir Ifor Evans in University College London [1956–1962] *(1962)*

A new era

The enormous popularity of Sir Gregory Foster as Provost was shown by the tumultuous reception he received in February 1926 on his return from a year's leave of absence in South Africa. Charabancs full of students provided an exuberant escort from his home to 'the largest number of students and staff ever gathered' in the Front Quad. There was much shouting of what had become – and was for some years to remain – the College chant:

> Foster, Foster, Gregory Foster,
> Gower Street, Gower Street, UCL.

While he had been away, his duties had been carried out by a triumvirate of Pro-Provosts: Walter Seton, the Secretary; H. E. Butler, the Professor of Latin; and Col. H. J. Harris, the Senior Tutor – known collectively as 'the world, the flesh and the devil'. Less than a year later, on the eve of the centenary celebrations which he had done much to plan, Seton died suddenly. He was succeeded by C. O. G. Douie, an extremely able administrator from the Ministry of Education and a civilised man of wide interests and tastes (Fig. 6.1).

Fig. 6.1 C. O. G. Douie, Secretary of the College, 1927–38, in conversation with Hugh Gaitskell in the Senior Common Room.

Fig. 6.2 Sir Allen Mawer, FBA, Foster's successor as Provost, 1930–42.

Fig. 6.3 The pre-war Ramsay Memorial Laboratory of Chemical Engineering.

Fig. 6.4 The Pewterers' Gate, dating from 1668 and believed to have been designed by Sir Christopher Wren, is UCL's second oldest architectural feature. The Gate was removed from its original position at Pewterers' Hall in the City to its present site, at the rear of what is now the UCL Medawar Building, in 1932 by Sir Albert Richardson. It is one of the several 'follies' around the College buildings for which Richardson, Professor of Architecture at UCL, was responsible.

Fig. 6.5 A plan showing the pre-Second World War expansion of the College into most of the 'rectangle' bounded by Gower Street, Torrington Place, Gordon Street and Gower Place.

At the end of 1929 Foster retired as Provost to concentrate on being Vice-Chancellor of the University of London under its new Statutes. The second Provost was Sir Allen Mawer, a former graduate student of the College who had gone on to become Professor of English at Newcastle and then at Liverpool (Fig. 6.2). Mawer's great passion was English place names, and he did more than anyone to put their study on a rigorous basis (p.192).

The major innovation in the Faculty of Engineering between the wars was the creation of the Department of Chemical Engineering in 1923. The first Professor of the subject in the country was E. C. Williams who, after putting the Department on its feet, became Research Director for Shell in California. Both the new Chair and the laboratories that followed were a memorial to Sir William Ramsay, who had died in 1916 (Fig. 6.3). Half the money raised by the Memorial Fund was put towards the new Department, which also received substantial support from industry. The first temporary accommodation was opened in 1924 in the old St Pancras Vestry Hall; next door the site of 21 and 23 Gordon Street was being used for the building

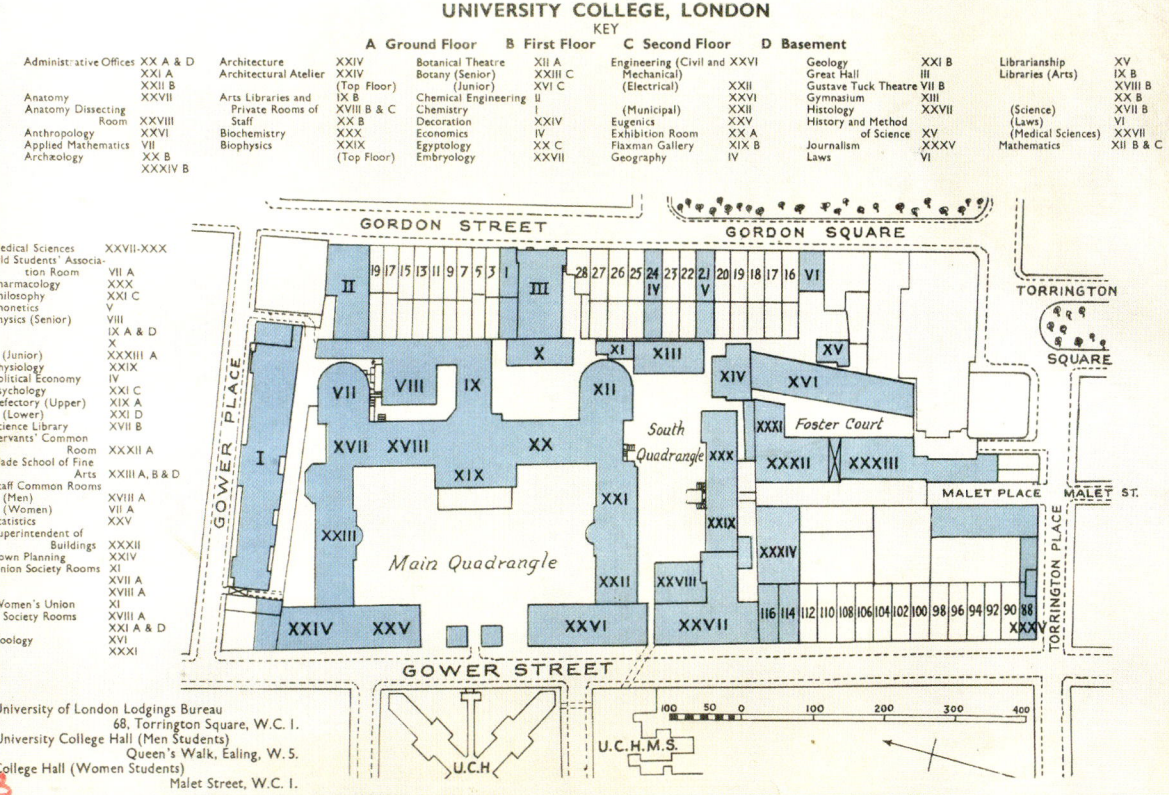

of completely new laboratories, designed by A. E. Richardson – the first of many College buildings for which he was to be responsible (Fig. 6.4). Postgraduate courses started from the beginning of the new Department, albeit with a good deal of improvisation; the undergraduate degree dates from 1938. The new laboratories, which opened in 1931, were to suffer severe bomb damage in the Second World War (Fig. 6.5).

Further expansion of the College buildings was made possible by the bankruptcy in the depression of the early 1930s of Shoolbreds, a once-famous department store in Tottenham Court Road. Their workshops and stables lay immediately to the south of the College site, and D. M. S. Watson decided that, suitably converted, they could contain adequate premises for the Department of Zoology and Comparative Anatomy which was outgrowing the quarters created for Lankester in the North Wing (Fig. 6.6). Since succeeding to the Jodrell Chair in 1921, Watson had nurtured plans for a Zoology expansion parallel to Elliot Smith's development of human biology in the enlarged Department of Anatomy. The Rockefeller Foundation provided another endowment for this purpose. The acquisition of Shoolbred's Mews in 1931 was more than half funded by the sale, in advance, of rather less than one-third of the buildings to the National Central Library, then being established with Carnegie money. In this skilful manoeuvre, the College's well-placed Highland connections were deftly deployed, as was, apparently, the necessary Talisker whisky over lunch. The rest of the utilitarian buildings, erected by Shoolbreds in the 1890s, were straightforwardly reconstructed as laboratories and teaching rooms by A. E. Richardson. Watson continued his important contributions to Zoology and Palaeontology until his retirement from the Jodrell Chair in 1951, and afterwards as an Honorary Research Associate (Fig. 6.7). His resignation in 1965 ended 53 years of continuous service to the College.

When the National Central Library building was re-acquired by the College in 1967, mainly for use as an annexe to the Library, it was renamed the 'D. M. S. Watson Library'. Both this and the western part of the Foster Court buildings, at that time housing the Departments of Geography, English, Scandinavian Studies and Egyptology (the latter in the former stables), were long overdue for replacement. Plans were drawn up by Anthony Cox in 1972 for a major redevelopment involving a large new School of Medicine as proposed by a Royal Commission chaired by Lord Todd in 1968. Much thought was given to these proposals in the 1970s, but eventually the government withdrew its funding. The subsequent building developments took place elsewhere; the Foster Court buildings continued to be adapted and re-adapted for use by various academic departments. This area of the campus is now known as Malet Place.

Fig. 6.7 D. M. S. Watson, FRS, Jodrell Professor of Zoology, 1921–51.

Developments in Psychology, Phonetics and Linguistics

In the earliest years of the College, John Conolly and John Elliotson as Professors of Medicine had taken an interest in psychological problems. However, the origins of a more systematic approach to the subject are to be found in the Department of Philosophy in the 1890s. James Sully, who succeeded Croom Robertson as Grote Professor, was in fact more of a psychologist than a philosopher. He was a prime mover in the creation of the British Psychological Society, founded at UCL in 1902. A laboratory for Experimental Psychology was established in 1897. Housed originally in a small room that doubled as a library store, it was the first such laboratory in the UK, which in this respect lagged behind Germany and the United States. The new laboratory was equipped with apparatus brought from Freiburg and put under the charge of W. H. Rivers, though he left after a year to take part in the famous Cambridge anthropological expedition to Torres Straits.

Fig. 6.6 The new quarters for the Department of Zoology created out of the former Shoolbreds' warehouse and mattress factory. They formed part of the addition to UCL named Foster Court, after Sir Gregory. He died just before the properties were acquired in 1931.

In 1903 William McDougall was made Reader in Experimental Psychology. However, significant work in the new subject really began in 1907 with his successor, the German-trained Charles Spearman, and with the move to more spacious quarters in the South Wing. Spearman became Grote Professor in 1911 and later, in 1928, the Chair of Psychology was established for him, by which point the lab had grown into a Department of Psychology. One of Spearman's earliest interests was in the concept of 'general intelligence' and in ways of measuring it through the application to psychological problems of the techniques of correlation developed by Galton and Pearson (Fig. 6.8). J. C. Flugel joined Spearman as his Assistant in 1909 and remained a member of the Department for virtually the rest of his life. He resigned as Assistant Professor of Psychology in 1943, finding life in wartime Aberystwyth intolerable, but became a Special Lecturer on the Department's return to London until his death ten years later in 1955. For many

Fig. 6.8 A cartoon showing members of staff in the Department of Psychology hunting for 'G' or 'General Intelligence', the origins of the concept of IQ. Featured are (left to right) S. J. F. Philpott, a member of staff from 1920 to 1950, Professor Spearman and J. T. Roper, the Department's technician.

Fig. 6.9 Sir Cyril Burt, FBA, Professor of Psychology, 1932–50.

Fig. 6.10 Daniel Jones, creator of a new Department as Professor of Phonetics, 1921–49.

years he gave pioneering lectures on Freudian psychoanalysis, and also wrote an interesting book on *The Psychology of Clothes*.

The lines of research opened up by Spearman were developed by his successor, Sir Cyril Burt, Professor of Psychology 1933–50 (Fig. 6.9). In 1913 Burt had been appointed by the London County Council to be the first official psychologist to an education authority; in 1924 he became Professor of Education at the Institute of Education, where he showed strong commitment to training educational psychologists. Burt conducted classic research on 'delinquent' and maladjusted children – research that involved his becoming for a time a member of a criminal gang who accepted him as 'Charlie the parson'. His work on intelligence testing was one of the influences on the re-organisation of secondary education after the 1944 Education Act, which saw the introduction of the 11 plus examination.

Burt's thesis that differences in intelligence are to a considerable extent genetic, and that general intelligence is a fixed and measurable entity, has become the focus of much controversy since his death in 1971. In the 1970s he was accused in the press of inventing not only some of his data, but also two mythical female collaborators, Margaret Howard and Jane Conway. While these charges were rejected at the time by his many admirers, subsequent research has confirmed the allegations of fraudulent scholarship.

The study of phonetics may be said to go back to the work of Alexander Melville Bell, who lectured on speech at UCL between 1866 and 1870 and who devised a phonetic script which he called 'visible speech'. He was assisted in his work by his son Alexander Graham Bell, then a student at the College and later the inventor of the telephone, but it was not until 1907 that systematic teaching began with the appointment of Daniel Jones (Fig. 6.10). At first the courses were under the auspices of the Departments of English and Modern Languages, and were mainly offered to those intending to become language teachers. Jones worked alone for ten years, but by 1918 the subject had expanded to include not only more and more languages but also the historical aspects of phonetics. Experimental Phonetics had also obtained a toe-hold with the creation of a small laboratory in 1911. With encouragement from Gregory Foster, the subject expanded rapidly after the First World War; by 1921 Jones had become its first Professor and there were nine full-time assistants. By the time Daniel Jones retired in 1949, he had created a thriving Department with a worldwide reputation.

The Department was afterwards enlarged to include Linguistics as well as Phonetics. The first step came in 1953 when the Communications Research Centre was set up as an experiment in interdisciplinary studies; it sought to involve linguists, biologists and all interested in any form of communication, both verbal and non-verbal. The enterprise was years ahead of its time, anticipating developments to be hailed as new and exciting a decade later in other universities. Its weakness was perhaps that it included too much; when M. A. K. Halliday was appointed Director in 1963, he recommended narrowing the focus to human communication. In 1965 the Department of Linguistics was created, including the Communications Research Centre; six years later, it was merged with Phonetics.

Allen Mawer's main academic work, which he sustained after becoming Provost, was the methodical survey of English place names. His initial interest came from his work on the Scandinavian influence on early England; from the inception of the English Place Names Society, which he inspired, he acted as its Director and was General Editor of its county by county survey. At UCL he found an energetic assistant in A. H. Smith, who came to the Department of English in 1930 and worked as one of its most devoted members for 37 years, becoming Quain Professor of English in 1949. Smith was the man who kept the Place Names Survey moving, so that it remained a very vigorous element in UCL. He also acted as Director of Scandinavian Studies and was an active secretary of the Communications Research Centre in its early days, fostering two areas that grew into independent departments in the course of the 1960s. It was also in his Department that the study of Medieval Archaeology was started by the appointment of D. M. Wilson, later Sir David and the Director of the British Museum from 1977 to 1992; the subject itself later moved into Scandinavian Studies, then into History and finally into the Institute of Archaeology after its merger with UCL.

Interwar politics and protest

National and international politics began to intrude significantly into student life from the late 1920s (Fig. 6.11). An International Society was started to promote discussion of international, political and economic relations and to bring international students together. Following the formation of the National Government in 1931 – widely seen on the Left as a betrayal of socialist principles – the Gower Socialist Society was one of a number of Marxist student societies founded at British universities (Fig. 6.12). The first official political students' club at UCL, it won recognition only after a battle with the College authorities, evolving into one of the most active student societies in the run up to the Second World War (Fig. 6.13). In common with universities

Fig. 6.11 A satirical cartoon from the University College Magazine of 1934. It depicts Mawer as Provost accompanied by R. W. Chambers and C. J. Sisson, Professors of English, defeating the growing political forces of the 1930s.

Fig. 6.12 A cartoon depicting students in the lower refectory, supposedly well known for its 'Bohemian atmosphere', as reproduced in UCL magazine *New Phineas* in 1939.

Fig. 6.13 A student demonstration in 1933 reveals the growing political influences of the period.

Fig. 6.14 Hugh Gaitskell, later leader of the Labour Party, taught economics at UCL between 1928 and 1939.

elsewhere, Armistice Day emerged as the focus of a growing antiwar movement in the early 1930s. On 11 November 1932 (a year before the more famous 'King and Country' debate at Oxford) UCL students passed the motion, by 101 votes to 47, 'In the event of the Government declaring war, the British student should not support the Government'. From 1936 the Union Lounges held regular collections of tinned foods and clothing for victims of the Spanish Civil War, and at least four UCL students served with the International Brigades in Spain. A Conservative Society was formed in the session 1938–39 in response to the view that 'socialist ideas are having an unchallenged sway in College'.

One member of the staff with strong political interests was Hugh Gaitskell (Fig. 6.14). He came as an Assistant in Political Economy in 1928 and rose to be Reader and acting Head of the Department, as well as Tutor to the Higher Civil Service students. He attended a dining club, the *Tots and Quots*, which met in Soho for scientific argument; it had been founded by G. P. (Gip) Wells, later Professor of Zoology. In 1945 Gaitskell was offered the Chair of Political Economy, but declined it in order to stand for Parliament. He became Chancellor of the Exchequer, 1950–51, and subsequently leader of the Labour Party until his premature death in 1963.

Gaitskell also served as Vice-Chairman of the UCL Co-operating Committee of International Student Service (ISS) – the body through which members of UCL raised money and offered support to refugee students fleeing Nazi persecution. Sir Bernard Katz was one of several such refugees to enrich the College's life. He came to UCL in 1935 to study for a PhD with A. V. Hill, subsequently becoming UCL's first Professor of Biophysics, 1952–78; in 1970 he won the Nobel Prize. UCL likewise supported the work of the Academic Assistance Council (later known as the Society for the Protection of Science and Learning) to support exiled research and teaching staff. In June 1933 the Professorial Board approved a set of provisions for the acceptance of such refugee academics, who were to be supported financially by philanthropic donations. It has been estimated that about 100 refugee scholars spent some time at UCL in the years before 1945; among them was Hans Kalmus, who left Prague in 1939 and eventually became Professor of Biology at the College.

Most of these exiles were scientists, but a few worked in the humanities. A. D. Momigliano, for example, came as an exile from fascist Italy; his prodigious writings weave a powerful counterpoint between the ancient world and the modern, between ideas and social reality, between historical problems and their historiography. In the years and months before the Second World War, the bleak international situation drove many College students to reflect on, and proudly articulate, the principles underlying their education. In September 1939 an editorial in the College magazine *New Phineas* boldly declared:

> War or no war there must be no sacrifice of culture ... We as students will always be ready to fight for liberty and for democracy. First then we must protect our student liberty and be prepared to fight for democracy in the Universities. War or no war we shall demand the perpetuation of our cultural heritage. U.C. students will be in the vanguard of this demand.

The College tradition of producing the cycle of 'Little Plays of St Francis' – written by Laurence Housman, the brother of A. E. Housman – began in 1925 at the suggestion of Walter Seton. They became an annual event for the Dramatic Society until 1950. The *University College Magazine* noted in 1938 that 'unless you have seen the Little Plays you can hardly claim to know the college'. Housman himself was closely involved, granting the College the right to produce the plays free of royalty. In 1937 a performance was televised and UCL's Dramatic Society became the first amateur group to appear on television.

Fig. 6.15 J. B. S. Haldane in 1941 sitting at his desk

J. B. S. Haldane, who took his forenames from John Burdon Sanderson, his great-uncle, came to UCL as Professor of Genetics in 1933 and became the first Weldon Professor of Biometrics in 1937 (Fig. 6.15). He had made his name by a series of papers showing mathematically how Darwin's theory would actually work in terms of Mendelian genetics. Haldane was regarded by many as a near-genius. He was also famous as one of the great popularisers of science, and moreover he had already shown his splendid patrician pugnacity against all forms of imposed authority. Throughout the 1930s his politics moved leftwards; he began a remarkable series of scientific articles in the *Daily Worker*, though he did not actually join the Communist Party until 1942. His highest public fame came over the Lysenko controversy when he stubbornly defended the Party's line, despite private misgivings about both Lysenko's theories and the Stalinist regime's exploitation of them.

Haldane's achievement as a scientific theoretician was formidable, but his achievement as Professor at UCL was limited by his own perversity. Cantankerous to a degree, he became notorious for mismanaging business, terrorising secretaries and abusing administrators. In 1958 he made an improbable, though in the event successful, move to India. The departure was vintage Haldane, complete with bogus political motive (revulsion at the Suez adventure, though he had in fact already decided to go), allegations of bad faith by the College (promises made to him about the development of his Department had, he claimed, never been fulfilled) and a silly little scandal (his second wife Helen Spurway, once a student, later a lecturer in the Department, insisted on going to prison after an incident outside the Marlborough Arms in which she trod on a police dog's tail). Haldane's stature as a scholar survives all the aberrations; the College honours his memory in the Haldane Room, today a meeting room that served for a time as the Joint Staff Common Room.

College servants

In any history of UCL the College Servants – including Beadles, stewards, porters, housekeepers and the so-called 'morning women' – who kept UCL running day to day should not be forgotten. Since the late nineteenth century there had been social clubs and outings for these staff members (Fig. 6.16), and in the 1930s the Servants' Association ran its own magazine (Fig. 6.17). The students organised annual collections for servants' Christmas 'boxes' and held parties for servants' children each year. Easiest of all to distinguish were the Beadles, who wore a traditional uniform complete with a top hat. Beadles were originally responsible

Fig. 6.16 The College Servants' Association on one of its earliest annual outings in the 1890s.

for maintaining order and discipline in College, but by the twentieth century their role had shifted somewhat to ensuring the smooth running of the College. They were held in high regard. Beadles staffed the main lodge, ran the post and locker system and acted as toastmasters at dinners; each faculty also had its own Beadle, who sat in a 'Beadle box'. Ron, the much-loved Union Beadle of the 1960s and 1970s, was, in his own words, 'matchmaker, bouncer, book-keeper and bookmaker'. In the twenty-first century the tradition survives only in the Beadle who leads graduation processions.

Fig. 6.17 The front cover of the College Servants' Association Magazine.

UCL in exile: the Second World War

The Second World War did more damage to UCL than to any other British university or college. In September 1940 a bomb hit the buildings, entirely destroying the Great Hall and the Carey Foster Physics Laboratory (Fig. 6.18). The Gustave Tuck and the Applied Mathematics Theatres were gutted, as was the Library north of the Dome. Serious damage was also done to other parts of the building. In April 1941 another air raid led to considerable destruction by fire of the main building south of the Dome, and of the Dome itself.

The academic work of the College had already been dispersed. The crisis of 1938 had led to arrangements being made for evacuation (Fig. 6.19). In 1939 new entrants

Fig. 6.18 The site of the Great Hall and the Carey Foster Physics Laboratory after the bombing of September 1940.

were refused and the Departments immediately scattered to Aberystwyth, Bangor, Cardiff, Swansea, Sheffield, Southampton, Oxford, Cambridge and Rothamsted in Hertfordshire (Fig. 6.20). The Faculty of Medical Sciences was subsequently reunited at Leatherhead, and an administrative headquarters was formed at Stanstead Bury, near Ware, in Hertfordshire. The much reduced College continued in this extraordinarily far-flung way for the duration of the war. A College magazine, *New Phineas*, was founded to attempt to 'unite the scattered *ethos* of U. C.'; its first edition was illustrated by a cartoon of a Beadle looking around glumly for any sign of students (Fig. 6.21).

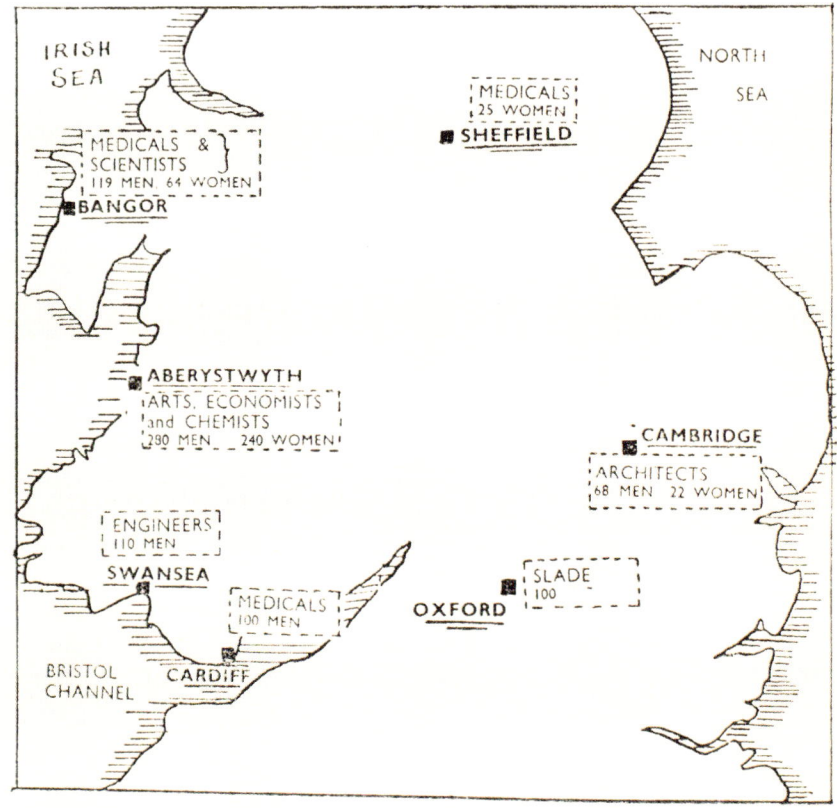

Fig. 6.19 A map showing the distribution of UCL students during the Second World War evacuation.

Fig. 6.20 (overleaf) Arts students in exile in Bangor during the Second World War.

Fig. 6.21 A cartoon from student magazine *New Phineas* in 1939. It portrays a Beadle on the lookout for students in the evacuated UCL.

Fig. 6.22 Bartlett students in Cambridge in 1943. Professors H. O. Corfiato and Sir Albert Richardson are seated in the front row.

The decision to clear the College buildings was not taken without opposition. J. B. S. Haldane was in his element when he refused to budge; he continued his work for a time, 'subject' as he reported gleefully, 'to a certain amount of siege by the College authorities'. The Library suffered most drastically from the air raids. Its manuscripts and rare books were evacuated to the solid rock cellars of the National Library of Wales at Aberystwyth, but some 100,000 books and pamphlets were destroyed as a result of the 1940 attack. The heaviest losses were to the Science Library, the English, German, Scandinavian and Phonetics collections, and the Mocatta Library. John Wilks, the Librarian from 1926 to 1954, had been a pupil of Robert Priebsch, the Professor of German, himself a noted bibliophile; together they had built up the best working library of German scholarship outside the German-speaking countries. It is ironic that this was one of the collections largely destroyed. Towards the end of the war all the main College deeds were flooded at Stanstead Bury; still preserved in the College safe, they have formed an unreadable solid mass ever since. Fortunately Jeremy Bentham spent the war safely in Stanstead Bury before returning to Gower Street in 1946.

The difficulties of life for the remaining students and staff in the dispersed elements of the College were considerable. In Physics, for example, sent to the University College of North Wales at Bangor, there were various demarcation disputes with the host department. It became necessary for Orson Wood, the Tutor to Science students, to improvise a laboratory in a converted bicycle shop in the High Street, blocking up the windows so that students could work unobserved by passers-by. Soon after the Faculty of Engineering moved to Swansea, the students claimed that their lodgings were disturbed by so many air raids that they might as well move back to less makeshift accommodation in London. There were some compensations, however, such as the 'attractive and interesting' Cardiff women students who did not go unnoticed by the Londoners.

In Oxford the Slade was amalgamated with its 'half-sister', the Ruskin Drawing School, under the joint direction of Randolph Schwabe as Slade Professor and Albert Rutherston, the Ruskin Master of Drawing who was himself, like his brother Sir William Rothenstein, a former Slade student. The Slade students, predominantly women, were considered to have contributed much to the gaiety of Oxford during the grim war years; students from The Bartlett were accommodated in Cambridge (Fig. 6.22). In this war, as in the last, many of the official war artists were former Slade students. They included Paul Nash, Percy Wyndham Lewis, Stanley Spencer, Christopher Nevinson, Rosemary Allan, Leila Faithfull and Ray Howard-Jones.

Fig. 6.23 Bombing raids in the Second World War caused huge damage to UCL. This photograph shows the gutted South Cloisters in April 1941.

R. W. Chambers visited the students in exile in Aberystwyth and Bangor. He gave them brilliant lectures on the history of the College, but, on the way to deliver another such lecture in Swansea, he collapsed and died – it was said of a broken heart following the destruction of so much of the Library he had created and of the College he had loved. Sir Allen Mawer died a few weeks later in 1942, on his way from Stanstead Bury to a committee meeting in London. He had suffered from the strain of much travelling in his efforts to hold the scattered fragments of the College together. However, the war did present new opportunities for some, notably women. The President of the Women's Union, for example, urged students to seize these unprecedented wartime opportunities and regretted that women had let men take the lead in student prewar life. Many thousands of UCL students and staff, past and present, served in the armed forces and on nursing, civil defence and other war duties. The College's Second World War Roll of Honour, unveiled in the library on 11 November 1952, lists 173 who lost their lives in the conflict.

Reconstruction

Dr David (later Sir David) Pye became Provost in 1943 of a deserted and ruinous College in which 'there was hardly a square foot of glass' (Fig 6.23). He was an engineer with a considerable academic and administrative reputation. In Cambridge he had done innovative work on the internal combustion engine and, as Director of Scientific Research for the Air Ministry, on the development of jet propulsion. Pye proceeded to nurse the College through an extremely difficult move back to the blitzed buildings and the planning of its postwar rebuilding. 'Refectory accommodation in 1939 was totally inadequate,' propounded the first plan for reconstruction, produced in June 1943. 'Common Rooms were equally so and were inconveniently scattered. It is regarded as an essential feature of the replanned College that the amenity accommodation shall be conveniently grouped round a central position.' These confident hopes of 1943 were never to be realised in the postwar world.

The first step in providing accommodation for the College after the return to its ruined buildings in 1945 was the construction of concrete huts in every available gap. Four were built in the Front Quad. Two were for the Union, which proposed naming them 'Cripps Cottage' and 'Bentham Bungalow'; they were used for debates, chamber music concerts and a full range of revived student activities. Other huts in Foster Court and on the bombsites to the rear of the college housed the Refectory, the Library and several academic departments. Once economic

Fig. 6.24 Sir Albert Richardson, Professor of Architecture, 1919–46.

conditions permitted, the main building was finely restored and improved by Sir Albert Richardson (Fig. 6.24). H. O. Corfiato, Professor of Architectural Design, 1937–46, and subsequently Professor of Architecture, 1946–60, also contributed to the College's rebuilding activity (Fig. 6.25). However, it was not until 1951 that the General Library was re-opened, and the building as a whole was only fully re-occupied in 1954.

Despite all the material difficulties, the academic work of the College was rapidly resumed after the war. The Mathematics Department of 1949, run by the outstanding Harrie Massey (p.239), included many future eminent Professors at UCL (Fig. 6.26), among them M. J. Seaton, FRS (first right, front row), L. Castillejo, FRS (first left, third row), C. A. Rogers, FRS (third from right, third row) and Sir Robert Boyd, FRS (third from left top row); Egon S. Pearson, son of Karl Pearson and Professor of

Fig. 6.25 H. O. Corfiato, Professor of Architectural Design, 1937–46 and of Architecture, 1946–60, photographed in the Senior Common Room after the war.

Fig. 6.26 The Department of Mathematics in 1949 when Massey was still its head.

Statistics, 1935–60 (Fig 6.27), also taught in the Department over many years. Among UCL's other long-serving staff were J. W. Jeaffreson, an inspiring teacher of French from 1919 to 1949 (Fig. 6.28), Sir Christopher Ingold, FRS, Professor of Chemistry 1930–61 and N. Eumorfopoulos, demonstrator and research assistant in Physics from 1884 to 1942 (he served in an honorary capacity for the last 22 years). In 1949 Kathleen Lonsdale, the crystallographer who in 1945 had been one of the first two women to be elected to the Fellowship of the Royal Society, was appointed as the first woman Professor at UCL (Fig. 6.29); she remained Professor of Chemistry there until 1968. A Quaker and committed pacifist, Lonsdale had refused to register for civil defence during the war; she served a month in Holloway prison for refusing to pay the fine for this. Lonsdale returned to UCL in 1946 and was made a Dame of the British Empire in 1956, also becoming the first female president of the British Association for the Advancement of Science in 1967.

The great Tudor historian Sir John Neale, Pollard's effective successor since 1927, powerfully continued to dominate the Department of History (Fig. 6.30). His *Queen Elizabeth* (1934) remains one of the greatest of all historical biographies, painstakingly researched yet fresh. Neale was also a popular College figure – the first edition of the *UCL Student's Song Book* (1926) was dedicated to him. In other Departments new heads were appointed to build up their subjects: the philosopher

Fig. 6.27 E. S. Pearson, FRS, Professor of Statistics, 1935–60. The son of Karl Pearson, he was one of the three men it took to succeed 'K.P.' in his various fields.

A. J. Ayer, for example, and H. C. Darby, whose great work was the reconstruction of the geography of eleventh-century England from the Domesday Book. A new Chair of Anthropology was established for Daryll Forde while the Elliot Smith tradition of research was continued by N. A. Barnicot, who later became the country's first Professor of Physical Anthropology. In Town Planning Lord Holford (as he was to become) succeeded Sir Patrick Abercrombie, who had produced notable reports on the planning of Greater London; Holford himself was the planning consultant for the City of London's postwar rebuilding.

Student life also revived postwar, as the activities of clubs, societies and intervarsity sports resumed; the launching of a new college newspaper Pi, in February 1946, was a deliberate attempt to weld together various student interests. The Department of English helpfully possessed a printing press (Fig. 6.31). On 1

Fig. 6.28 J. W. Jeaffreson, who taught French at UCL, 1919–49.

Fig. 6.29 The crystallographer Dame Kathleen Lonsdale, FRS, Professor of Chemistry, 1949–68.

Fig. 6.30 Sir John Neale, FBA, Astor Professor of English History, 1927–56, photographed in the Senior Common Room in the later 1940s.

April 1946 the Men's and Women's Unions were amalgamated into a new joint Union (Fig. 6.32). Hannah Steinberg, the outgoing Vice-President of the Women's Union Society and 'probably the most well-known person in College, after the porter at the gate', served as Acting President of the joint Union during the period of transition (Fig. 6.33).

One of the first initiatives of the new union was an exchange programme with the University of Tübingen in the French zone of Germany; exchanges of correspondence, literature and student delegations were part of UCL's contribution to the de-Nazification process. The Union's religious societies were particularly active in the postwar years – perhaps surprisingly, 'considering the ungodly reputation of the College' – and the now-famous UCL Film Society was also formed in 1948. The first all-night ball since the war began was held in March 1950 in a hall in Leyton that could accommodate 1,000 dancers. A new Tutor to Women Students, Miss Eleanor Megaw, was appointed to fill a post that had been vacant for some time. In 1959 the old Seaman's Hospital in Gordon Street was converted to create a new, supposedly temporary home for the Students' Union – a base it has never in fact left.

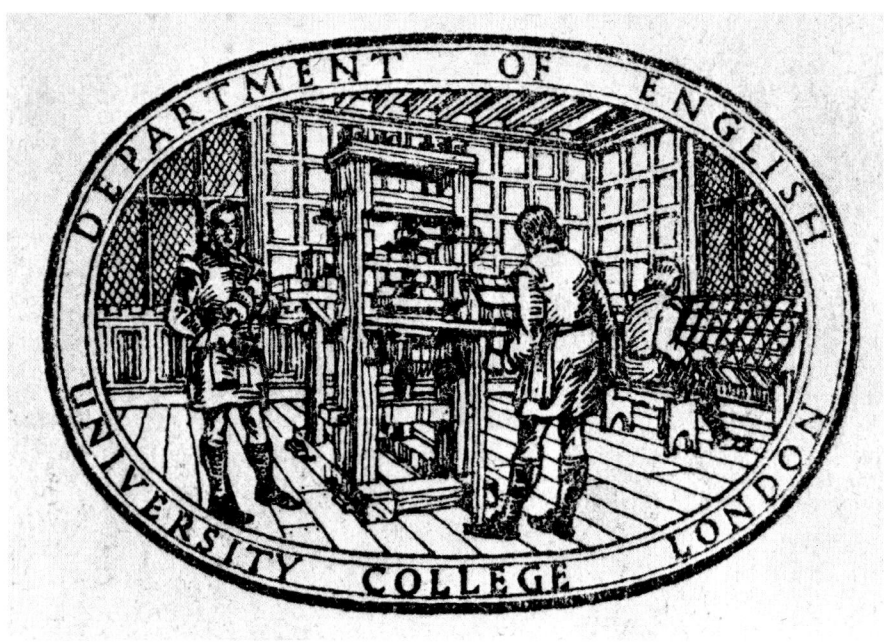

Fig. 6.31 A colophon from the printing press in the Department of English.

Fig. 6.32 The last committee of the Women's Union Society prior to its amalgamation with the all-male Union Society to form 'The Union' in 1946.

Fig. 6.33 This cartoon from *Pi*, the student newspaper named after Sir David Pye, depicts Hannah Steinberg, Vice-President of the Women's Union Society. She served as Acting President of the joint Union and later became Professor of Pharmacology. Steinberg played an important role in supporting other women academics at UCL in the 1970s and 1980s.

CHAPTER 7

The Evans and Annan Years

1951–78

> The leafless trees in Gordon Square stood black and gaunt against the facade of Georgian houses. The sky was cold and grey. It looked like snow. I hunched my shoulders inside my coat and set off briskly in the direction of the English department … Access to the English Department was through a small courtyard at the rear of the College. There seemed to be a lot of young people about, and I had to linger some moments before I caught the eye of Jones, the Beadle. I always make a point of catching the eye of beadles, porters and similar servants. Jones did not disappoint me: his face lit up.
>
> 'Hallo, sir. Haven't seen you for some time.'
> 'Come to see Mr. Briggs, Jones. There seem to be a lot of people about?'
> 'Undergraduates, sir,' he explained.
>
> *David Lodge,* The British Museum is Falling Down *(1965)*

Sir Ifor Evans

In 1951 Sir David Pye retired as Provost owing to ill health. He was succeeded by Sir Ifor Evans (Fig. 7.1), who was destined to preside over UCL in a period that saw rapid growth and change on an even greater scale than that witnessed in the Gregory Foster era. Sir Ifor Evans had himself been a student of English at the College in 1917; he had led an active subsequent career as Professor of English at Southampton and Sheffield, as Education Director of the British Council during the war and as Principal of Queen Mary College after it. For 15 years Evans was to devote himself to UCL and its many problems of overcrowding and rebuilding at a time when national policy was demanding still further expansion. He faced all the difficulties fairly and firmly, displaying a patience, tact and charm that minimised disappointment following difficult decisions. He was not only much admired in the College, but also much loved. He did this while remaining a well-known literary critic, writer and broadcaster, as well as serving the *Observer*, the Arts Council and a good many other advisory bodies.

In the fine 'testimonial' presented to Sir Ifor Evans on his retirement in 1966, signed by nearly a thousand of his colleagues, he was addressed as 'an outstanding

Fig. 7.1 Sir Ifor Evans, later Lord Evans of Hungerford, the fourth Provost, 1951–66, as painted by Sir William Coldsteam. The portrait took 73 sittings over two years and Evans later confessed that he had wondered if he would live to see it completed.

benefactor to the College, not only by your power to shape and order its affairs, but, to a singular degree, by being the cause of benefactions in others'. The government, through war damage compensation and through the University Grants Committee (UGC), provided substantial sums for the acquisition of property and for new buildings. But a good deal of the money for the expansion of the 1950s and 1960s had to be raised in the traditional way, through appeals and gifts. In Evans' day

Fig. 7.2 The steel framework under construction for the large new Engineering Building designed by H. O. Corfiato, Professor of Architecture, 1946–60.

Figs 7.3a and 7.3b The new refectory, opened in 1961, and The Lower Refectory, extended later in the brutal concrete of the post-Richardson phase of the College's rebuilding.

this flow was faster than ever. The first appeal, coinciding with the centenary of Sir William Ramsay's birth, provided for a new storey on the Chemistry building. The second brought in £400,000 from industry for the Engineering Building on Torrington Place (Fig. 7.2). Lord Marks gave £160,000 towards a new refectory and the start of the Central Collegiate Building. Lord Samuel gave another £100,000; the Wolfson Foundation gave generously too; and through these and other benefactions the College's facilities and its accommodation for students began to be revolutionised. The new refectory opened in 1961, a welcome change from the 'austere air-raid shelter appearance' of the former facilities (Figs 7.3a and 7.3b). Some of the postwar huts (Fig. 7.4) were demolished to make way for the Central Collegiate Building, opened in 1968. The rest were not demolished until 1990.

The Arts at UCL

The Faculty of Arts followed a very different course from that of Science during the decades after the Second World War. It was larger than other Faculties, consisting by the late 1980s of 21 Departments, varying considerably in size (Fig. 7.5). Of these,

Fig. 7.4 A characteristic view of UCL during the early 1960s showing postwar huts. Some of these were later demolished to make way for the Central Collegiate Building, but the rest were not removed until 1990.

Fig. 7.5 The strawberry tea in the Front Quad on the occasion of the Assembly of Faculties in 1962. This annual gathering occurred every year between 1908 and 1966, apart from those in the Second World War. It was merged with the Union's Foundation Week in 1966.

some had already gone over to the Course Unit system or to some other form of College-based degree, while others still strove to maintain the traditional University of London Final Examination, together with intercollegiate teaching. The Faculty of Arts also retained, to a far greater degree than elsewhere in College, the tradition of individual (rather than group) research projects. The achievements of some of its more prominent members, therefore, give a flavour of its character.

T. B. L. Webster, a brilliant and prolific writer on the relations of art and literature in ancient Greece, was the founder of the University's Institute of Classical Studies; he must take credit also for offering Michael Ventris his only academic post as Honorary Research Associate in Greek after the latter's revolutionary discovery that Linear B tablets were written in an early form of Greek. Daryll Forde, originally a geographer who migrated to prehistoric archaeology and thence to social anthropology, created a Department of Anthropology. This reflected in its structure Forde's own range of interests; it was unique in offering to undergraduates courses in material culture as well as both physical and social anthropology.

A second great age for the Department of Egyptology began with the appointment of W. B. Emery as Professor in 1951. His digs in Saqqara, the necropolis of Memphis, led to the discovery of the sacred ibises, falcons, baboons and the mothers of the Apis bull. Emery's excavations were extended by his successors H. S. Smith, who worked on the temple complexes of the gods Anubis and Bastet, and G. T. Martin, who discovered the tombs of the General Horemheb and of Tutankhamun's treasurer, Maya. Meanwhile Sir Eric Turner, Professor of Papyrology, 1950–78, was the only Professor of the subject in the UK at the time (Fig. 7.6). He inspired and organised a methodical publication of the papyri discovered in Oxyrrhynchus in Egypt, thus transforming knowledge of the comic playwright Menander of Athens, whose works had been lost since antiquity. The Department became part of the Institute of Archaeology in 1993. It remains a leading centre for research and teaching in the archaeology and cultural heritage of Egypt and the Middle East, albeit with a greater sensitivity to the contemporary circumstances of the region – including the legacy of colonialism and the ethical challenges of archaeological research – than was previously shown.

Brian Woledge, appointed Fielden Chair of French in 1939, was the man responsible for widening the Department's range to include Renaissance and twentieth-century studies; his own work on early medieval literature was a pioneering application of computer analysis to the study of medieval texts. The Department of History developed an impressive range of interests. Following in Pollard's footsteps, two more specialist Institutes were generated in the 1960s – one for Latin America Studies, inspired by R. A. Humphreys, the first Professor of Latin American History, and one for United States Studies, under H. C. Allen,

Fig. 7.6 Sir Eric Turner, FBA, Professor of Papyrology 1950–78, was at the time the only Professor of the subject in the UK.

Fig. 7.7 A. D. Momigliano KBE, FBA, Professor of Ancient History, 1951–75. His wide interests were reflected in his work, celebrated for the correspondences it perceived between past and present, ideas and social reality.

Fig. 7.8 Sir William Coldstream, Slade Professor of Fine Art, 1949–75.

Fig. 7.9 The Slade Antique Room, a vital teaching tool for generations, was abolished in the 1960s to reflect changing fashions in art teaching.

Hale Bellot's successor as Commonwealth Fund Professor of American History. Alfred Cobban, a member of the Department from 1937 until his death in 1968, dealt lucidly and memorably with modern French history and political ideas. The prodigious writings of A. D. Momigliano, Professor of Ancient History, 1951–75, provided a powerful counterpoint between the ancient world and the modern, between historical problems and their historiography (Fig. 7.7).

Sir William Coldstream, Slade Professor from 1949 to 1975, had been a Slade student himself in the late 1920s (Fig. 7.8). After a period in film production, he joined with Claude Rogers and Victor Pasmore to found the influential Euston Road School in 1937. As a painter, Coldstream is best known for portraits showing the scrupulous concern for empirical observation that is the hallmark of the Slade tradition (Fig. 7.9). As Professor, however, tolerance and open-mindedness were the key words, and the School's work broadened to include new studies and a wider range of styles and experiments. Sculpture already had an established tradition, to which Reg Butler as Director of Studies between 1966 and 1981 added (Fig. 7.10). However, but among the developments in Coldstream's time were postgraduate work in many areas, new facilities for wood, metal and photographic work and the extension of a full range of print-making facilities. In 1960 UCL became the first university in England to have a unit specifically dedicated to the study of film, headed by Thorold Dickinson. In the 1970s the Slade also became a leader in integrating computers into the art curriculum.

Meanwhile, as a committee man of wholly individual and quite devastating style, Coldstream became widely known and loved inside the College and extremely influential in art education outside it. It was in fact the Coldstream Report on art education which led to the expansion of art history teaching in the 1960s at UCL and elsewhere. The first Professor of the History of Art to become full-time – his part-time predecessors had included Sir Ernst Gombrich – was Leopold Ettlinger in 1964. Ettlinger, like Gombrich a refugee scholar, had left Nazi Germany in 1938 to work at the Warburg Institute; he created six joint-degrees with Art History and set up a department independent from the Slade. This Department of Art History expanded dramatically under Professor John White between 1971 and 1990, making the most of the many opportunities London offered for bringing classes face to face with the art of all periods.

In 1965 UCL, with help from the Max Rayne Foundation, acquired the former offices of the National Union of General and Municipal Workers in Endsleigh Gardens. The building was given to the Faculty of Laws (Fig. 7.11), which had been expanding rapidly and was previously inadequately housed in the Torrington Place building. It had become one of the strongest areas of College in terms of student demand for places. While maintaining its traditional interests in Jurisprudence

Fig. 7.10 Reg Butler teaching sculpture in the Slade. A conscientious objector during the Second World War, Butler went on to become one of the best known sculptors during the 1950s and 1960s.

Fig. 7.11 The Faculty of Laws building, purchased in 1965 and previously the offices of the General and Municipal Workers. Later renamed Bentham House, it is seen here in the 1990s before the remodelling of 2016–18.

Fig. 7.12 The moot room of the Faculty of Laws contributes an important element to the experience of undergraduate lawyers at UCL.

and Roman Law, the Faculty was also at the forefront of new developments in the undergraduate teaching of law (Fig. 7.12). After 1967 it possessed what was for many years the only Professor of Air and Space Law; it was the first in the country to develop courses for undergraduates on International Air Law and Economic Law; and it was also the first to offer options in Russian and Soviet Law, using these as a vehicle for the comparative study of law.

The momentum of expansion

The growth of student accommodation at UCL after the war was one of its greatest successes, as was necessary to keep pace with the increase in student numbers. From the end of the Second World War until the early 1960s student numbers remained relatively stable at around 3,500–4,000. The vast majority of these were undergraduates, with women making up around one-quarter of the student body. In line with national trends in UK higher education and following important changes

Fig. 7.13 Ramsay Hall, a large hall of residence only five minutes walk from the main UCL campus, was opened in three stages between 1964 and 1987.

Fig. 7.14 The front cover of the *UCL Students' Handbook* for 1965 shows a new local landmark, the Post Office Tower, which was completed in that year. Beloved by generations of UCL students, the BT Tower was referred to in the lyric 'lights will guide you home' from the Coldplay song 'Fix You'. It refers to the location of Ramsay Hall, close by the BT Tower, where the band met in 1996.

to student fees and grants, numbers grew rapidly from the mid-1960s, passing the 5,500 mark by the end of that decade. There was steady growth through the 1970s, followed by more rapid expansion in subsequent decades.

In 1947 there were just 47 student places available in UCL accommodation; by 1961 there were 350 and by 1978 there were 1,500, in addition to nearly 500 students living in the intercollegiate halls of the University of London. From 1952 Bentham Hall for men and, from 1954, Campbell Hall for women provided 250 places between them through the conversion of existing properties not far from the College site. A breakthrough came in 1961, when the College became the first university to attempt the provision of self-catering houses for students, first in Gordon Street and later in Bedford Way. But the long-term solution was to be found in purpose-built halls, and a series of extraordinary benefactions made the programme possible. The 'Anonymous Donor' provided for Ramsay Hall, the first phase of which was opened in 1964 (Fig. 7.13), and for Ifor Evans Hall, opened in 1968.

As student numbers increased in the 1950s and 60s, so did the need for informal advice on etiquette, what to wear, navigating London's nightlife and living in the capital on a limited budget. An annual publication, the *UCL Students' Handbook* offered tongue-in-cheek guidance from those at the sharp end; the cover featured here dates from 1965 (Fig. 7.14). Lord Samuel gave the airspace above a block of shops in Oxford Street for the building of Goldsmid House, opened in 1968 as UCL's first purpose-built self-catering hall. Meanwhile the Max Rayne Foundation gave £50,000 a year for ten years to support the building programme and in particular Max Rayne House, opened in 1970.

Students' comfort was also increased when in 1960 the College agreed to open the Union facilities – apart from the bar – on Sunday afternoons and evenings. The Student Union's new sportsground at Shenley was finally opened in 1958 on land purchased in 1939 to replace Perivale. In 1971 new changing rooms were built, and in 1977 a new bar was added. The excellence of the facilities at Shenley came to contrast with the limited accommodation of the Union building itself.

Noël Annan came to UCL in 1966 from Cambridge, where he had been a lecturer in politics since 1948 and Provost of King's College since 1956 (Fig. 7.15). He became a Life Peer in 1965. A formidable reputation as scholar, administrator and orator preceded him, though it took the College time to adjust to a profound change of style from that of his predecessor. Events were to sharpen the contrast between the two periods, as the years of expansion gave way to economies, frozen posts and competition for diminishing funds. The years which followed required above all skilled diplomacy – not only to deal with severe cuts in establishment, but also to cope with the threat of student unrest and far-reaching changes in the organisation and role of the College's non-academic staff. In 1966, as in 1951, UCL was fortunate in finding the right man to manage the problems of the time.

The momentum of expansion continued for a while. The first stage of the new Chemistry Building was completed in 1969 (Fig. 7.16); it was formally opened as

Fig. 7.15 Lord Annan, the fifth Provost, 1966–78, as painted at the end of his period of office by his friend Rodrigo Moynihan.

Fig. 7.16 The new Chemistry Building under construction in Gordon Street, shortly before its completion in 1969.

the Christopher Ingold Laboratories in 1970 for teaching purposes, though the old Chemistry Laboratories of 1915 continued to be used for research until the top floor was added to the new building in 1984. The Student Health Service, founded in 1945 and inadequately housed in Gower Street until 1973, received a new building thanks to a benefaction from the Wolfson Trust. The last major building of the Annan years was Wates House, built through a substantial donation from the Wates Foundation and opened in 1975 as a new home for the Bartlett School of Architecture – the only Department in the Faculty of Environmental Studies, which had been created in 1969. Its name was changed in 1992 to the Faculty of the Built Environment, but in normal speech it continued as always to be called 'The Bartlett'.

Science and Engineering

UCL continued to be the home of many distinguished scientists and engineers. For a long time, the College had the unusual distinction of having several Nobel

Fig. 7.17 Sir Peter Medawar CH, FRS, Jodrell Professor of Zoology and Comparative Anatomy.

Fig. 7.18 A cartoon of Sir Andrew Huxley, FRS, Jodrell Professor of Physiology, 1960–69 and Royal Society Research Professor in Physiology, 1969–83. He won the Nobel Prize in 1963 for his work on the transmission of nerve impulses.

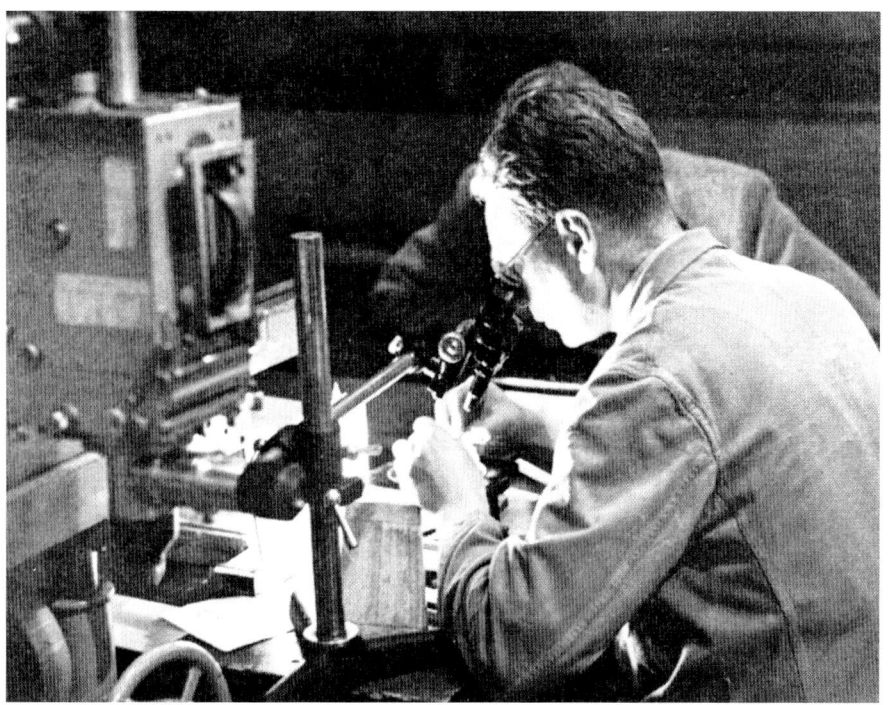

Fig. 7.19 A second Nobel Prize winner working in the College was Professor Sir Bernard Katz, who won his prize in 1970. He was the first Professor of Biophysics, 1952–78.

Prize winners in Physiology or Medicine on the academic staff. Sir Peter Medawar, Jodrell Professor of Zoology and Comparative Anatomy, 1951–62, was awarded the Nobel Prize for Physiology or Medicine in 1960 (Fig. 7.17), while in 1963 Sir Andrew Huxley, Jodrell Professor of Physiology, 1960–69, received his Nobel Prize for work on the transmission of nerve impulses (Fig. 7.18). Sir Bernard Katz, the first Professor of Biophysics at UCL, 1952–78, was also awarded a Nobel Prize in 1970 (Fig. 7.19). In Engineering the Chair of Photogrammetry and Surveying, established in 1946, was the only one of its kind in the country; the separate Department was created in 1961 under E. H. Thompson, who held the Chair from 1951 until his death in 1976. Mechanical Engineering had been a separate Department since the restructuring of the Faculty after the war. With Professor R. E. D. Bishop at the helm from 1957 to 1981, however, it developed particular interests concerned with the sea and the Navy, as the prewar emphasis on photoelasticity and the study of bodies at rest swung instead towards dynamics and the management of vibration. In 1967 the Department took over the teaching for the Royal Corps of

Fig. 7.20 The Observatory at Mill Hill, taken over by UCL when the Department of Astronomy was set up in 1951.

Fig. 7.21 Sir Harrie Massey, FRS was one of the most outstanding of many scientists at UCL during the postwar years. He achieved fame not only through research, but also in shaping leading departments in their fields.

Naval Constructors from the Royal Naval College at Greenwich; this resulted in the creation of a very successful postgraduate course, based on a radical reappraisal of naval architecture. The first British postgraduate course in Ocean Engineering followed in 1972, established with an eye to the need for specialist engineers caused by the exploitation of the North Sea for gas and oil.

The Department of Physics and Astronomy was formed by amalgamation in 1972, establishing the largest and most far-flung of all College departments. The Observatory at Mill Hill had been part of UCL since 1951 (Fig. 7.20), having been originally built to house a 24-inch reflector presented to the University of London in 1928, with a second dome added in 1938. Space research had begun in the Department of Physics in 1956, when a group led by R. L. F (later Sir Robert) Boyd (pp.211 and 213) was set up. Following the successful launch of the Ariel I satellite in 1962 it became one of the most powerful research groups in Britain, taking full advantage of the American space research programme. Sir Harrie Massey was the instigator of this and other research groups, including a particularly fertile one concerned with particle physics (Fig. 7.21). In the 1960s and 1970s UCL scientists working on a collaborative project on the Gargamelle bubble chamber at the European Organisation for Nuclear Research (CERN) in Geneva were involved in the discovery of the weak neutral current.

In the 1960s the Survey of Spoken English (later renamed the Survey of English Usage) became one of the College's major research projects (Fig. 7.22). It arrived

Fig. 7.22 The Survey of Spoken English, one of UCL's major research projects through the 1960s.

together with its originator, Professor Randolph (later Lord) Quirk, FBA, from Durham in 1960. Its purpose was to provide a corpus of 'the grammatical repertoire of adult educated speakers of British English, using the evidence both of written and spoken language'.

UCL and changing social attitudes

Although the numbers of women academics increased after the war, there were just a handful of female Professors at UCL. Mary Douglas, Professor of Social Anthropology, 1970–78, joined UCL as a lecturer in Anthropology in 1951 (Fig. 7.23). One of the most influential social anthropologists of the second half of the twentieth century, Douglas is credited with establishing Anthropology as a discipline at UCL. She was well known for her writings on human culture and symbolism, and for challenging orthodoxies in many fields of learning. Her groundbreaking book *Purity and Danger: an Analysis of Concepts of Pollution and Taboo* examined how cultures define themselves through their rituals of purity. Hannah Steinberg, a well-known figure in College since the 1940s, was made Professor of Psychopharmacology

Fig. 7.23 Mary Douglas, Professor of Social Anthropology 1970–79.

in 1970–89. The Slade appointed Tess Jaray, a former student, as its first woman lecturer in 1968.

Until the late 1960s UCL had three common rooms for academic staff: the Women's Common Room, the Joint Staff Common Room (founded in 1947) and the Men's Common Room, which was the largest and most impressive room. Attempts at desegregation in the 1950s had failed, but a new campaign between 1966–69 was spearheaded by Professor Brian Woledge and David Colquhoun, then a young lecturer and later the A. J. Clark Chair of Pharmacology. On the third attempt in 1969 the men's committee voted to admit women and the common rooms were reorganised. The former Women's Common Room was re-named the Margaret Murray Room, although this name only survived until 1989.

Student life underwent many changes between the early 1950s and the late 1970s. Social and political causes gained an importance they had not had held since the 1930s. In November 1956 members of UCL organised a silent march of 1,300 London students from the Royal Albert Hall to the Soviet Embassy in protest over the Soviet invasion of Hungary, and students went on to play a part in the significant relief effort for Hungarian students that was organised across British universities. A high proportion of students were moved by causes such as CND – UCL had one of the most active College branches in the country in the early

1960s – and anti-apartheid. Like many universities in the late 1960s, UCL faced a degree of student unrest. Students were engaged in some heated discussion over their lack of representation on UCL's governance structures, eventually gaining representation on the College Committee and Professorial Board. In October 1969 Richard Saville, a second-year UCL student, was beaten by porters as he tried to enter Senate House at the head of a 2,000-strong protest over links between the University of London and University College, Rhodesia.

Despite solidarity with discrimination overseas, the experience of the growing number of overseas students, particularly the so-called 'colonial students' from the Caribbean and West Africa, was not always positive at this date. Black and Asian students sometimes faced isolation, racism and discrimination on campus. One wrote to *Pi* explaining how a girl had 'slammed the door' in his face when he dared to ask her if she was going to lunch. A Welfare Committee was set up to help foreign students adjust to life at UCL, and the *Students' Handbook* urged students to feel 'proud of our cosmopolitan society'. International students often experienced greater collegiality in their own clubs, such as the Afro-Caribbean Society, founded in the 1956–57 session, but which failed to attract British members. However, liberalising social attitudes were reflected in students' participation in the earliest Women's Liberation Movement marches and in the formation of UCL's 'Gay Soc' – a pioneering group which was the moving force behind the NUS's wider gay rights campaign in the early 1970s.

Royal Charter and sesquicentenary

In November 1977 UCL received a new Royal Charter (Fig. 7.24). This was in succession to the Deed of Settlement of 1826, the first Charter of 1836, the Acts of Parliament of 1869 and 1905 and the University of London's Act of 1926, which had previously governed the College. The changes introduced by the 1977 Charter were largely formal and titular, but they restored the College's status as an independent corporation, abandoning the 'incorporation' into the University of London. Under the terms of the new Charter, the College Committee resumed its nineteenth-century name of College Council as well as its formal responsibility as UCL's governing body. Sir Bernard Waley-Cohen had served as the Committee's Chairman since 1971 and before that as Treasurer, 1962–70, following a family

Fig. 7.24 The Royal Charter issued to the College in November 1977.

ELIZABETH THE SECOND by the Grace of God of the United Kingdom of Great Britain and Northern Ireland and of Our other Realms and Territories Queen, Head of the Commonwealth, Defender of the Faith:

TO ALL TO WHOM THESE PRESENTS SHALL COME, GREETING!

WHEREAS an humble Petition has been presented unto Us by Our most dearly beloved Mother Queen Elizabeth The Queen Mother, Chancellor of Our University of London, Sir Cyril Philips, then Vice-Chancellor of Our University of London and by the College Committee of University of London, University College: praying that We should grant a Charter of Incorporation for the purpose of re-constituting University of London, University College as a College of the University of London:

AND WHEREAS We have taken the said Petition into Our Royal Consideration and are minded to accede thereto:

NOW THEREFORE KNOW Ye that We by virtue of Our Prerogative Royal and of Our especial grace, certain knowledge and mere motion have willed and ordained and by these Presents do for Us, Our Heirs and Successors will and ordain as follows:—

1. University of London, University College is hereby re-constituted as a college of the University of London by the name and style of "University College London", hereinafter referred to as "the College".

2. The Council, the Academic Board, the Fellows and Honorary Fellows, the Academic Staff and Students of the College and all such other persons as may pursuant to this Our Charter and the Statutes and Regulations of the College become Members of the Body Corporate are hereby constituted and shall for ever hereafter be one Body Corporate and Politic by the name of "University College London" with perpetual succession and a Common Seal.

3. The objects of the College shall be to provide education and courses of study in the fields of Arts, Laws, Pure Sciences, Medicine and Medical Sciences, Social Sciences and Applied Sciences and in such other fields of learning as may from time to time be decided upon by the College and to encourage research in the said branches of knowledge and learning and to organise, encourage and stimulate postgraduate study in such branches.

4. The College, subject to this Our Charter and to the Statutes and Regulations of Our University of London (hereinafter referred to as "the University") shall in furtherance of the foregoing objects but not otherwise have the following powers:—

(1) To take over from the University the properties and liabilities hitherto entrusted to vested in or incurred by the University on behalf of the College by virtue of its incorporation in the University.

(2) To provide courses of instruction and facilities for research in the branches of knowledge and learning mentioned in Article 3 of this Our Charter, and for postgraduate study in such branches.

(3) To provide, maintain, alter and improve for the use of the Students

tradition of service that had begun in the College's earliest days. The new Charter was 12 years in the making; if the old constitutional machinery had been put to any serious test during this time, 'the creaking would have been heard from here to Timbuctoo', according to Arthur Tattersall, the Secretary of the College, 1964–78. Tattersall headed the administration of the College through the 1960s and 1970s in a wise, humane fashion, and was strikingly successful in maintaining close relations between the administration and the College community.

As soon as it was granted, however, the new Charter began to be revised to provide for re-amalgamation with the Medical School. Professorial Board was also re-named under the new Charter, becoming the Academic Board (Fig. 7.25), but it remained the controlling body on academic matters. All Professors, a group of elected non-Professors and representatives of the student body comprised its membership.

The Queen Mother's visit in November 1977 marked the start of a series of celebrations for the sesquicentenary of the College, leading up to a great exhibition on 'UCL Past and Present' in May 1978, opened by Shirley Williams as Secretary of State for Education. The sesquicentenary was celebrated confidently, but it was a time of increasing financial uncertainty for universities in general and for London colleges in particular. Many UCL staff members were active participants in the Association of University Teachers (AUT) campaign over the inadequacy of university teachers' salaries (Fig. 7.26). Students were also engaged in protest against cuts in government spending on education. In March 1977 there was a short, sharp confrontation, in which the students occupied some administrative rooms for two days and the Slade School for rather longer. Such incidents have been very rare and peacefully resolved; the campaign against cuts by successive governments has continued intermittently ever since, but with little or no success.

Fig. 7.25 The Professorial Board assembling in June 1977, later renamed as Academic Board under the new Charter. Student members can be seen in the foreground.

Fig. 7.26 (overleaf) Allan Maccoll, Professor of Chemistry, 1963–81 and long-term supporter of the AUT, protesting at cuts in government spending on education in November 1977.

CHAPTER 8

The Years of Expansion

1978–2003

> The Council and the Academic Board have given unanimous support to an active policy aimed at preserving UCL's integrity in the face of current university enquiries. They both see the College as an administratively integral and topographically compact academic institution, strong in the humanities and law, fine arts and architecture, physical sciences and engineering, life sciences and medicine. They are determined to maintain this integrity, which allows an intimate spirit of collaboration within and among all those fields on UCL's 'Half Kilometre Square'. Furthermore, they see no case for attempting to widen that organisation in ways that would change the academic balance or the topographical compactness.
>
> *Sir James Lighthill*, UCL Annual Report, 1979–1980

Sir James Lighthill

In 1978 Lord Annan resigned as Provost in order to become the first full-time Vice-Chancellor of the University of London in preparation for the constitutional changes brought about by the University's new 1978 Act of Parliament. For the following academic year, 1978–79, Professor Harold Billett was Acting Provost (Fig. 8.1). He had been a member of the staff since 1946, Professor of Mechanical Engineering from 1965 and a Vice-Provost since 1973. Professor Billett presided calmly and wisely over the College in an interregnum between two contrasting, commanding Provosts.

Sir James Lighthill was chosen as Provost in 1979 (Fig. 8.2). Like Lord Annan, he came to UCL from Cambridge with a formidable reputation, though an utterly different one. A brilliant mathematician, he was Lucasian Professor of Applied Mathematics at Cambridge at the time of his appointment. Lighthill was a product of Winchester and Trinity College, Cambridge; he had been a Professor at Manchester at 26, a Fellow of the Royal Society at 29 and Director of the Royal Aircraft Establishment at Farnborough from 1959 to 1964. As Provost he found 'something of an advantage', as he put it, in being an applied mathematician who had worked for many years on various applications of mathematics in the sciences, engineering and medicine. There were few academic subjects of which he did not have some knowledge, and there were no areas of the College on which he did

Fig. 8.1 Professor Harold Billett, Acting Provost, 1978–79.

Fig. 8.2 Sir James Lighthill, FRS, the sixth Provost of the College, 1979–89.

Fig. 8.3 The Engineering Building, 1987. Funded by donations from industry, it opened in 1961.

not have considerable impact in the nine years that he devoted to UCL. In 1988 Sir James Lighthill expressed the hope that the history of the College in the 1980s would be judged by the quality of the professorial appointments made during his Provostship – over a hundred of them altogether. He put academic excellence first, but he also had many problems to deal with.

Already in 1979–80 a savings target of three per cent of the recurrent grant from the University Grants Committee had to be imposed; further problems were caused by the UGC's insistence that 'non-EEC students' should be charged fees on a new, higher scale. These were followed by what the *Annual Report* called a 'traumatic sequence of body-blows'. In the 1981 budget Margaret Thatcher's government announced a substantial cut in the resources to be provided for the university system as a whole; as a result UCL found that its grant for 1981–82 was to fall 15 per cent short of the amount needed to maintain its 1980–81 levels of activity. Retrenchment was not easy, given that staff costs accounted for nearly 80 per cent of all College expenditure. Lighthill introduced a 'seven-point plan' for economies and was vigorous in hammering out painful plans for coping with the cuts. UCL adhered firmly to its policy of 'no redundancy', but an extensive early retirement scheme was launched, with a target of 160 retirements among members of the academic staff by 1984.

The target was achieved (though for many academics, it was only a technical retirement) and substantial one-off as well as ongoing economies were made in various different ways. At the same time the College embarked on a vigorous drive

Fig. 8.4 UCL's Pearson Building, dating from 1919, viewed from UCH Hospital. The photograph was taken shortly after the completion of the extension to the Pearson Building in 1985.

to increase its income from non-governmental sources. Along with the research councils and charitable foundations, industry was an increasingly important source of support, as all three have been ever since. The economies enabled UCL to complete key building projects despite the financial situation, notably the Engineering Building in 1987 (Fig. 8.3) and the extension of the Pearson Building, formerly the Bartlett Building and dating from 1919, in 1985 (Fig. 8.4).

In the event, during a period of enormous financial difficulties, UCL was so successful in obtaining alternative new funding that the number of staff in academic departments actually rose from 1,976 in 1978–79 to 2,014 in 1982–83. Despite the 'massive cuts' that marked the beginning of the decade, the 1980s turned out to be a remarkable period of growth, though most notably in the area of staff employed on research contracts. The financial problems also led to a significant increase in the power of the Deans, who for some years came to exercise considerable control over the budgets of the Departments within the seven Faculties. One permitted expense in 1986 was a grand dinner to commemorate the 160th anniversary of the College's foundation. It was attended by the College Council, shown here a month later in March 1986 (Fig. 8.5).

Progress on gender equality was also slow (Fig. 8.6), although some progress was made during the 1980s. In 1979 there were just four female Professors at UCL out of a total of 123, and in that year Hannah Steinberg was one of five women academics who founded the Academic Women's Achievement Group (AWAG) following a meeting with Lord Boyle, Chair of the Committee of Vice-Chancellors and Principals (Fig. 8.7). One of the first such women's academic groups in the UK, the group soon

Fig. 8.5 The College Council in March 1986. Sir Peter Matthews, Chair of Council, is seated in the centre, with Sir James Lighthill on his right and Ian Baker on his left.

Fig. 8.6 UCL's all male senior leadership team in 1986. It consisted of the Deans of the seven Faculties, the Provost, two Vice-Provosts and the Secretary of the College.

Fig. 8.7 The Academic Women's Achievement Group met regularly from 1979 to discuss and celebrate women's achievements in academic positions and to campaign on remaining issues. Believed to be the earliest such group to be established, meetings were attended by a wide range of female academics at UCL.

expanded beyond UCL to campaign for greater representation of women at senior levels in higher education and on related issues such as nursery provision. In the early 1980s women held around 12 per cent of academic posts in British universities, and there was also a large gender pay gap. In 1987 the group celebrated the fact that the number of women Professors at UCL had risen from four to 11 out of a total of 151 – more than double the national average of three per cent. Their contributions to UCL were substantial. Professor Leslie Aiello, for example, now Professor Emeritus of UCL, taught in the Department of Anthropology from 1976, including six years as Head of Department. She also served as Head of the Graduate School 2002–05 (Fig. 8.8). Her colleague Barbara Adams, archaeologist and museum curator, worked for 36 years at the Petrie Museum. Appointed in 1965, she took on the immense task of conservation, storage, re-identification, sorting and display, almost single-handedly rescuing the collection from its postwar confusion (Fig. 8.9). Thus, while limited, women's progress at UCL could be described by Steinberg as 'miles ahead' of rivals such as King's College or the University of Cambridge, and the College began to capitalise on this record in its student prospectus. In 1985 UCL established its first Committee on Equal Opportunities.

Fig. 8.8 Professor Leslie Aiello, whose 30-year career at UCL was celebrated in 2005, made a significant contribution to teaching and research in the Department of Anthropology.

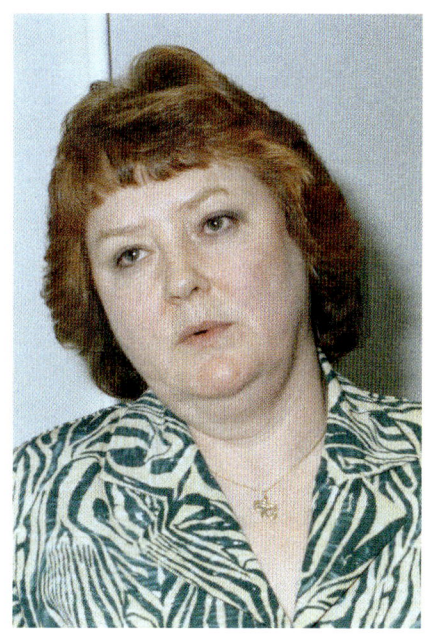

Fig. 8.9 Barbara Adams, archaeologist and museum curator, was for more than 36 years a curator at the Petrie Museum. Her role in restoring and conserving the Petrie Collection, which she rescued almost single-handed after the Second World War, was invaluable, as were her celebrated enthusiasm, energy and skill.

Mergers and restructuring

Some of UCL's expansion derived from the intense period of restructuring upon which the University of London embarked under the Vice-Chancellorships of Lord Annan, 1978–81, and his successor, Professor Sir Randolph Quirk, 1981–85 (Fig. 8.10). Lord Flowers' report in 1980 on medical education in the University was followed by an investigation into the organisation of all other subjects, conducted by Sir Peter Swinnerton-Dyer. A period of anguish and mergers ensued, coinciding with the 'cuts'. For many parts of the University of London this process was dismaying and hurtful, but UCL was on the whole a beneficiary. In 1982–83 a number of geologists were translated from Queen Mary College to enhance the Department of Geology (to be renamed Geological Sciences in 1985 and Earth Sciences in 2002) under Professor Michael Audley-Charles; Bedford College's Department of Dutch moved

Fig. 8.10 Sir Randolph (later Lord) Quirk, FBA, Professor of English, 1960–81. He became Vice-Chancellor of the University of London, 1981–85.

to the College *en bloc*; the Department of Italian was strengthened by transfers from Bedford, as was the Department of Mathematics, which came to include Professor P. M. Cohn, FRS, as well as Dr Bill Stephenson. The Bioengineering Centre in the Department of Mechanical Engineering was established in 1980, after the transfer from Roehampton of a DHSS group integrating engineering and medical research. The D. M. S. Watson Library, after the restructuring of University library provision, became the Bloomsbury Science Library for a while after 1985. But the biggest changes of all were in Medicine. In April 1980 the University College Hospital Medical School – a separate school of the University of London since 1907 – was reunited with the College, forming the Faculty of Clinical Sciences within a new UCL School of Medicine.

Between 1986 and 1999, no fewer than 12 previously separate institutions joined the expanding UCL. The first was the Institute of Archaeology which amalgamated

Fig. 8.11 (overleaf) The Institute of Archaeology, which merged with UCL in 1986, has been housed in this building in Gordon Square since 1948.

Fig. 8.12 The formal inauguration of the new University College and Middlesex School of Medicine was marked by a visit from HRH The Princess Royal in November 1987.

with the College in August 1986 (Fig. 8.11), retaining its separate identity as a Department within the Faculty of Arts. The Institute of Archaeology had been founded in 1937 as an institute of the University of London; it had developed into the leading centre for archaeological research as well as undergraduate teaching in the field. Complex discussions with Westfield College did not lead to a merger, but in 1987 there was an outbreak of medical amalgamations. This saw the Middlesex Hospital Medical School (founded in 1745, rebuilt in 1935 and possessor of its own medical school since 1835) join with three of the constituent parts of the former British Postgraduate Medical Federation – the Institute of Urology, the Institute of Orthopaedics and the Institute of Laryngology and Otology. The 'University College and Middlesex School of Medicine' was inaugurated in 1987

Fig. 8.13 A student in her room at Astor College, Middlesex, part of UCL's increasing stock of student accommodation.

Fig. 8.14 The Sesquicentenary Appeal, delayed in the hope of better times to come, was finally launched in October 1981 in the presence of HRH The Princess Royal. Here Sir James Lighthill presents Lord Goodman, a Fellow of UCL since 1965.

(Fig. 8.12), although the first students at the joint School had been admitted in 1983, before the completion of the complex period of planning for full integration. These mergers brought close connections with the Royal National Orthopaedic Hospital at Stanmore and the Royal National Throat, Nose and Ear Hospital in Gray's Inn Road. By the mid-1980s the enlarged UCL contained over 7,000 students, of whom 3,000 were women. Fortunately the amalgamation of the Middlesex Hospital Medical School enabled its residence, opened in 1967, to become much needed student accommodation for UCL in the renamed Astor College (Fig. 8.13). Postgraduate numbers were also at record levels, accounting for nearly 30 per cent of all students at this date.

During this period of expansion, UCL also acquired a new look. In 1979–80 the stone-cleaning of the Front Quad improved the outward appearance of the College dramatically, and in 1983–85 the Front Quad was closed to enable the building of a new main front entrance. The Sesquicentenary Appeal, delayed in the hope of better times to come, had been finally launched in October 1981 in the presence of HRH Princess Anne – on the day that she was installed as Chancellor of the University of London in succession to the Queen Mother (Fig. 8.14). The centrepiece of the Appeal was the long-proposed 'filling of the gap' to complete the Gower Street entrance to the Front Quad with two pavilions designed by Sir Hugh Casson (Fig. 8.15). The unsightly postwar huts were finally removed, and the College came to present a handsome front to the world.

In November 1985 the Queen unveiled an inscription above the entrance in the Portico, which records that the Quadrangle started in 1827 was deemed complete in 1985 (Fig. 8.16). In her speech in the Donaldson Library she wryly commented, 'I confess that, sometimes, when I lay a foundation stone I am prey to faint worries about when, or even whether, the building will be finished. I wonder if, on that April afternoon in 1827 when he laid the first stone here, the Duke of Sussex had those same worries. Even if he did, I doubt if he would have guessed that it would be his great-great-grand niece, 158 years later, who would see the end of the process he began'.

The Kathleen Lonsdale Building, containing the old Chemistry Laboratories, was elegantly reconstructed, also in 1985. The renovated building was to house the Sandoz Institute for Medical Research, a signal example of co-operation with a major pharmaceutical company. All these changes, combined with some modest gardening expenditure as part of a 'greening of UCL' programme, significantly improved the rectangle site, which Sir James Lighthill liked to call the 'half-kilometre square'.

Fig. 8.15 This sketch of the new pavilions by Sir Hugh Casson was hung in the Royal Academy's Summer Exhibition of 1981. The elegant structures were designed to 'fill the gap' on either side of the lodges and complete the entrance to the Front Quad.

Fig. 8.16 HM The Queen arriving at UCL on 13 November 1985. She is shown being introduced to Ian Baker, the retired general who was Secretary of the College, 1982–91.

Fig. 8.17 Sir Derek Roberts, FRS, the seventh Provost, from April 1989.

Fig. 8.18 (overleaf) The Bloomsbury Theatre, originally opened as the Collegiate Theatre in 1968, and renamed in 1982. This photograph was taken in 1989.

Sir Derek Roberts

In April 1989 Dr Derek Roberts, FRS, was chosen to succeed Sir James Lighthill as Provost (Fig. 8.17). The appointment attracted much attention in the press, especially since the union representing academic staff, the AUT, was threatening a boycott of examination marking following the Government's refusal to make an adequate salary settlement on top of its insistence upon the abolition of 'tenure' by legislation. Sir Derek Roberts, as he soon became, had held several visiting professorships (including one in the College's Department of Electronic and Electrical Engineering), but he was not an academic. His life had been spent in industrial scientific research, and at the time of his appointment as Provost he was Joint Deputy Managing Director and Technical Director of the General Electric Company (GEC). His appointment, welcomed throughout the College, was also seen as a sign of the times. Mergers started up again, and a sharp difference in style was observed between the first round of mergers under Lighthill and the second round under Roberts. Lighthill held elaborate negotiations first and then agreed the mergers; Roberts decided to merge first and negotiate afterwards.

The times were indeed changing. An exhaustive report in 1985, in connection with Sir Alex Jarratt's investigation of the efficiency of universities, had pronounced that 'the overall governance of UCL, in terms of its organisational structure and decision processes, is generally effective'. A new managerial and public relations style was becoming evident. David Bowles, the College's Finance Secretary and Accountant since 1978, became Director of Finance and Planning in 1989. In that year an Alumnus Day was held on an entirely new basis. *UCL Universe* replaced the old *Annual Report* and a glossy news magazine, *UCL NEWS*, was launched in October.

Some of these developments had been foreshadowed before 1989. Dr Stephen Montgomery had been appointed Director of External Relations in 1985, and in 1988 the former ASU (Academic Services Unit, established in 1978) had been re-launched as UCLi, UCL Initiatives – a concerted effort to link UCL expertise to industrial and commercial opportunities. UCL Ventures, UCL's first technology-transfer company, was formed in 1989; it later merged with Freemedic PLC, the commercial arm of the Royal Free Hospital Medical School, to form UCL BioMedica. By the end of 1990 major new buildings were underway. UCL was choosing not to sit on its laurels.

For many years the totally inadequate stage in the gymnasium, originally built for University College School in 1878, had to serve for the many student dramatic productions. Among them were the annual opera, a major feature of UCL life since 1951. The Music Society's policy has been to produce little-known operas, and it has a number of premieres to its credit. In 1968 a purpose-built theatre was opened as the Collegiate Theatre, to be re-named in 1982 as the Bloomsbury Theatre (Fig. 8.18). It provided first-rate facilities for student activities and performances, as well as for visiting professional groups. The gym itself was finally pulled down in 1990–91, making way for new buildings for medical research.

Another measure of changing times was the promotion of David Bowles, the much-respected Director of Finance and Planning, to Vice-Provost in 1991. As Director of Finance and Planning he was succeeded by Marilyn Gallyer, who also succeeded him as Vice-Provost in 1996. Both finance and planning came to play an increasingly prominent role in UCL's decision-making. Many old-style committees of elected and appointed academics (as well as, since the 1970s, elected student representatives) gave way to more modern managerial structures. Under a Provost who believed in – and practised – quick decision-making, directors and managers appeared to proliferate; members of the academic staff, however, who generally still preferred to talk of 'administrators', progressively lost the sense of contributing to College decisions. The growing number of unfilled elective places on the Academic Board provided an unhappy index of diminishing affection for UCL as a whole.

The drive to polish UCL's external image, however, continued to grow apace. After expert advice from Dr Henry Drucker, who had raised millions for Oxford, a new and more professional Development Office was established under Rachel Hall as its first Director, 1994–98. Fundraising moved into a higher gear, and better relations with UCL alumni were carefully cultivated on a global scale. In 1996 Professor Tim Biscoe became a Pro-Provost – a new office created in 1990 for senior

Fig. 8.19 A monument to the first Japanese students to study at UCL in 1863 and 1865. Inscribed in Japanese and English, the monument was unveiled outside the Bernard Katz Building in September 1993. Beside it stands Professor John White, Pro-Provost, 1990–95.

members of the College given special responsibilities for a specific area, in Biscoe's case relations with East Asia. On the newly created terrace outside the Bernard Katz Building, opened for the Eisai Research Laboratory in May 1993, a monument to the pioneering Japanese students of 1863 and 1865 (p.92) was erected to symbolise UCL's enduring links with Japan (Fig. 8.19). The very successful Language Centre at UCL was opened in 1991 in the refurbished former premises of the once famous medical bookshop H. K. Lewis & Co Ltd on the corner of Gower Street and Gower Place (Fig. 8.20). The Lewis building was refurbished again in 2011 as a new social space for the students' union.

In the 1980s and 90s UCL moved towards a new era of corporate public relations, with a strong emphasis on international co-operation and global links.

Fig. 8.20 UCL's Language Centre opened in 1991. It was based in UCL's Bloomsbury heartlands, on the site of a former bookshop.

Many individual members of staff also developed high media profiles in this period. Lawrence Gowing, Principal of the Slade School of Art, 1975–85, was an associate member of the Royal Academy and a trustee of the Tate Gallery, the National Portrait Gallery and the British Museum (Fig. 8.21). He was the author of several art monographs and catalogues and organised major exhibitions on Turner, Matisse and, in 1988–89, Cézanne, the last travelling from the Royal Academy to the Musee d'Orsay and the National Gallery of Art, Washington. Steve Jones, Professor of Genetics, achieved popular fame for his 1991 Reith Lectures on 'The Language of the Genes', and has maintained a strong media presence as a writer and broadcaster ever since (Fig. 8.22). Professor Lewis Wolpert, since 2010 Emeritus Professor of Biology as Applied to Medicine at UCL, also became well-known as a broadcaster

Fig. 8.21 Sir Lawrence Gowing, the Slade Professor of Fine Art.

Fig. 8.22 Professor Steve Jones, Professor of Genetics, achieved popular fame through his 1991 Reith Lectures on the 'The Language of the Genes'. He has been a well-known broadcaster and writer ever since.

Fig. 8.23 Another member of academic staff who became well known as a writer and broadcaster in the 1980s and 1990s is Professor Lewis Wolpert, FRS, now Emeritus Professor of Biology as Applied to Medicine.

and writer for the general public through the 1980s and 1990s (Fig. 8.23). In 1998 he became one of the first Fellows of the Academy of Medical Sciences and was elected a Fellow of the Royal Society in 1999.

University of London reform and 'round two' of mergers

Lord Annan may have thought in 1978 that the 'harness of attachment' which long chafed between UCL and the University of London had been turned into 'bands of silk'. Nevertheless, between 1929 and 1993 the grant from the UGC and its short-lived successor, the Universities Funding Council, had not been paid directly to UCL, but to the University of London, whose Court Department had the responsibility of dividing the annual grant between the constituent colleges, schools and institutes. It had long been believed by many at UCL that this system worked to the disadvantage of the larger colleges, and also that the system caused delay in the planning process.

Both Lighthill and Roberts, in their different styles, maintained heavy pressure on a University that was in any case engaged in reform. The outcome of the sound and fury was that after 1993 the Higher Education Funding Council for England (HEFCE) grant was paid directly to UCL and to the other colleges, placing them on the same footing as all other English universities. The University of London rewrote its statutes in 1994, abolishing the Court Department and central control of finance and planning; there was to be no more top-slicing for federal activities. The first 'graduation ceremony' at UCL was held in September 1992 (Fig. 8.24). The degrees awarded were still of the University of London, but the former centralised 'presentation ceremonies' in the Royal Albert Hall gave way to devolved occasions organised by the colleges.

In 1992 the UCL Graduate School was formed. It was a response to the increasingly clear separation of government funding for teaching and for research; at the same time there was a widespread feeling that the growing number of research students needed more support from the College in social life, in skills training and in interdisciplinary stimulus than the individual departments had been offering. The first Head of the Graduate School was Professor Tim Biscoe, Jodrell Professor of Physiology and Vice-Provost, 1990–92. By 2003 the Graduate School had become a well-established presence within UCL, providing over 2,700 research students with a source of funding for travel, conference-going and research expenses.

In 1995 there were two mergers. The Institute of Ophthalmology, founded nearly 50 years previously in conjunction with the Moorfields Eye Hospital in the City Road, brought into UCL what became the largest single site for eye research as well as eye care in the world. The National Hospital's College of Speech Sciences, which had evolved from the speech therapy clinic established in 1918 at the West End Hospital for Nervous Diseases, became the Department of Human Communication Science in the Faculty of Life Sciences.

The Institute of Child Health (ICH) merged with UCL in 1996. It was formally established in 1945 on the initiative of senior staff at the Great Ormond Street Hospital for Sick Children. Collaboration between curing patients and teaching students in fact goes back to the earliest days of Great Ormond Street Hospital, when the founder Charles West and Sir William Jenner, also a UCL Professor, accepted students from its foundation in 1852. Regular courses were established by the end of the nineteenth century. From 1947 the ICH formed part of the British

Fig. 8.24 The first 'graduation ceremony' at UCL held in September 1992, replacing presentation ceremonies of the University of London in the Royal Albert Hall. The first UCL 'graduation' was proudly reported in UCL *Alumnus* magazine.

Postgraduate Medical Federation, the umbrella created by the University of London for various postgraduate medical institutes – several of which came to be such a major element in the expanded UCL. The ICH's first Director, who served between 1945 and 1963, was Professor (later Sir) Alan Moncrieff (Fig. 8.25); he presided over its early development and encouraged specialisations in tropical medicine and in child growth. In 1990 Roland Levinsky became Dean, and it was he who oversaw a period of re-organisation, expansion and eventually merger with UCL. Today the UCL Great Ormond Street Institute for Child Health, under its Director Professor Rosalind Smyth, forms the largest concentration of children's health research in Europe.

The Institute of Neurology merged with UCL in 1997. It had been established in 1950 and retains its close links with the National Hospital for Neurology and Neurosurgery in Queen Square, now part of UCLH NHS Foundation Trust (Fig. 8.26). The Institute is now the major national centre for postgraduate training and research in neurology and allied disciplines, and a key component of the Faculty of Brain Sciences at UCL.

Fig. 8.25 Sir Alan Moncrieff, first Director of the newly founded Institute of Child Health, 1946–64.

Fig. 8.26 The National Hospital for Neurology and Neurosurgery, built in 1884, as viewed from Queen Square Gardens. Above it towers the building of the UCL Institute of Neurology, completed in 1978.

The merger of the Royal Free Hospital Medical School with UCHMS in 1998 brought together three of the great medical institutions of nineteenth-century London. The creation of the Royal Free Medical School derived directly from the struggle by women in Britain to be accepted for medical degrees and to qualify as doctors. In the summer of 1874, on the initiative of Sophia Jex-Blake (Fig. 8.27) and with the somewhat reluctant support of Elizabeth Garrett Anderson (Fig. 8.28), the London School of Medicine for Women opened with 14 students – Jex-Blake among them – in a house in Henrietta Street, later extended to have a Hunter Street frontage. At first no hospital would agree to accept the students, but in 1877 the Royal Free, in nearby Gray's Inn Road, came to the rescue (Fig. 8.29). The following year the position was secured by the University of London's decision to open its degrees to women. Garrett Anderson emerged in 1883 as the Dean, as she was to be for the rest of the century. In 1898 'London (Royal Free Hospital) School of Medicine for Women' became its official name, although for all practical purposes it remained the 'London School of Medicine for Women' until men were admitted as students for the first time in 1948.

Fig. 8.27 A photograph of Sophia Jex-Blake by Margaret G. Todd. It is dated to the 1880s or 1890s, by which time Jex-Blake had succeeded in establishing the London School of Medicine for Women.

Fig 8.28 Dr Elizabeth Garrett Anderson, photographed in the 1880s. She served as Dean of the London School of Medicine for Women, 1883–1902, becoming the first woman to hold such a post.

Fig. 8.29 Pioneer women students of Medicine being taught Anatomy in the Hunter Street building that in 1898 became the London (Royal Free Hospital) School of Medicine for Women.

The current hospital and medical school in Hampstead was established between 1974, when the hospital moved, and 1982, when the pre-clinical departments completed their move. Less than ten years later the Tomlinson Report recommended the merger that took place in 1998, so creating what is today known as UCL Medical School (Fig. 8.30). As a recent history by Neil McIntyre reports, some academic staff at the Royal Free were less than enthusiastic about the merger, and felt that the speed at which UCL signage appeared on parts of the Hampstead building was unseemly. The former University College Hospital, originally opened in 1906, was vacated by the NHS in 1996. It was restored as the Cruciform Building to provide teaching and research facilities for medical students at a cost of £50 million. The sum was, raised through contributions from the Wellcome Trust, the Wolfson Foundation and HEFCE, with additional initial funding raised through a private finance initiative.

The Eastman Dental Clinic, next to the Royal Free Hospital in Gray's Inn Road, was opened in 1931 by the American Ambassador in the presence of Neville Chamberlain. George Eastman, the American pioneer of popular photography, provided most of the funding. The Clinic was dedicated to providing dental care for children from the poor districts of central London. In 1948 the Eastman Dental

Fig. 8.30 The Royal Free Hospital, Hampstead and its Medical School, since 1999 amalgamated with the UCL Medical School.

Institute, now independent of the Royal Free Hospital, became the postgraduate dental institute of the British Postgraduate Medical Federation; in 1999 it joined the enlarged UCL.

That same year, 1999, also saw an important non–medical merger. The School of Slavonic and East European Studies (SSEES) had been founded in 1915 by Tomáš Masaryk at King's College London (Fig. 8.31), with a much-publicised lecture on 'The Problem of Small Nations in the European Crisis'. The School became an independent institute of the University of London in 1932, relocating to the newly-built Senate House in 1939. After the First World War Masaryk became the first President of Czechoslovakia. Between 1922 and 1932 Russian literature at the School was taught by D. S. Mirsky, an émigré prince who commuted from his residence in France. Later in the 1930s, reconciling himself to the new order, he returned to Soviet Russia, only to die in a labour camp in Siberia in 1939. Masaryk's interests in questions of national identity and self-determination, rooted in language, history, culture and society, continue to inform the School's activities with as much relevance today.

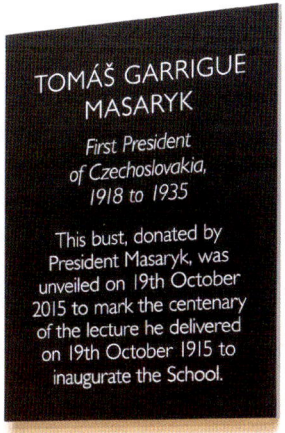

Fig. 8.31 Tomáš Masaryk, founder of the School of the School of Slavonic and East European Studies in 1915. After the First World War he became the first President of Czechoslovakia.

Sir Chris Llewellyn Smith

Derek Roberts' term as Provost had been extended to 1999; his leadership was regarded as indispensable to the unprecedented process of expansion in the late 1990s. His successor was the physicist Chris (soon to be Sir Chris) Llewellyn Smith (Fig. 8.32). He had been Professor of Theoretical Physics at Oxford, on secondment since 1994 as Director of the Europe-wide CERN research organisation, based at Geneva and concerned with the basic particles of matter. Professor Llewellyn Smith, on the advice of his predecessor, was the first to add the title President to that of Provost, so clarifying the status of the post – particularly useful when visiting universities in the US. He was shrewd enough to have recognised from the beginning the problems inherent in running an institution whose size and complexity was in danger of outrunning its existing system of administration. Llewellyn Smith appointed three Vice-Provosts, each to have an area of responsibility (initially these were Humanities and Social Sciences, Medical Sciences and Science and Engineering) within which each exercised some of the Provost's powers; this left

Fig. 8.32 Professor Sir Chris Llewellyn Smith, physicist and UCL's eighth Provost, 1999–2002.

Llewellyn Smith himself with more time to concentrate on planning, fund-raising and the relations of UCL with the outside world. Some sceptical academics felt that the new Provost was in fact taking on the role, not only the title, of an American University President.

Under Chris Llewellyn Smith, UCL was successful in research bids in the Joint Infrastructure Fund ('JIF') competition. The College also received further funding for scientific research, especially in Biomedicine, from the Science Research Investment Fund ('SRIF'). The total funding obtained from these sources was of the order of £100 million. The plans had to be submitted within a short time frame, but problems were overcome triumphantly and a major building programme was soon underway. It was to be Professor Llewellyn Smith's legacy to UCL, alongside his concern to see that these enhancements for the scientific side of UCL did not leave the non-laboratory subjects behind.

What should by rights have been a period of triumph rapidly soured. Early in the new millennium it was discovered that the financial situation was far worse than had previously been calculated. Previous efforts at savings, it was now realised, had failed to take enough factors into account and a new, more stringent savings programme was adopted. Despite this, the deficit went up and morale in the College went down. At the same time the Provost's proposals for academic re-structuring also attracted opposition. By the summer of 2002 the Chairman of Council, Lord Young, had been approached by some senior members of the College who conveyed extreme anxiety about the situation; they felt that there was no effective strategy in place and that the necessary decisive action was not being taken. Lord Young's discreet consultation among senior academics led him to advise the Provost that the College and the Council had lost confidence in his leadership. A statement was issued saying that Sir Chris was resigning to return to his research work. The news of this prompt action was received with some misgiving in parts of UCL, but by August the previous Provost, Sir Derek Roberts, had been pressed to return for one more year as Provost while the search for a successor was carried on.

Between 1978–79 and 2002–03 UCL's turnover increased from £20 million to nearly £500 million per annum, of which rather less than one-third was provided by the Government through HEFCE. Over one-third came from research grants and contracts, some from the research councils, but far more from industry and charitable funds. It was a difficult task to remain competitive internationally at a time when successive British governments in the 1990s failed to increase spending in line with the expansion in student numbers. In real terms academic salaries fell, while academic workloads increased. The situation had been summed up by Sir Derek Roberts in the *UCL Newsletter*, written after his first retirement as Provost in 1999.

> The level of excellence in research and teaching which is maintained at UCL is a direct result of the excellence and dedication of the staff. I find it remarkable that members of staff do perform at such a high level given the miserable way they have been treated by successive governments for two decades. The erosion of academic salaries, with respect to other professions, is a national disgrace. It was so when I came to UCL, and my biggest regret about my time here is that no improvement has been achieved – instead the converse is true.

The efforts of the Development Office and the new emphasis on fund-raising and on alumni relations became global in scope. Outstanding success in research and intellectual achievement helped to attract funding for capital projects, but the income from fees and grants needed to underpin such a programme of expansion never reached the proper level. Somewhat paradoxically, UCL in the early 2000s was the scene of extensive building activity, while financial deficits continued to demand ever more stringent efforts to contain day-to-day expenditure. The staff and students who had to suffer the inconvenience of the building works were to be denied even the comfort of feeling that it was the price to be paid for financial security.

Growth in student numbers

The last decade of the twentieth century saw a near doubling of student numbers, from just over 9,000 in the 1990–91 academic year to nearly 17,000 by 2000–01. There was also a steady increase in the percentage of women, and by 1997 the number of women students had reached parity with men. Expansion was not achieved without some misgiving. More students meant more income, but also more pressure on limited resources and space. The unit of resource per student fell. In many areas the overcrowding became too serious to overlook readily. Nevertheless, as quality assessments and research assessments both consistently proved, the highest academic standards were maintained. As part of a broader modernisation programme, UCL invested heavily in computer provision across its offices, libraries, laboratories and halls of residence; such PC cluster-rooms provided a new type of working environment for students and academics. These changes were also driven by rising student expectations, especially after the introduction in 1998 of the up-front undergraduate tuition fee of £1,000.

Unsurprisingly, the expansion in student numbers led to increasing demand for accommodation. New halls of residence included Langton Close, converted from the former nurses' home of the old Royal Free Hospital in 1994 and named after

Fig. 8.33 Among the students of the 1990s were the band Coldplay, who met in UCL's Ramsay Hall in 1996. They were Chris Martin (Greek and Latin), Will Champion (Anthropology), Jonny Buckland (Mathematics) and Guy Berryman, who studied at UCL for a year.

Fig 8.34 Mark West, photographed in his Beadle outfit as a young man in the early 1990s. Mark is a long-serving member of the security team who became UCL's Head of Security in 2010. Today Beadles are only seen on ceremonial occasions.

one of its significant benefactors, Alfred Langton. Schafer House, named after the famous physiologist, was purpose-built in 1995; John Dodgson House, named after the much-loved Dean of Students, was built in 1996; James Lighthill House, named after the former Provost, was built in 1998; and Frances Gardner House, named after a memorable Dean of the Royal Free Hospital Medical School, opened in 2004. By 2003 there were some 3,500 places available in UCL student accommodation, with over 500 further places in University of London intercollegiate halls.

The Students' Union celebrated its centenary over the academic year 1993–94, beginning with a 'rededication ceremony' and ending with a Centenary Ball. By this date there were over 100 arts, cultural, political and special interest societies and over 40 sports clubs for students to join. In the 1980s the commercial activities of the Union had expanded greatly, and by the 1990s it ran a large number of cafés, bars, club nights, shops and services in Bloomsbury. It also offered an extensive programme of cheap entertainments, designed to stretch a student's 'grant cheque and still leave enough money for beer' (Fig. 8.33). Other objects of student affection were the 'Top Hat Beadles', whose imposing presence as representatives of tradition survived into the 1990s (Fig. 8.34). As times changed, so did forms of student organisation. The role of President had been abolished by the Union in 1975 and

Fig. 8.35 Professor Wendy Davies, FBA, Professor of History from 1985 to her retirement in 2007. A former UCL student herself, the History department benefited greatly from her leadership in the 1980s. Professor Davies served as Dean of the old Faculty of Arts, 1991–94, and became the first Dean of the new Faculty of Social & Historical Sciences. From 1995 she was UCL Pro-Provost (European Affairs).

replaced with three sabbatical posts which would become equal in status. This 'cabinet approach' had expanded to include six officers by 2000.

Nor was UCL a stranger to academic reorganisation during the 1990s. In 1994–95 the old Faculty of Arts was divided, with Professor Wendy Davies, Professor of History since 1985, becoming Dean of the new Faculty of Social and Historical Sciences (Fig. 8.35). Developments took place within the Slade, such as the 1995 establishment of its Centre for Electronic Media in Fine Art. Turner Prize-winning alumni who studied at the Slade from the 1970s to the 1990s include Martin Creed, Douglas Gordon, Antony Gormley and Rachel Whiteread, the first female winner. In 1995 Professor Robert Hazell (Fig. 8.36) founded the Constitution Unit, the UK's leading research centre on constitutional change. The Unit in turn became part of the School of Public Policy. This completely new development, founded in 1997, rapidly built up an impressive political science research portfolio and an active postgraduate teaching programme. One research group originally housed within the School of Public Policy was the Jill Dando Institute of Crime Science, created in 2001 in memory of the television journalist murdered outside her home in 1999. It

Fig. 8.36 Professor Robert Hazell, founder and Director of the Constitution Unit. Established in 1995, this became the UK's leading research centre on constitutional change.

was the first institute in the world devoted specifically to reducing crime. Under its first Director Professor Gloria Laycock, the Institute's mission was to change crime policy and practice.

The Committee for UCL

At first the second coming of Roberts restored confidence. But early in the new academic year 2002–03 a proposal was made – initially on television by Sir Richard Sykes, the industrialist who had recently become Rector of Imperial College – that UCL and Imperial should merge. The proposal implied that the new institution would continue to be divided between the Bloomsbury and South Kensington sites, but that Sir Richard would become the head of the whole enterprise, with the search for a new Provost consequently being deferred. The main arguments in favour were that the size of the joint institution would place it among the most powerful universities in the world, second only to Stanford in research spending, and that this initiative would be strongly supported by the Government, which

was looking for ways to make UK universities more globally competitive. A rapidly devised structure of sub-boards and internal committees immediately began examining the implications for both UCL and Imperial, reporting to a specially established joint board. UCL's Council insisted that there should be a tight deadline for this intense period of consultation, and that a decision one way or the other should be made by Christmas 2002.

Strong resistance within UCL quickly emerged. There was a sense of disbelief among many staff members who formed a 'Committee for UCL', with the Housman Room becoming a sort of 'headquarters of the resistance'. A website was set up by Professor David Colquhoun to encourage comment and discussion (Fig. 8.37), and before long this attracted vigorously critical statements and signatures from staff, students and distinguished alumni. It became clear that the proposed merger was not seen in UCL as the pooling of two equivalent institutions, but rather as the covert destruction of the tradition of independence and radicalism that had been an inheritance from the 1820s. Talks were called off by the end of 2002, and the search committee for the new Provost resumed its interrupted work. The consequences of the failure of this dramatic initiative were in some ways very positive. This crisis had revealed a sense of community and purpose within UCL that many had thought lost in the years of expansion.

Fig. 8.37 David Colquhoun, Professor of Pharmacology, served on the academic staff of UCL for five decades. In 2002 he created the 'Committee for UCL' website as part of a concerted campaign to prevent the merger between Imperial College and UCL. He is seen here in a mixed-media portrait produced in 2016 by UCL Artist-in-Residence Kristina Clackson Bonnington for the exhibition 'Women at UCL: Presence and Absence'.

CHAPTER 9

London's Global University

UCL in the twenty-first century

The ninth Provost: Sir Malcolm Grant

The discussions concerning the proposed merger between Imperial College and UCL in 2002, and their subsequent breakdown, have come to be seen as something of a turning point in the road leading to UCL's renewal as 'London's Global University'. A key aspect of establishing stability and restoring confidence after this tumultuous period was the appointment of Professor Malcolm Grant as UCL's President and Provost from September 2003 (Fig. 9.1). Originally from New Zealand, Grant was a barrister, environmental lawyer and academic. He came to UCL after completing a year as Pro-Vice-Chancellor at the University of Cambridge, where he was also Professor of Land Economy. The new Provost was no stranger to UCL, however, having been a Professor of Law from 1986 to 1991, and towards the end of this period serving as Vice-Dean in the Faculty of Laws. Alongside his role as Provost, Malcolm Grant chaired the Russell Group of Universities from 2006 to 2009, during which time it appointed its first director-general and emerged as an influential voice in higher education policy. In 2003 Professor Grant was awarded a CBE for services to planning law and local government, and in 2013 he was knighted for services to higher education.

The new Provost made a vigorous start to tackling some of UCL's intractable problems, receiving a warm welcome from an academic community pleased to feel a renewed sense of purpose. In February 2004 he launched a much applauded consultation throughout UCL on the basis of a 'Green Paper'; in June, after extensive debate in Departments and Faculties, in Committees and Union meetings, the corresponding 'White Paper' was approved by both Academic Board and Council. One key recommendation was to reinforce UCL's standing as a university of global consequence. Another was to place UCL's finances on a sounder footing by focusing investment in areas of world-leading excellence and increasing annual and endowment income through a major capital campaign. A second White Paper, 'Modernising UCL', followed in 2007.

Widespread staff and student resistance to the proposed merger soon gave way to renewed interest in UCL's founding principles of radicalism, independence and widening access. It was on these core ideas that UCL began to draw, to shape not only institutional strategies but also those of marketing and communication. This went hand in hand with the desire to promote a greater sense of UCL as a single institution. There was concern that the UCL brand was not as well recognised –

Fig. 9.1 Professor Sir Malcolm Grant, UCL's ninth Provost and President who served from 2003 until 2013, pictured on the steps of the Portico. Sir Malcolm is a barrister and a member of the Bench of Middle Temple.

Fig. 9.2 The commitment to international relationships implicit in the phrase 'London's Global University' is evident in this drinks reception of January 2009. Attended by 200 UCL staff and students from China, it marked the Chinese New Year of the Ox. Special guests included Minister Counsellor Tian Xiaogang (Education) and Minister Counsellor Chen Futao (Science and Technology), from the Chinese Embassy and Lord Tim Clement-Jones, Vice Chair for the All-Party Parliamentary China Group.

either at home or overseas – as that of competitors, especially Oxford, Cambridge, Imperial or LSE. On his early visits to East Asia, for instance, Malcolm Grant was alarmed by UCL's lack of profile outside specialist academic communities, a finding confirmed by extensive 'external perception' research. UCL was swift to respond. It became one of the first UK universities to publish an international strategy in 2004, and the Provost himself coined the new strapline 'London's Global University' (Fig. 9.2). Council also approved a major rebranding of UCL, which became evident in extensive new signage around the Bloomsbury campus.[3]

Changes in governance and financial management – such as the creation of executive faculty Deans with the power to manage budgets and an expanded portfolio of non-executive Vice-Provosts to oversee specific areas of work – were important to Grant's early reforms. A programme of voluntary severance and early retirement within UCL's staff helped to achieve much-needed savings, and UCL ended the decade running a budget surplus. There was also a successful devolution of financial support from the finance division to faculty offices. The grouping of faculties into three schools, colloquially known as SLASH, BEAMS and SLMS, was designed to cut costs in administration as well as to encourage greater interdisciplinarity in teaching and research.[4] In 2011 SLMS – the School of Life and Medical Sciences – was restructured from two faculties into four, comprising Brain Sciences, Life Science, Medical Sciences and Population Health Sciences. Further restructuring took place at department level, such as the amalgamation of six modern languages departments into the School of European Languages, Culture and Society (SELCS), part of the Faculty of Arts and Humanities.

During Malcolm Grant's era success was reflected in UCL's rapid rise up the world university rankings. In 2007 it entered the top ten of the then *Times* Higher – QS World University Rankings, rising from 25th place the previous year. While UCL senior management remain rightly aware of the problems inherent in such league tables, UCL has maintained its position in the top ten of the QS World University Rankings ever since; in 2017 it celebrated retaining seventh place for three consecutive years. UCL also has a number of subject areas in the QS top five. For instance, UCL Institute of Education retains its position as the world number one in Education, while Archaeology, Architecture/Built Environment and Anatomy and Physiology all rank in the top five globally.

Professor Michael Arthur: towards UCL 2034

In September 2013 Professor Grant stepped down (Fig. 9.3), to be replaced as Provost and President by Professor Michael Arthur, Vice-Chancellor of the University of Leeds since 2004. Michael Arthur is a hepatologist with research interests in liver cell biology; he had spent much of his career at the University of Southampton, where he was made Professor of Medicine in 1992. He was awarded the Linacre Medal of the Royal College of Physicians in 1994 and became a Fellow of the Academy of Medical Sciences in 1998. At Leeds, Professor Arthur had overseen a programme of sustained improvement in research, innovation and education that led to the university consolidating its position among the top 100 universities in the world. He has a significant profile in higher education as well as medicine, serving for a time as Chair of both the Worldwide Universities Network and the Russell Group of Universities (Fig. 9.4).

The new Provost's unique contribution to date has been to push UCL to think on a much longer timescale than is usual in higher education institutions, focusing on

Fig. 9.3 Jeremy Bentham was recorded as 'present but not voting', in acknowledgement of one of the most popular Bentham legends, when he made a surprise appearance at Malcolm Grant's last ever UCL Council meeting on 9 July 2013. This photograph shows Bentham being moved for the occasion.

Fig. 9.4 Professor Michael Arthur, President and Provost since 2013. He is the first clinical academic to hold this position in the history of UCL.

a 20-year period, rather than one of five or ten years. Upon arrival, Michael Arthur instigated a strategic review of activities which aimed to consolidate and build on the successes of the Grant years and secure the UCL's future for decades to come. The resultant 'UCL 2034' strategy is structured around six principal themes and underpinned by a mission that identifies UCL as:

> A diverse intellectual community, engaged with the wider world and committed to changing it for the better; recognised for our radical and critical thinking and its widespread influence; with an outstanding ability to integrate our education, research, innovation and enterprise for the long-term benefit of humanity.

Building on the previous Provost's concept of UCL as London's Global University, UCL 2034 also places a greater significance on UCL's London location than has any previous strategy. UCL now presents itself as being 'at the centre of a cluster of organisations that will make London the premier destination for higher education,

Fig. 9.5 UCL decorated to celebrate the London 2012 Olympic and Paralympic Games in August 2012. Featured in the foreground is the installation piece 'Bloom', designed by Alisa Andrasek and Jose Sanchez. This so-called 'urban toy', a reconfigurable system of 60,000 recyclable plastic cells, is in the official London 2012 colour of neon pink.

research and innovation'. London's emergence as a global city paralleled UCL's own resurgence, and the university seeks to help fulfil London's post-Olympic legacy, in part through the creation of its own new campus on the former Olympic Park (Fig. 9.5).

As UCL shares in London's highs, so it has shared in its lows. UCL was directly affected by the terrorist attacks of 7 July 2005 (Fig. 9.6). Gladys Wundowa, a member of the cleaning staff for 16 years, was killed on the number 30 bus after finishing her early morning shift, and Miriam Hyman, an Art History graduate, was also among the 52 people who died. In the years since the bombs UCL has honoured both victims through a number of memorial events; an Indian bean tree in the Front Quad is also dedicated to Gladys Wundowa. Academics such as Professor Chris Brewin have been in involved in providing and evaluating NHS mental health support to victims.

Under Michael Arthur, it has been recognised that establishing financial sustainability for UCL is essential. The Provost and his team believe it is necessary as part of UCL's response to recent changes in the ways universities are funded, as well as a response to current uncertainties around Britain's impending departure

Fig. 9.6 Professor Malcolm Grant presides over a minute's silence in the UCL Quad on 8 July 2005, the day after the London terrorist attacks.

Fig. 9.7 Rapid of expansion of student numbers in the 2000s led to severe overcrowding on campus. A number of temporary buildings, such as the marquee in the Main Quad, were erected to provide an interim solution.

from the European Union. A significant capital investment programme, underway since the end of Malcolm Grant's period, has been extended and plans for a new campus in East London more fully developed. This new development in Stratford will be part of the London 2012 Olympic Legacy, which has strong support from the Government and current and past Mayors of London. The major capital programme will be enabled by support from the Government and investing budget surpluses; it is underwritten by a low-interest loan made by the European Investment Bank. A programme to transform and enhance professional services has also been launched to cope with the demands of institutional growth. In line with a tradition of robust academic critique which goes back nearly two centuries at UCL, some members of the academic community have expressed their concerns over the pace of these changes via a series of special meetings of Academic Board.

Growth in student numbers has continued apace at UCL (Fig. 9.7). At the start of Grant's period of office in 2003, UCL had 17,000 students, a number which by 2017 had more than doubled to just under 40,000, of whom 58 per cent were women. The

Fig. 9.8 Since 2005 UCL has awarded its own degrees rather than University of London degrees. Here a group of students celebrate graduation on the steps of the Portico in 2017.

increase has been driven by a number of factors including institutional mergers, the launch of new degree programmes and a sustained recruitment drive for international students, as well as the removal of the government-imposed cap on undergraduate student numbers from 2015. The merger with the Institute of Education in 2014, for instance, added 5,600 students and turned UCL into a majority postgraduate institution; 54 per cent of all students are now postgraduates.

London, and UCL in particular, has long attracted students from across the world. However, as UCL climbed up the world league tables, so its attractiveness to students and faculty from around the world increased. There was a big growth in numbers of both international and EU students; in 2003–4 the percentage of UCL students domiciled outside the UK was 27 per cent, a figure that had increased to 42 per cent by 2016–17.[5] UCL now has the highest absolute number of international students of any UK university. In addition, by 2017 almost half (47 per cent) of UCL's academic, research and teaching staff were not UK nationals. This changing staff and student profile has influenced the internationalisation and diversification of the curriculum in a number of ways.

In 2005 UCL won the power to award its own degrees rather than University of London degrees (Fig. 9.8). This change was part of an ongoing reassessment of the relationship between the College and the federal university that was also taking place across other member institutions. The emergence of the colleges as leading universities in their own right by the 1990s led to a relaxation of central academic control. To date only Imperial College has officially left the University (in 2007), while the previously independent City University joined the federation in 2016, changing its name to City, University of London. The University of London Act 2017 has paved the way for member colleges to claim university title in their own right while remaining within the federation. In 2017 Council took the decision to move forward with this claim, thus aiming to rectify the historic anomaly that UCL is a university in all but name. The University of London Union (ULU), established in 1921 and representing 120,000 students in 2014, was abolished in that year, with its Malet Street building being rebranded as Student Central.

UCL now has the largest research student community in the UK and the largest number of funded Centres for Doctoral Training. In 2014–15 the College awarded over 1,000 doctorates for the first time, a near doubling over the previous decade. The Graduate School, originally set up under Derek Roberts, has developed into the UCL Doctoral School, although much of the responsibility for student support and training remains with faculties and departments. In 2015 a new Institute of Advanced Studies in the Humanities and Social Sciences (IAS) was founded to improve multi-disciplinary collaboration, particularly across subject areas that had been part of the old Faculty of Arts. With a suite of rooms at the heart of the main Wilkins Building, IAS is a research-based community of doctoral students and academics from across UCL, as well as visiting scholars from the UK and overseas. It offers a vibrant programme of events and activities.

Much of the growth in both student and staff numbers was serendipitous – indeed, a culture of planning has sometimes been seen as anathema to UCL. On Michael Arthur's arrival, for example, there was no central planning function. The rapid expansion resulted in huge pressure being placed on the ageing Bloomsbury estate, particularly on teaching space and student facilities, causing frustration for students and staff members alike. The situation has begun to be addressed with, for example, the new Student Centre on Gordon Street, next to the Bloomsbury Theatre. This fills in the last remaining Second World War bombsite on campus, and will provide individual and group study spaces managed by UCL Library Services for 1,000 students. In addition, since 2012 many more learning spaces for medical students have been created, among them the Cruciform Hub, the Royal Free Hub within the Royal Free Hospital and the Whittington Hub in the Highgate Wing.

Research excellence

UCL's growing reputation in the 2000s was further reflected in its successes in the UK's research assessment exercises and in its ability to attract significant research funding. UCL's total research grant spend in 2015–16 was £441 million, an increase of 73 per cent since 2009–10. In addition, UCL is to date Europe's top performing university in accessing funding from the EU's major Horizon 2020 programme. Professor David Price, Vice-Provost (Research) since 2007 (Fig. 9.9), has helped to shape an innovative cross-disciplinary research agenda at UCL, and led it through the 2008 Research Assessment Exercise (RAE) and the 2014 Research Excellence Framework (REF). The results of both these assessments demonstrated UCL's depth and breadth of research excellence. In 2014 UCL was the top-rated university in the UK for 'research power' (a measure of average research score multiplied by staff numbers submitted). Professor Price has argued that as a leading international university, UCL has an obligation to ensure that its output of new knowledge is used to address the many complex problems besetting humankind and the Earth in the twenty-first century. Global challenges such as climate change, urbanisation or pandemic diseases, for instance, will not be solved by experts working in isolation from one another. UCL's first institution-wide research strategy, published in 2008, proposed the innovative – and now widely copied – Grand Challenges programme as a lever to promote the necessary cross-disciplinary thinking in research.[6]

Fig. 9.9 Professor David Price, Vice-Provost (Research), a key figure in shaping UCL's cross-disciplinary research agenda and achieving successful research assessments in 2008 and 2014.

Fig. 9.10 A view of the current University College Hospital, the third on the site, taken in 2016.

This strong cross-disciplinary emphasis has also resulted in the establishment of a range of new hubs designated to facilitate collaborative research between different departments and faculties, including the UCL European Institute, the Centre for Behaviour Change and the Energy Institute. One example of the sort of innovative, cross-disciplinary research in which UCL has come to excel is the collaboration between Deborah Padfield, a visual artist based at the Slade, and Professor Joanna Zakrzewska and other clinicians at UCLH, which explores the value of visual images in the diagnosis and management of chronic pain (Fig 9.10).

External factors, notably the growing levels of investment available for biomedical research in the 2000s, were particularly significant factors in UCL's growth. This was something from which UCL was uniquely well positioned to benefit, following the completion of the merger of its three medical schools in 1998 and the integration of several postgraduate institutes. UCL's reputation in medicine was further enhanced when, in 2009, UCL Partners was designated as one of the first academic health science partnerships in the UK. Today UCL Partners works through over 40 organisations across the NHS, higher education and local authorities to support improvements in health provision and care, encompassing a population of six million people in north London and the surrounding counties.

An important new development in this area is the Sainsbury Wellcome Centre for Neural Circuits and Behaviour (Fig. 9.11). The Centre – funded through a £100

Fig. 9.11 The Sainsbury Wellcome Centre for Neural Circuits and Behaviour. The building that houses this centre for global experts was designed in consultation with neuroscientists from across the world; it is one of the first buildings designed to incorporate knowledge from neuroscience into its fabric from inception. The design of the wavy facade reflects the experimental and theoretical research that takes place inside.

million donation from Gatsby, the charitable foundation set up by David Sainsbury – brings together world-leading scientists to investigate how brain circuits process information to create the neural representations that guide behaviour. The Centre, with additional support from the Wellcome Trust, opened in its award-winning new buildings in 2016; here it was joined by staff from the Gatsby Computational Neuroscience Unit, established by Gatsby 18 years previously. In 2013 the Leonard Wolfson Experimental Neurology Centre, a specialist £20 million research centre funded by the Wolfson Foundation, also opened to investigate exciting new therapies for neurodegenerative diseases such as Alzheimer's and Parkinson's. More recently in 2017 the UCL Huntington Disease Centre, UCL Institute of Neurology, was officially opened by Provost Michael Arthur. The Centre will make significant contributions to research into Huntingdon's disease.

The Francis Crick Institute is perhaps the most significant development in biomedical research at UCL to date (Fig. 9.12). UCL had been involved in discussions over the proposal to find a new home for the Medical Research Council's (MRC) National Institute for Medical Research since 2004. After much negotiation, and many early morning meetings in Malcolm Grant's offices, plans evolved to form a new partnership between the MRC, Cancer Research UK, Wellcome, UCL, Imperial College London and King's College London to set up and operate a new, independent, biomedical discovery institute. The Crick opened in 2016 in a state-of-the-art building behind the British Library in King's Cross. It brings together 1,500 scientists dedicated to understanding the fundamental biology underlying health and disease. Their aim is to translate discoveries into new ways to prevent, diagnose and treat illnesses such as cancer, heart disease, stroke, infections and neurodegenerative diseases.

Although the Biomedical and Life Sciences have tended to dominate the headlines in recent years, and now form around 60 per cent of UCL's academic activity, UCL has research strength across many disciplines. In the Faculty of Arts and Humanities, for example, Professor Mary Fulbrook's important research into the Holocaust and the continuing significance of Nazi persecution in Germany has attracted significant funding and scholarly recognition. In 2016, building on the ground-breaking historical research of Professor Catherine Hall and colleagues, the Centre for the Study of the Legacies of British Slave-ownership was established at UCL with funding from the Hutchins Center at Harvard.

Fig. 9.12 The Francis Crick Institute is a biomedical discovery institute dedicated to understanding the fundamental biology underlying health and disease. In 2016 it moved into a brand new, state-of-the-art building in Central London, enabling 1,500 scientists and support staff to work collaboratively across disciplines. The Crick is the biggest biomedical research facility under a single roof in Europe.

UCL is also committed to making its world-leading research more accessible to audiences outside universities. The UCL Public Engagement Unit was created in 2008 as one of six in the UK to be funded by HEFCE, Research Councils UK (RCUK) and the Wellcome Trust through the beacons for public engagement programme. The unit has supported and funded a range of activities, with a focus on better connecting UCL academics with communities and organisations in London and with socially excluded groups. There is now a public engagement strategy in place and public engagement is recognised in academic staff promotion criteria. UCL Public Policy is an initiative of the Vice-Provost (Research), set up in 2011 to strengthen links between UCL researchers and policymakers in government, business or the third sector. UCL also seeks to provide leadership on the 'open access' agenda; UCL Press was launched in 2015 (led by UCL Library Services) as the UK's first fully open access university press, with all books, journals and monographs freely available online. Since 2013 the UCL Festival of Culture (originally known as the Festival of the Arts) has provided a public showcase for UCL's research in the Arts, Humanities and Social Sciences (Fig. 9.13).

Growth in research income since 2003 has substantially increased the size of the research staff population at UCL. However, many of these staff members are on short-term contracts and face the precarious task of finding continuous employment in an increasingly competitive higher education field. UCL today places great importance on developing the opportunities for early-career researchers, and is committed likewise to ensuring equal opportunities and maximising diversity.

Another area in which UCL has made significant progress since 2003 is in commercialisation and enterprise activities. In 2006 Malcolm Grant commissioned an external review of UCL's work in this area which led to the creation of the post of Vice-Provost (Enterprise). The position was initially held by Professor Mike Spyer, a neuroscientist and long-term Board member of UCL's technology transfer company, UCL BioMedica. The review recommended broadening the remit of UCL BioMedica to include disciplines such as computing and engineering alongside the biomedical sciences, and it was subsequently renamed UCL Business (UCLB).

Under Professor Spyer, and his successor Professor Stephen Caddick between 2010 and 2015, UCL developed a strong reputation for excellence in enterprise. There has been continuing success in the commercialisation of research through UCLB, which makes connections between UCL academics and industry. The company has overseen the development of many licences and spin-out companies, ranging from

Fig. 9.13 Henrietta Simpson, *(Don't) Fall On Me*, submission to the Graduate Degree Show of 2016.

gene therapy treatments to rail safety systems to computer software. In contrast to older forms of tech 'transfer', UCLB is moving towards a model of 'technology commercialisation' in which the academics stay involved as the process moves, for example, though clinical trials to developing products for patients. UCL's recently announced £50 million investment fund is a significant boost to its enterprise agenda, while student entrepreneurship is promoted through a range of activities including competitions, awards and a popular 'boot camp'.

Global impact

The first two decades of the twenty-first century have seen the growth of far larger and more professionally managed fundraising campaigns than ever before, reflecting a concerted attempt to re-position UCL as a major fundraising university. Between 2004 and 2012 the 'Campaign for UCL' raised £316 million, exceeding its original £300 million target two years early. Although a Development Office had existed since the mid-1990s, UCL's income from philanthropy remained modest relative to its student numbers, research income and international reputation until the mid-2010s. UCL was underperforming compared to Oxford, Cambridge and some North American universities, which often launch 'billion dollar' campaigns managed by very large staff teams. Since joining UCL, however, Michael Arthur has committed around one-quarter of his time to fundraising and alumni relations activities. In 2016 he signalled the growing importance of philanthropy to UCL by raising the Development Office to Vice-Provost level. Lori Houlihan became UCL's first Vice-Provost (Development), overseeing a 75-strong team and generating £10 in donations for every £1 invested in the office.

In September 2016 UCL launched 'It's All Academic' – its biggest-ever philanthropy and engagement campaign, associated with the UCL 2034 strategies (Fig. 9.14). Alongside an appeal seeking to raise £600 million by 2020, this Campaign also has specific targets around promoting engagement with alumni through new activities such as an annual public engagement festival and a new alumni social network. The Campaign launch in China, home to UCL's fastest-growing group of alumni, was a very grand affair with a televised ball and reception.

The growing importance of China to UCL is reflected in the new strategic partnership between UCL and Peking University (PKU), which was formalised in 2016 and aims to work together to address global challenges. The partnership includes a joint MBA programme and collaborative working in a number of areas, such as the International Centre for Chinese Heritage and Archaeology and the

Fig. 9.14 Provost Michael Arthur launches 'It's All Academic', UCL's large-scale campaign for philanthropy and engagement, in 2016. Aligned with UCL's long-term strategy UCL 2034, the campaign focuses on four main themes that reflect the unique contribution and culture of UCL: health, students, London and disruptive thinking.

Confucius Institute at UCL Institute of Education, which develops Chinese language teaching in UK schools.

Since the start of Michael Arthur's period as Provost and the appointment of Dr Dame Nicola Brewer as Vice-Provost (International) in 2014 (Fig. 9.15), UCL's international strategy has undergone a shift in direction, following an extensive consultation with staff and students. As well as setting targets to increase the proportion of international students, the College's 2004 international strategy had opened the way for UCL to establish a number of small overseas campuses. The first of these, the UCL School of Energy and Resources Australia, was set up in partnership with the State of South Australia in 2009, offering postgraduate education in the energy and resources sectors (Fig. 9.16). In 2010 UCL signed a five-year agreement with the University of Nazarbayev in Kazakhstan to deliver a foundation year and a course in English for Academic Purposes. In 2012 UCL became the first British university to open a campus in Qatar, establishing a centre for the study of cultural heritage in partnership with the Qatar Foundation. Drawing

Fig. 9.15 Dame Nicola Brewer, Vice-Provost (International) since 2014. Brewer was a senior diplomat at the Foreign and Commonwealth Office before joining UCL in May 2014. She was British High Commissioner to South Africa, Lesotho and Swaziland from May 2009 to September 2013.

Fig. 9.16 In 2009 UCL hosted a life-sized fibreglass kangaroo sculpture as part of a public arts project, reflecting its special relationship with South Australia following the opening of the UCL campus in Adelaide.

upon the expertise of the UCL Institute of Archaeology, UCL Qatar offered MA programmes in museum and library studies. Although not an overseas campus, in 2011 the Yale–UCL Collaborative was established as a research, education and clinical collaboration, originally in cardiovascular medicine but subsequently expanded to other disciplines.

UCL 2034 commits UCL to 'delivering global impact'. Its rise in the world university rankings since the first international strategy was published has fundamentally changed the ways in which the College believes it can have global impact. There has thus been a strategic shift away from an overseas campus model to one of 'partnerships of equivalence', in which benefits flow both ways and global impact is achieved through partnership working. The contract with Kazakhstan was therefore not renewed, and in 2015 a new partnership was signed between UCL Engineering and the University of South Australia, committing the two institutions to work together to deliver teaching and research. The collaboration with PKU is the first of a proposed small number of core strategic partnerships which UCL is developing through its global engagement strategy, launched in 2015 for a first five-year phase.

The global engagement strategy also commits UCL to an ambitious increase in the proportion of students taking up international mobility opportunities such as a period of study abroad, including short-term overseas experiences, and to increasing the diversity of the international student population. These two objectives aim to cultivate students' global outlook, preparing them for global lives and careers. Since 2012 competence in a modern foreign language has likewise been a requirement for graduation at UCL. The year 2012 also saw the introduction of UCL's Global Citizenship Programme – a free, two-week optional scheme which runs in the period after summer examinations. Attracting around 1,000 students, the programme gets participants to work in small, cross-disciplinary teams on real-world problems, such as global health or urbanisation, while also developing a range of skills and meeting people from across UCL.

The student experience

These are just a few examples of a growing emphasis on improving the quality of the 'student experience' in recent years. By the late 2000s it had become apparent that UCL's stellar research success was not yet being mirrored in the quality of education it offered to students. A series of poor results in student surveys, notably the National Student Survey (NSS) of third-year students, forced some institutional rethinking about undergraduate teaching, with concerns over the amount of assessment and quality of student feedback at the fore. The introduction of variable undergraduate tuition fees provides a context in which student satisfaction is taken ever more seriously.[7] The UK Government's new Teaching Excellence Framework (TEF), which seeks to assess higher education teaching through a series of proxy measures, has also been influential; UCL's silver grade in the first round of this assessment in 2017 was received with relief and a renewed commitment to ongoing improvement.

During Professor Grant's period in office several steps were taken to improve the student experience. These included an improved student records system, a single timetable for undergraduate programmes across all faculties and an increase in library opening hours. Changing technology has also had a significant impact on teaching and learning at UCL, as across all higher education institutions. In 2008, for example, UCL was one of the first UK universities to launch an iTunes platform, something previously taken up only by universities in the US. All courses now provide students with access to a virtual learning environment known as 'moodle'; UCL has its own YouTube channel, and there have been experiments with new teaching techniques such as the 'flipped lecture'. This has been used particularly in the Department of Mathematics and on the BSc Arts and Sciences – UCL's new liberal arts degree launched in 2012 in order to foster interdisciplinary thinking.

Under the UCL 2034 strategy there has been a concerted effort behind the better integration of research and education, with UCL seeking to offer a distinctive 'research-based' education. To many academic staff, this is nothing new. Students at UCL have always benefited from the research expertise of their lecturers and Professors. Moreover, in some areas, such as the Department of English, longstanding traditions of tutorial-based teaching continue to thrive. To its advocates, however, research-based education means something more: a commitment to enabling students to participate actively in research and enquiry at every level of the curriculum, as encapsulated in the 'Connected Curriculum', an institution-wide strategy adopted in 2014.

An ongoing, top-down attempt is therefore underway to develop undergraduate teaching in line with the UCL Education Strategy 2016–21, led by Professor Anthony Smith as Vice-Provost (Education) in partnership with the UCL Arena Centre for Research-based Education. There is a concerted effort, for instance, to increase the proportion of teaching staff who hold the nationally recognised fellowship of the Higher Education Academy. However, it would be wrong to ignore the many bottom-up shifts, with staff-driven changes to many degree programmes across all disciplines, often anticipating rather than following this agenda. One example is in Engineering, where experiments with changes to the Civil Engineering programme preceded a more thorough overhaul of the engineering curriculum across seven departments. The Integrated Engineering Programme (IEP) was launched in 2014 with a focus on problem-based, real-world learning from year one and a compulsory, immersive module called 'How to Change the World' in year two. A second example is on the multidisciplinary BSc Philosophy, Politics and Economics, a programme launched in 2015 and based in UCL Political Science. It offers final-year students three disciplinary perspectives on a specific global policy problem through a compulsory 'capstone' module.

UCL's museums and collections have also played a growing role in teaching and learning over the past decade (Fig. 9.17). By the late 1990s UCL's extensive cultural collections – including the Art Museum, Petrie Museum and Grant Museum, as well as over 6,000 specimens and objects comprising the Pathology Collection and Galton Collection of scientific instruments and memorabilia – were facing an uncertain future. This was in part because many of these collections were no longer routinely used in teaching. Professor Michael Worton, then Vice-Provost (Academic and International), was a significant player in helping to restructure the collections (Fig. 9.18), all originally housed within different academic departments, into a central department known as 'UCL Museums and Collections' (rebranded as UCL Culture

Fig. 9.17 Students from UCL's BA Education Studies degree having a teaching session in UCL's Art Museum in 2016. Since the mid-2000s UCL's museums and collections have been used more extensively for teaching and learning across a range of disciplines.

Fig. 9.18 Professor Michael Worton first joined UCL as a lecturer in French in 1980 and retired in 2013. Since 1998 Vice-Provost (latterly 'Academic and International'), he was responsible for developing and promoting UCL's international strategy as well as overseeing teaching and learning. In 2011 he was awarded the Chevalier de la Legion d'Honneur.

Fig. 9.19 (below) Students examining bones and other objects in the UCL Grant Museum in 2007 as part of a UCL Widening Participation summer school.

Fig. 9.20 (opposite) The UCL Academy is a new mixed school, taking pupils aged 11–18. It opened in September 2012 with 180 Year 7 students (first years) and 125 students in Year 12 (Sixth Form) and grew year on year, reaching capacity in September 2015. The Academy specialises in maths and science, and enjoys a close relationship with UCL.

in 2016). This step was important in enabling the development of a significant programme of research, teaching and public engagement. In particular, under the direction of Helen Chatterjee, now Head of Research and Teaching for UCL Culture, UCL has developed an international specialism in object-based learning (OBL).

The new emphasis on 'widening access' promoted by the Blair government led to great efforts in UCL to encourage well-qualified applicants from state schools. However, despite having Widening Participation strategies in place since 2001 (Fig. 9.19), progress has been slow, with the modest increase in the diversity of the undergraduate intake being neither sufficiently significant nor fast enough. Since 1999 UCL has enjoyed a partnership with City and Islington Sixth Form College aimed at supporting students in making applications to UCL. Various other initiatives are now in place, such as the Faculty of Laws' Widening Participation summer school for Sixth Form students interested in studying law at university.

In September 2012 the College became the first university in the UK to be the sole sponsor of an academy school. UCL Academy is a non-selective, mixed, state secondary school with 1,150 pupils in the London Borough of Camden (Fig. 9.20). Its successful establishment was driven by Professors Grant and Worton, in response

Fig. 9.21 The UCL School of Pharmacy, founded by the Pharmaceutical Society of Great Britain in 1842. The School merged with UCL in 2012.

to Lord Adonis's vision that universities should become involved in the running of schools. This initiative was not without controversy; there were objections from some opposed to academy schools on principle, and from others over its location in Swiss Cottage rather than Bloomsbury. However, the school now forms a core plank of UCL's London strategy. UCL academics deliver a regular programme of lectures and masterclasses, and Academy pupils have access to some UCL facilities. The Founding Principal, Mrs Geraldine Davies, was made an Honorary Fellow of UCL in 2017 in recognition of all that she did in translating UCL's vision into reality.

Mergers

The last decade has seen a number of important mergers at UCL, notably the School of Pharmacy in 2012 and the Institute of Education in 2014.[8] The School of Pharmacy was founded by the Pharmaceutical Society of Great Britain in 1842 as its College. It

Fig. 9.22a John Adams (centre), the first Principal of the London Day Training College and the University of London's first Professor of Education. He is seated with Margaret Punnett, the first – and for many years the only – female member of staff, who served as deputy for 31 years, and Percy Nunn.

became a School of the University of London in 1926, although the Pharmaceutical Society retained financial responsibility for the maintenance of the School until after the Second World War. Work began on a purpose-built School in Brunswick Square in 1938 but, owing to the interruption of war, this was not completed until 1960. In 2012 the School joined UCL's Faculty of Life Sciences, helping to make this Europe's largest grouping of biomedical research (Fig. 9.21).

The Institute of Education began life in 1902 as the London Day Training College. It was founded by the London County Council in conjunction with the University of London to train teachers (Fig. 9.22a). In 1932 it became a central activity of the University of London and acquired a new name, the Institute of Education. This signified its growing importance as an international centre of research and advanced studies in education as well as a provider of teacher training, and the Institute attracted significant funding from the Carnegie Corporation. Originally housed in Southampton Row, the Institute relocated to the newly-built Senate House in the late 1930s before moving to its new building in Bedford Way in 1975. This brutalist building, designed by Sir Denys Lasdun, remains one of the most

Fig. 9.22b The main building of the Institute of Education at 20 Bedford Way.

impressive examples of modernist architecture in the UK, housing the Institute of Education as well as other UCL departments in its northern section (Fig. 9.22b).

In July 2012 the Institute of Americas was created at UCL as a department of the Faculty of Social and Historical Sciences. The Institute is a multidisciplinary specialist institution for the study of Latin America, the United States, the Caribbean and Canada, and was originally based within the School of Advanced Studies at the University of London. As the UCL Institute of the Americas it has expanded its research base and postgraduate teaching, and in September 2018 launched a new History and Politics of the Americas BA, offering the only undergraduate degree of its kind anywhere in the UK. A year later, in 2013, Imperial College London's Translation Studies Unit moved to UCL, forming a new Centre for Translation Studies in the Faculty of Arts and Humanities. The new Centre offers highly specialist postgraduate and professional courses in scientific, medical and technical translation. In 2013 the Survey of London, founded in 1894 by Arts and Crafts designer Charles Robert Ashbee, became a part of The Bartlett, where it continues its 120-year tradition of producing detailed topographical and architectural surveys of London districts.

UCL has also acquired some important Medical Research Council institutes. The MRC Laboratory for Molecular Cell Biology was established at UCL in 2013 as a division within the Faculty of Life Sciences, having been originally set up in 1993 under the

Fig. 9.23 Professor John O'Keefe, winner of the Nobel Prize for Physiology or Medicine in 2014 for his work on the positioning function of certain cells in the brain.

Fig. 9.24 Professor John Hardy (UCL Institute of Neurology) was awarded the $3 million Breakthrough Prize in Life Sciences for research into Alzheimer's and Parkinson's diseases.

leadership of Professor Colin Hopkins as one of the first centres for cell biology in the UK. The unit carries out research into fundamental aspects of cell function and their links to human diseases. In June 2017 the MRC Prion Unit successfully transferred to UCL as part of a new UCL Institute of Prion Diseases within the Faculty of Brain Sciences. Although not formally part of the College, the Unit has been based at UCL since 1998, where it conducts research into prion molecular processes in human disease – notably neurodegenerative conditions such as Alzheimer's.

UCL has long been home to many world-leading academics, among them Nobel laureates and other prize winners, far too many to list in full here. Professor John O'Keefe, Director of the Sainsbury Wellcome Centre for Neural Circuits and Behaviour, won the 2014 Nobel Prize in Physiology or Medicine for the discovery of cells that constitute a positioning system in the brain –an 'inner GPS' – that enables us to orient ourselves (Fig. 9.23). In 2015 Professor John Hardy (UCL Institute of Neurology) was awarded the $3 million Breakthrough Prize in Life Sciences for his pioneering research into Alzheimer's and Parkinson's diseases (Fig. 9.24). This is the first time that the prize has been awarded to a UK researcher, reflecting UCL's world-leading position in dementia research.

Student life

UCL now has one of the UK's largest student communities and provides teaching in a very diverse range of subjects. Most students are based on the Bloomsbury campus, but others are located at teaching hospitals and institutes elsewhere in London. The students' union today supports 250 student clubs and societies, while medical students largely organise their social and sporting activities through RUMS (Royal Free, University College and Middlesex Medical Students Association), formed in the wake of the final medical school merger in 1998 (Fig. 9.25). UCL's student newspaper was founded after the Second World War; it continues today as *Pi Media* with a print magazine, an online news platform and a TV channel. UCL's Voluntary Services Unit runs one of the UK's largest student volunteering programmes with around 1,700 students campaigning, fundraising or volunteering for a wide range of charities and community organisations.

A longstanding tradition of student campaigning and protest continues to thrive at UCL. The invasion of Iraq in 2003 was met with a large-scale demonstration in the Front Quad which spilled over into Gower Street. Tuition fees have been an important cause since the late 1990s, and in 2010 a group of students staged an occupation of the Jeremy Bentham Room, in the heart of the Wilkins building, in protest over the proposed increase in tuition fees to £9,000 a year. In 2012 the students' union was involved, alongside staff members and local residents, in a solidarity campaign

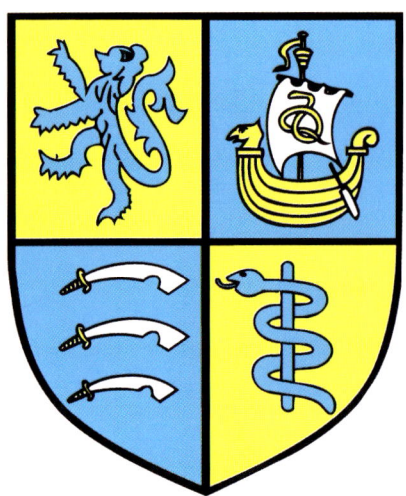

Fig. 9.25 The logo of RUMS, the Royal Free, University College and Middlesex Medical Students Association, formed in the wake of the 1998 merger between the three constituent medical schools. Its crest today represents the three schools. The ship represents UCH, the lion represents the Royal Free and the cutlasses represent the Middlesex; the Rod of Asclepius is the international symbol of medicine.

Fig. 9.26 A demonstration as part of the student rent strike of 2015. The cost of living in the capital is a recurring concern for students attending UCL and other London educational institutions.

against the negotiations with Newham Council for a new UCL campus to be built on the Carpenters Estate in Stratford. Students and staff similarly worked together on the successful campaign that led to a 2010 commitment to pay the London living wage to all staff at UCL, including contract cleaners.

A key area of student campaigning in recent years has been on the rising costs of living in London. What began with a rent strike by 1,000 students in protest over delayed building works and poor living standards at Hawkridge House and Campbell House in 2015–16 evolved into a wider campaign (Fig. 9.26). By summer 2017 this had achieved significant concessions from the College authorities. The 'UCL Cut the Rent' campaign secured rent reductions, the halving of accommodation deposits and the creation of a range of new bursaries, and has since inspired similar groups at other universities.

Equality and diversity

Today, besides a population of nearly 40,000 students, UCL has over 12,500 people on its payroll, 52 per cent of them women, making it the biggest employer in the London Borough of Camden. Progress on addressing inequalities and improving diversity among the staff has been relatively slow at UCL, as across higher education as a whole. However, since 2003 UCL has made serious attempts to improve and monitor staff diversity, currently working to the Equality, Diversity and Inclusion Strategy 2015–2020. The strategy has modest but achievable targets around increasing staff diversity at senior levels, primarily looking at disability, gender and race, alongside other goals such as improving the experiences of those with caring responsibilities. There are also a number of equality and diversity networks and groups, such as the Lesbian, Gay, Bisexual, Transgender and Queer Equalities and Advisory Group (LEAG) and the Out@UCL network.

Around one-fifth of UCL's staff overall come from a minority ethnic background, although this proportion varies considerably between faculties and roles, falling to just 12 per cent of academic staff and nine per cent of Professors. In particular there remains a problem around the low numbers of academics of Black African/Black Caribbean heritage at UCL, as elsewhere. There were just 85 black Professors out of 18,510 Professors across the UK in 2014 – the year in which Michael Arthur hosted a groundbreaking and widely reported discussion at UCL addressing the question 'Why isn't my Professor black?'. In August 2015 UCL was one of eight higher education institutions to receive the Race Equality Charter Bronze Award, marking some improvement in this field. Across UCL various attempts have been made to reflect diversity better in the curriculum, supported by a programme of 'Liberating the Curriculum' small grants.

UCL was one of the first universities to sign up to the Athena Swan Award, which recognises good employment practices for women working in higher education – originally in science and engineering, but since 2015 across all disciplines. UCL was awarded its first College-wide bronze award in 2006, which it has renewed on several occasions, and it was awarded a silver in 2015. At departmental level a number of silver awards have been made, and both the MRC Laboratory for Molecular Cell Biology and the Elizabeth Garrett Anderson Centre for Women's Health have won the much-coveted gold, making these beacons of 'achievement in gender equality'. In 2013 Professor Uta Frith, the first woman at UCL to become both a Fellow of the Royal Society (FRS)and a Fellow of the British Academy (FBA), founded UCL Women, a grassroots network for female academics in STEM subjects at UCL.

Michael Arthur has also shown strong support for women in leadership roles at UCL. In 2017 female Professors made up 28 per cent of the salaried Professoriate today, a modest improvement on the 22 per cent of 2003, while the gender pay gap at this level has also shrunk in recent years.[9] Following changes introduced by Michael Arthur, in 2017 three out of the seven Vice-Provosts and four out of the 11 Faculty Deans were women. In 2013 Susan Collins became the first female Slade Professor of Fine Art.

There are nearly 1,200 academic and clinical Professors at UCL today – meaning there are twice as many Professors in 2018 as there were students who started in 1828. As the bicentenary of the College's foundation approaches in 2026, it is clear that UCL's longstanding traditions of radicalism and independence are alive and well. UCL's connections to London, one of the world's leading global cities, have been renewed and strengthened on many fronts, now more important than ever. The ambitious plans for UCL's new campus in East London brings the old 'Cockney College' epithet back to life, while the far-reaching renewal and redevelopment of the Bloomsbury estate (Fig. 9.27) should provide solid foundations on which the achievements of the next century or two can be built.

Fig. 9.27 Students walking up Malet Place on the main UCL campus in the frost. The Bloomsbury site, the traditional heart of UCL, is being redeveloped to meet the needs of twenty-first century students.

From Bloomsbury to 'UCL East'

Towards the start of Professor Grant's period as Provost, a number of major estates projects were reaching a conclusion – notably the Andrew Huxley Building in 2004 (Fig. 9.28), as well as the London Centre for Nanotechnology at 17–19 Gordon Street and the School of Slavonic and East European Studies (SSEES) building in 2005 (Fig. 9.29). However, it was increasingly obvious that a serious capital programme was needed to address years of underinvestment across the campus. In 2011 Council approved the 'Bloomsbury masterplan', which set out a strategic vision for the development and improvement of the Bloomsbury estate over a period of 10–15 years, and which was aimed at maximising space on a cramped site and enhancing the student and staff experience. The first major project to be completed under this programme was the redevelopment of 22 Gordon Street to create a new home for The Bartlett faculty. From the outside this appears to be a new building, but is in fact built around the retained structure of the former Wates House, providing a link to the building's past and the history of architecture at UCL (Fig. 9.30).

Fig. 9.28 UCL's Andrew Huxley Building lit up at dusk. The Huxley Building, formally opened on 4 March 2005 by Lord Sainsbury, Minister for Science and Innovation, is home to UCL's new Molecular and Cellular Neuroscience Laboratories. It is named for Nobel Laureate Sir Andrew Huxley in honour of his contribution to UCL and Physiology.

Fig. 9.29 The UCL SSEES Building, opened on 19 October 2005, houses the UCL School of Slavonic and Eastern European Studies and its related research centres. Located on Taviton Street, the building is a model for environmentally friendly architecture.

Fig. 9.30 The refurbished UCL Bartlett School of Architecture, 22 Gordon Street, London. The refurbishment, designed by leading architects Hawkins/Brown, has doubled the space available in a modern, light-filled building, built on the structural concrete frame of its predecessor. The building was officially opened by The University of London Chancellor, Her Royal Highness The Princess Royal, on 16 December 2016.

Other projects completed in 2017 include the provision of a refurbished and extended main refectory in the undercroft of the Wilkins Building, a stunning new outdoor social and events space known as the Wilkins Terrace (Fig. 9.31), and the renovation of 15 Woburn Square to support the work of the Confucius Institute. In a move away from Bloomsbury, the UCL School of Management has a new home on the 38th floor of One Canada Square, Canary Wharf, with state-of-the-art teaching and research facilities. Ongoing work includes modifications to the Kathleen Lonsdale Building; the redevelopment of the Grade II-listed Bentham House for the Faculty of Laws and the refurbishment and the remodelling of the 1930s Faculty of Engineering building at 66–72 Gower Street. There is a strong focus on embedding environmental sustainability into this building and refurbishment programme.

However, the most significant project has to be UCL East, the creation of an entirely new 4.6 hectare campus in Stratford (Fig. 9.32). UCL had been seeking growing room outside Bloomsbury for a number of years. As the earlier, ill-fated Carpenters Estate proposal was quietly abandoned, the suggestion that UCL form a central component of a new Cultural and Education District on Queen Elizabeth Olympic Park was met with enthusiasm by the Mayor of London. UCL East is envisaged as a radical new model of how a university campus can be embedded in the local community (Fig. 9.33), and will sit alongside the V&A, the University of the Arts London and Sadler's Wells. The first UCL teaching space opened in 2018 in Queen Elizabeth Olympic Park's former broadcasting centre, now known as Here East, on which UCL acquired a 20-year lease. In October 2017 The Bartlett launched four innovative new programmes which will be delivered jointly at Here East and 22 Gordon Street. The first purpose-built UCL East building for the College is set to open in 2021, and will contain student accommodation alongside flexible research, innovation, teaching and engagement space.

Despite scepticism voiced by some members of UCL's academic community, including through Academic Board and the unions, a great deal of work has been undertaken to develop an academic vision for the new campus, drawing on expertise from across UCL, including experiments, arts, society and technology (EAST). Moreover the new campus will strengthen and build on existing UCL connections with communities in East London. For example, the UCL Centre for Access to Justice, an initiative of UCL Laws set up in 2012 by Dame Hazel Genn to combine legal education with *pro bono* advice, runs an innovative legal advice centre in the Guttmann Health and Wellbeing Centre in Stratford. A bold and imaginative project, UCL East reflects the pioneering spirit that has shaped UCL since its foundation and ensured its unique and remarkable legacy.

Fig. 9.31 A new public space in the Bloomsbury Campus, the Wilkins Terrace opened in 2017. Named for UCL's original architect William Wilkins (1778--1839), the Terrace forms a new pedestrian route from Gower Street to Gordon Street.

Fig. 9.32 UCL is developing an ambitious new campus on Queen Elizabeth Olympic Park, to the south of the Aquatics Centre and the ArcelorMittal Orbit. The new campus is part of a major regeneration development that aims to transform the area and bring educational, cultural and economic benefits to local communities.

Fig. 9.33 An illustrative model of the UCL East campus on Queen Elizabeth Olympic Park. The site will ultimately provide around 180,000 square metres of new floor space, equivalent to 25 Wembley football pitches. The two UCL East Phase 1 buildings are illustrated in the more detailed wooden models.

Appendix

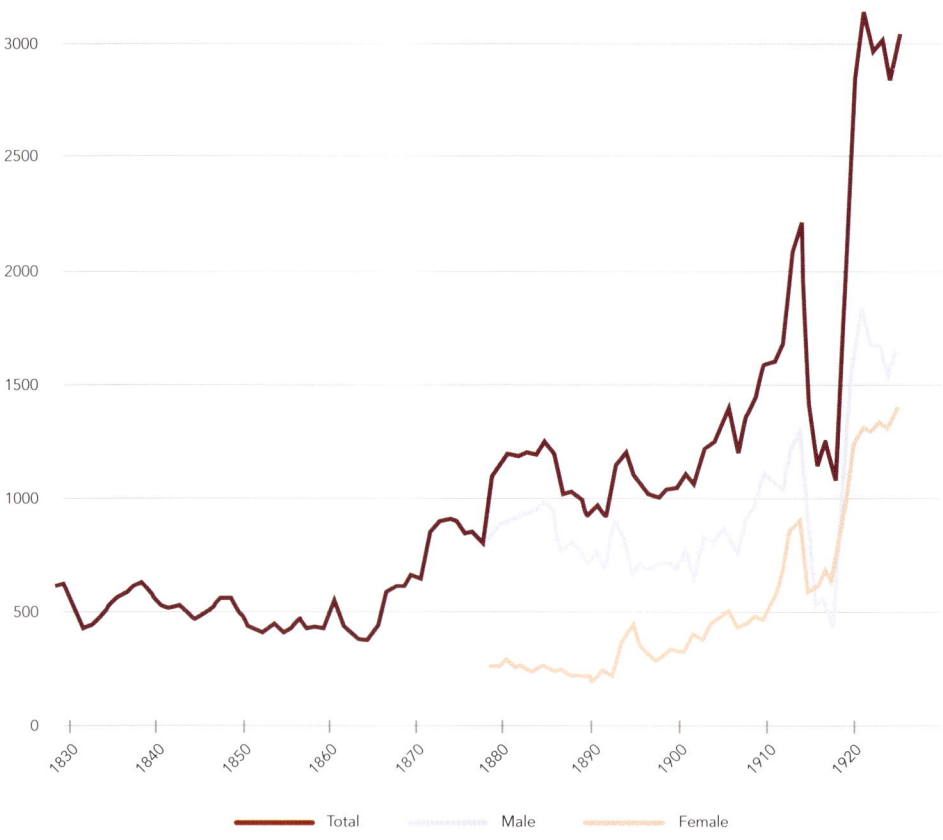

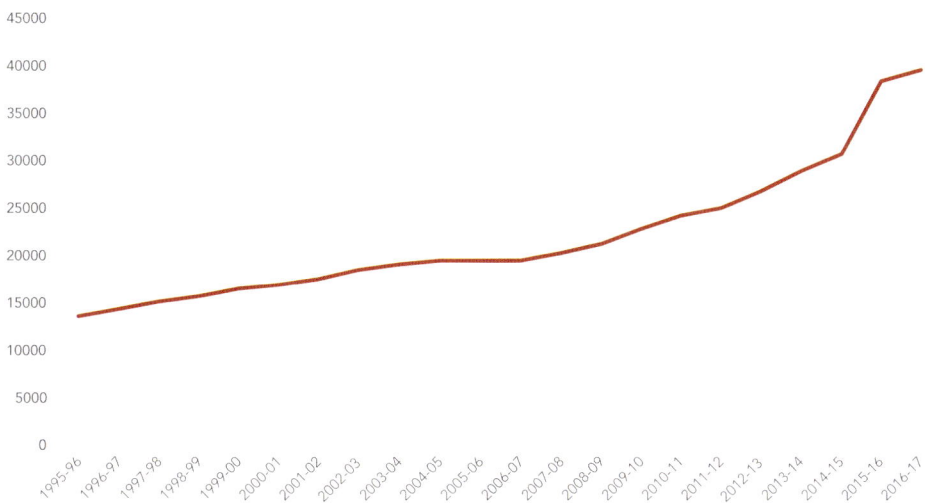

Total UCL students by year

APPENDIX

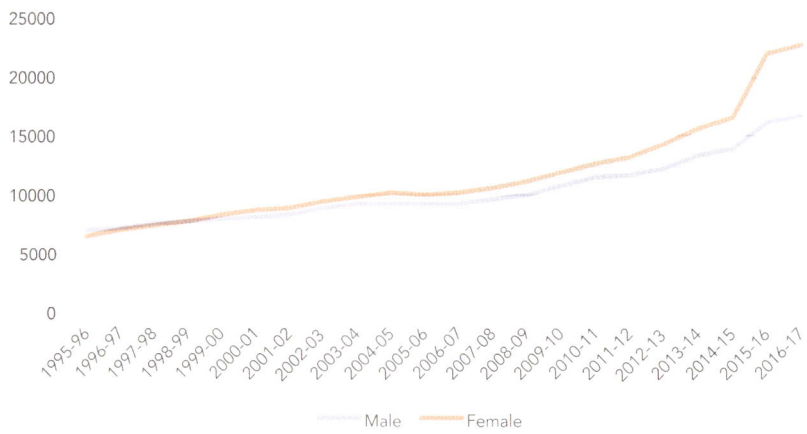

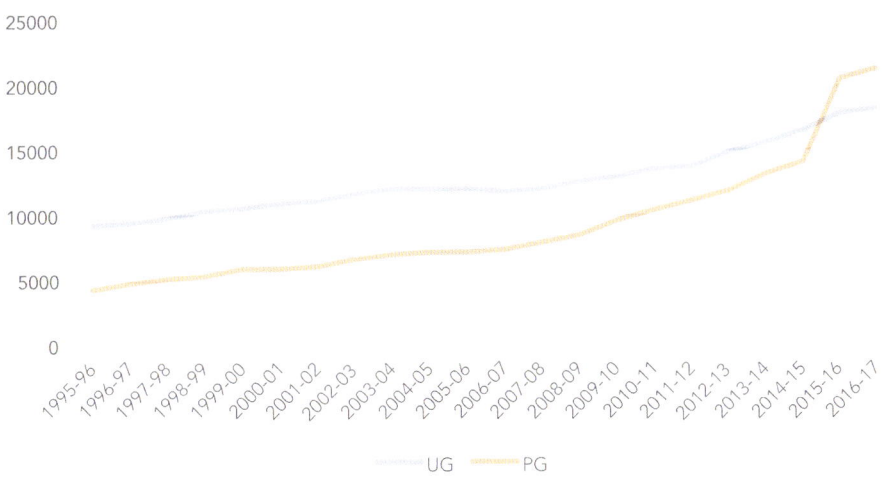

Further reading

Richard Aldrich, *The Institute of Education, 1902–2002: A Centenary History*. London: Institute of Education, 2002.

Lynne Amidon, *Illustrated History of the Royal Free Hospital*. London: Royal Free Hospital, 1996.

James Bates and Carol Ibbetson, *The World of UCL Union*. London: UCL Union, 1993.

Georgina Ferry, *Neural Architects: The Sainsbury Wellcome Centre from Idea to Reality*. London: Unicorn, 2017.

Gillian Furlong, *Treasures From UCL*. London: UCL Press, 2015.

H. Hale Bellot, *University College London 1826–1926*. London: University of London Press, 1929.

N. B. Harte, *The Admission of Women to University College London: A Centenary Lecture*. London: UCL, 1979.

Briony Hudson with Maureen Boylan, *The School of Pharmacy, University of London: Medicines, Science and Society, 1842–2013*. School of Pharmacy 2013.

Neil McInytre, *How British Women Became Doctors: The Story of the Royal Free Hospital and its Medical School*. London: Wenrowave Press, 2014.

Jeremy Melvin, ed. *175 Years of Architectural Education at UCL*. Bartlett School of Architecture, 2016.

Margaret Murray, *My First Hundred Years*. London: William Kimberm, 1963.

Ian Roberts, *History of the School of Slavonic and East European Studies 1915–1990*. London: SSEES, 1991.

Kathleen L. Sheppard, *The Life of Margaret Alice Murray: A Woman's Work in Archaeology*. Plymouth: Lexington Books, 2013.

Betsy Teasley Trope, Stephen Quirke and Peter Lacovara, *Excavating Egypt: Great Discoveries from the Petrie Museum of Egyptian Archaeology*, University College London. Atlanta, GA: Michael C. Carlos Museum, Emory University, 2005.

Notes

1. Since 1959 the Bentham Project at UCL has been engaged in the massive enterprise of preparing for publication Bentham's collected works and correspondence – 32 volumes of the new *Collected Works* have now been published. Since 2010 the Transcribe Bentham project has involved volunteers in transcribing several thousand previously unstudied and unpublished manuscripts, helping to create a free-to-access historical and philosophical resource of great significance.

2. The papers of the Society for the Diffusion of Useful Knowledge are now in UCL's Library, as are Brougham's own papers.

3. This chapter will use the term UCL, rather than 'the College', in line with current usage.

4. The three schools are the School of Laws, Arts and Humanities, and Social and Historical Sciences (SLASH), the School of Built Environment, Engineering and Mathematical and Physical Sciences (BEAMS), and the School of Life and Medical Sciences (SLMS). The Institute of Education now forms a single Faculty and fourth School.

5. In 2016–17 29 per cent of undergraduates were classified as 'overseas' students for fee purposes, rising to 32 per cent of postgraduate students.

6. The first Grand Challenge was Global Health, followed in 2009 by Sustainable Cities and in 2010 by Intercultural Interaction and Human Wellbeing. In 2015 Transformative Technology and Justice and Equality were added.

7. From 2006 universities were allowed to charge variable fees repayable after graduation up to £3,000. This cap was increased to £9,000 from the 2012–13 academic year.

8. Both these institutions have extensive published histories and this chapter can only provide a short summary; see Further reading.

9. Comparative data taken from 1 April 2003 and 1 April 2017.

Picture credits

The publishers would like to thank the following for permission to reproduce their material. Every care has been taken to trace copyright holders, but we will be happy to rectify any omissions in future editions.

1.1 Henry Tonks and Henry Clarence Whaite, *The Four Founders of University College: Lord Brougham, Jeremy Bentham, Thomas Campbell and Henry Crabb Robinson*, 1922. Oil. UCL Art Museum, University College London (UCL 5723); 1.2 UCL Digital Media; 1.3 UCL Library: College Collection; 1.4 James Lonsdale, *Henry Brougham, 1st Baron Brougham and Vaux*, 1821. Oil on canvas. Photo © National Portrait Gallery, London; 1.5 Virginia University Library; 1.6 Edinburgh University Library; 1.7 Goodman, *Sir Isaac Lyon Goldsmid*, c.1866. Oil. UCL Art Museum, University College London (UCL 5618); 1.8 UCL Library: College Archives; 1.9 UCL Library: College Archives; 1.10 UCL Library; 1.11 UCL Library: College Archives; 1.12 UCL Library: College Archives; 1.13 UCL Library: College Archives; 1.14 Guildhall Library; 1.15 Charles Walter Radclyffe, *London University College*. Lithograph. UCL Art Museum, University College London (UCL 3037); 1.16 British Museum, Department of Prints and Drawings.

2.1 UCL Library: College Archives; 2.2 Dean of Clinical Sciences; 2.3 UCL Library: College Collection; 2.4a Department of Physics; 2.4b UCL Library: College Archives; 2.5 UCL Library: College Collection; 2.6 Courtesy of the late Professor J. S Cummins; 2.7 John Linnell, *Sarah Austin (née Taylor)*, 1834. Chalk and pencil. Photo © National Portrait Gallery, London; 2.8 Sir Daniel Macnee, *John Ramsay McCulloch*, 1840 (exhib.). Oil on canvas. Photo © National Portrait Gallery, London; 2.9 W. E. Albutt, *View of University College, London*, c.1854. Engraving, hand-coloured. UCL Art Museum, University College London (UCL 2641); 2.10 Thomas Dick (after Thomas Charles Wagemen), *Leonard Horner*. Mezzotint on paper. National Galleries of Scotland; 2.11 UCL Records Office; 2.12 King's College London; 2.13 UCL Library: College Collection; 2.14 UCL Library: College Archives; 2.15 George Scharf, *University of London School. The Playground*, 1833. Lithograph, hand-coloured. UCL Art Museum, University College London (UCL 4484); 2.16 François Langlois, *Professor Thomas Hewitt Key*, c.1842. Oil. UCL Art Museum, University College London (UCL 5625); 2.17 UCL Library: College Archives; 2.18 Department of Physiology; 2.19 George Scharf, 'London/University College Hospital begun, 20 May 1833', 1833. Pen and black ink and brush with grey wash on paper. Photo © The Trustees of the British Museum, London; 2.20 UCL Library: College Collection; 2.21 George Sidney Shepherd, *London University from Old Gower Mews*, 1835. Watercolour over pencil heightened with green arabic and white. UCL Art Museum, University College London (UCL 4587).

3.1 UCL Library: College Collection; 3.2 Courtesy of Senate House Library, University of London, ULC/PC26/14; 3.3 UCL Library: College Collection; 3.4 Courtesy of the late Dr W. R. Merrington; 3.5 *Illustrated London News*, 1846; 3.6 Maull & Polyblank, *Thomas Leverton Donaldson*, c.1860. . Wellcome Library no.12646i. Wellcome Collection, London (CC BY); 3.7 UCL Library: College Collection; 3.8 Dr William's Library; 3.9 Courtesy of the late Dr W. R. Merrington; 3.10 UCL Library, MS ADD 81/2; 3.11 Courtesy of the late Dr W. R. Merrington; 3.12 *Punch*, 1847; 3.13 Thomas Sadler ed., *Diary, Reminiscences and Correspondence of H. C. Robinson*, 1869; 3.14 UCL Library: College Archives; 3.15 UCL Digital Media (photographer Mary Hinkley) ; 3.16 Charles George Lewis, printed by Jérémie Graf, after Charles Landseer, *Harriet Grote (née Lewin)*, c.1840. Lithograph. Photo © National Portrait Gallery, London; 3.17 F. W. Felkin, *From Gower street to Frognal*, 1909; 3.18 UCL Library: College Collection; 3.19 UCL Records Office; 3.20 Slade School; 3.21 *Illustrated London News*, 20 July 1878; 3.22 *Building News*, 10 September 1880.

4.1 Courtesy of Senate House Library, University of London, UoL/CH/10/2/7; 4.2 Courtesy of Senate House Library, University of London, UoL/CH/10/1/2; 4.3 H. S. Solly, *The Life of Henry Morley* (1898); 4.4 Department of Chemistry; 4.5 UCL Records Office; 4.6 Department of Physics; 4.7 Collection of J. A. North; 4.8 UCL Library: College Collection; 4.9 Collection of J. A. North; 4.10 Courtesy of Mrs Rosina Down; 4.11 UCL Library: College Collection; 4.12 UCL Library: College Collection; 4.13 UCL Library: College Collection; 4.14 Courtesy of the late Professor H. E. M. Barlow; 4.15 Courtesy of Professor K. J. Ives; 4.16 William Orpen, *Sir J. Ambrose Fleming, MA*, early twentieth century. Oil. UCL Art Museum, University College London (UCL 5611); 4.17 UCL Digital Media, object from the UCL Science Collection (photographer Mary Hinkley); 4.18 Department of Chemistry; 4.19 Henry Tonks, *Sir William Ramsay Receiving News of the Nobel Prize*, 1904. Watercolour over pencil with pen and ink. UCL Art Museum, University College London (UCL 8579); 4.20 Department of Chemistry; 4.21 Courtesy of the late Dr W. R. Merrington; 4.22 UCL Library, Pearson MS; 4.23 UCL Digital Media, object from the UCL Galton Collection; 4.24 Alfred Aaron Wolmark, *Dr. Marie C. Stopes*, 1904. Oil and resin. UCL Art Museum, University College London (UCL 5590); 4.25 UCL Digital Media, objects from the UCL Galton Collection; 4.26 Department of Chemistry; 4.27 Alphonse Legros, *Self-Portrait*, 1937. Etching. UCL Art Museum, University College London (UCL 1410); 4.28 Frederick Brown, *Self Portrait*, 1911. Oil. UCL Art Museum, University College London (UCL 5606); 4.29 Slade School; 4.30 Slade School; 4.31 Slade School; 4.32 Gwen John, *Portrait Group*, c.1897. Watercolour and pen over pencil. UCL Art Museum, University College London (UCL 3451); 4.33 George Charles Beresford, *Augustus John*, 1902. Photo © National Portrait Gallery, London; 4.34 Slade School; 4.35 Petrie Museum of Egyptian Archaeology; 4.36 Henry Wallis, *Excavating in Egypt: Professor Petrie at Thebes*, 1895. Watercolour. UCL Art Museum, University College London (UCL 2674); 4.37 Winifred Mabel Brunton, *Miss Margaret Murray*, 1917. Watercolour. UCL Art Museum, University College London (UCL 262); 4.38 Francis Dodd, *A. E. Housman*, 1926. Charcoal on paper. Photo © National Portrait Gallery, London; 4.39 Courtesy of the late Dr W. R. Merrington; 4.40 Courtesy of the late Dr W. R. Merrington; 4.41 UCL Union; 4.42 UCL Library, College Collection; 4.43 UCL Library, College Collection; 4.44 UCL Digital Media (photographer Mary Hinkley).

5.1 William Orpen, *Professor Gregory Foster*, early twentieth century. Oil. UCL Art Museum, University College London (UCL 5632); 5.2 UCL Records Office; 5.3 Sir Rickman Godlee, *The Past, Present and Future of the School for Advanced Medical Studies of University College London* (1906); 5.4a Courtesy of the late Dr W. R. Merrington; 5.4b UCL Library, College Archives; 5.5 UCL Library, College Collection;

5.6 UCL Library, College Collection; 5.7 UCL Records Office; 5.8 UCL Records Office; 5.9 UCL Library, College Collection; 5.10 UCL Library, College Archives; 5.11a *Windsor Magazine*, 234 (1914); 5.11b UCL Library, College Archives; 5.12 UCL Library, College Collection; 5.13 UCL Library, College Archives; 5.14 UCL Records Office; 5.15 UCL Digital Media; 5.16 UCL Digital Media; 5.17 UCL Library, College Collection; 5.18 UCL Library, College Collection; 5.19 Department of Physics; 5.20 UCL Library, College Archives; 5.21 Courtesy of the late Professor Sir Alan Parkes; 5.22 *Sphere*, 23 July 1921; 5.23 UCL College Collection, Senior Common Room photographs; 5.24 E. G. Coker and L. N. G. Filon, Jubilee Commemoration of Work on Photoelasticity, 1909–37 (1959); 5.25 Courtesy of the late Professor H. E. M. Barlow; 5.26 Department of History; 5.27 UCL Library, College Collection; 5.28 UCL Records Office, centenary Rag Magazine; 5.29 UCL Records Office, centenary Rag Magazine; 5.30 Department of History; 5.31 UCL Records Office, centenary Rag Magazine; 5.32 UCL Library, College Collection; 5.33 E. Levine, *The Origin and Growth of the Mocatta Library, Museum and the Gustave Tuck Lecture Theatre* (1933).

6.1 UCL Digital Media; 6.2 Courtesy of the British Academy; 6.3 Department of Chemical and Biochemical Engineering; 6.4 UCL Digital Media (photographer Mary Hinkley); 6.5 UCL Library, College Archives; 6.6 UCL Library, College Collection; 6.7 Department of Biology; 6.8 Department of Psychology; 6.9 Department of Psychology; 6.10 Department of Phonetics and Linguistics; 6.11 UCL Library, College Collection; 6.12 UCL Library Services, Special Collections; 6.13 UCL Library, College Collection; 6.14 UCL Library, College Collection; 6.15 Photo Hans Wild/The LIFE Picture Collection/Getty Images; 6.16 Department of Physics; 6.17 UCL Library Services, Special Collections; 6.18 UCL Records Office; 6.19 UCL Library Services, Special Collections; 6.20 UCL Library, College Collection; 6.21 UCL Library Services, Special Collections; 6.22 The Bartlett School of Architecture; 6.23 UCL Records Office; 6.24 *Sphere*, 23 July 1921; 6.25 UCL Library, College Collection; 6.26 Courtesy of H. L. Davies; 6.27 UCL Library, College Collection; 6.28 UCL Library, College Collection; 6.29 UCL Library, College Collection; 6.30 UCL Library, College Collection; 6.31 Department of English; 6.32 Courtesy of Professor Hannah Steinberg; 6.33 Courtesy of Professor Hannah Steinberg.

7.1 William Coldstream, *Lord Ifor Evans*, 1958–60. Oil. UCL Art Museum, University College London (UCL 5608) © The estate of Sir William Coldstream/Bridgeman Images; 7.2 UCL Records Office; 7.3a UCL Records Office; 7.3b UCL Records Office; 7.4 UCL Records Office; 7.5 UCL Records Office; 7.6 UCL Library, College Collection; 7.7 Department of History; 7.8 Slade School; 7.9 Slade School; 7.10 Slade School; 7.11 UCL Digital Media; 7.12 UCL Digital Media; 7.13 UCL Digital Media; 7.14 UCL Library Services, Special Collections; 7.15 Rodrigo Moynihan, *Lord Annan*, 1979. Oil. UCL Art Museum, University College London (UCL 5617) © the artist's estate; 7.16 UCL Publications Department; 7.17 Department of Biology; 7.18 Department of Physiology; 7.19 Courtesy of the late Professor Sir Bernard Katz; 7.20 Department of Physics; 7.21 Department of Chemistry; 7.22 UCL Digital Media; 7.23 Department of Anthropology; 7.24 UCL Records Office; 7.25 UCL Library, College Collection.

8.1 Andrew H. Freeth, *Professor Harold Billet*. Watercolour and guache. UCL Art Museum, University College London (UCL 3092) © Martin, Tony and Richard Freeth; 8.2 UCL Digital Media; 8.3 UCL Digital Media; 8.4 UCL Digital Media; 8.5 UCL Digital Media; 8.6 UCL Digital Media; 8.7 Courtesy of Professor Hannah Steinberg; 8.8 UCL Digital Media; 8.9 UCL Digital Media; 8.10 UCL Digital Media; 8.11 UCL Digital Media (photographer Mary Hinkley); 8.12 UCL Publications Department; 8.13 UCL Residence Office; 8.14 UCL Digital Media; 8.15 © Hugh Casson RA, Casson Conder Partnership; 8.16 UCL Digital Media; 8.17 UCL Digital Media; 8.18 UCL Digital Media; 8.19 UCL Digital Media (photographer Mary Hinkley); 8.20 UCL Digital Media; 8.21 Slade School; 8.22 UCL Digital Media (photographer Mary Hinkley); 8.23 UCL Development Office; 8.24 UCL Development Office; 8.25 *Professor Sir Alan Aird Moncrieff*. Oil. UCL Art Museum, University College London (UCL 0034); 8.26 UCL Digital Media (photographer Mary Hinkley); 8.27 Margaret G. Todd, *Sophia Louisa Jex-Blake, c.1880s–1890s*. Photo © National Portrait Gallery, London; 8.28 Elizabeth Garrett Anderson, c.1880s. Wellcome Library no.12277i. Wellcome Collection, London (CC BY); 8.29 London Metropolitan Archives, City of London (London School of Medicine for Women Collection, H72/SM/Y/01/009); 8.30 © Tim Geach/Alamy Stock Photo; 8.31 UCL Digital Media (photographer Mary Hinkley); 8.32 UCL Digital Media; 8.33 Courtesy of EMI records (photographer Tom Sheehan); 8.34 Mark West; 8.35 Celtic Inscribed Stones Project; 8.36 UCL Digital Media (photographer Mary Hinkley); 8.37 Kristina Clackson Bonnington.

9.1 UCL Digital Media (photographer Tony Slade); 9.2 UCL Digital Media (photographer Tony Slade); 9.3 UCL Digital Media (photographer Mary Hinkley); 9.4 UCL Digital Media (photographer Tony Slade); 9.5 UCL Digital Media (photographer Mary Hinkley); 9.6 UCL Digital Media (photographer Tony Slade); 9.7 UCL Digital Media (photographer Mary Hinkley); 9.8 UCL Digital Media (Student Group from 2007); 9.9 UCL Digital Media (photographer Mary Hinkley); 9.10 UCL Digital Media (photographer Mary Hinkley); 9.11 UCL Digital Media (photographer Mary Hinkley); 9.12 UCL Digital Media (photographer Mary Hinkley); 9.13 Slade School; 9.14 Office of VP Development, credit Kirsten Holst; 9.15 John G Maloney Photography (submitted by Jenni Bozec); 9.16 UCL Digital Media (photographer Mary Hinkley); 9.17 UCL Digital Media; 9.18 UCL Digital Media (photographer Mary Hinkley); 9.19 UCL Digital Media (photographer Mary Hinkley); 9.20 UCL Communications and Marketing (CAM); 9.21 UCL School of Pharmacy; 9.22a IOE Archive; 9.22b UCL Digital Media (photographer Mary Hinkley); 9.23 UCL Digital Media (photographer Mary Hinkley); 9.24 UCL Institute of Neurology; 9.25 UCL Records Office; 9.26 Photo courtesy UCL Cut the Rent; 9.27 Photo courtesy of Nora Baha; 9.28 UCL Digital Media (photographer Mary Hinkley); 9.29 UCL Digital Media (photographer Mary Hinkley); 9.30 Digital Media (photographer Mary Hinkley); 9.31 UCL Digital Media (photographer Mary Hinkley); 9.32 UCL Communications and Marketing (photographer Matt Clayton); 9.33 © Stanton Williams.

Index

Illustrations are indicated in *italic*

Abercrombie, Sir Patrick 214
Aberystwyth 202, *202*, 208, 210
Academic Assistance Council (later Society for the Protection of Science and Learning) 196
Academic Board (previously Professorial Board) 244, 251, 267, 293
Academic Women's Achievement Group (AWAG) 255, 256
academy schools 316, 317–18
Access to Justice, Centre for 330
accommodation, student 69–70, 71, 89, 151, 225, 231–2, 232, 262, 263, 284–5, 323, *323*, 330
Adams, Barbara 256, 257
Adams, Prof. John 319
Afro-Caribbean Society 242
Aiello, Prof. Leslie 256, 257
Air and Space Law 231
Airy, Anna 156
All Saints' Church 178
Allan, Rosemary 208
Allen, Prof. H. C. 227
alumni 130, 267, 283, 310
Alumnus (magazine) 275
Alumnus Day 267
American History 173, 229
Americas, History and Politics of the (BA degree) 320
Americas, Institute of 320
Amos, Prof. Andrew 43
Amos, Prof. Maurice Sheldon 43
Amos, Prof. Sheldon 43
anaesthetic, use during operations 70–2; *see also* ether
Anatomy 159–65, 279; *see also* Anatomy and Physiology; Comparative Anatomy
Anatomy and Physiology 47, 57, 94, 145, 159, 295
Anatomy Building 159
Anatomy Museum 57, 96; *see also* Grant Museum
Ancient History 228, 229
Andrade, Prof. Edward Neville da Costa 130, 166
Andrasek, Alisa, 'Bloom' 297
Andrew Huxley Building 326, *326*
Animal Genetics, Department of 114
Annan, Lord Noël 235, *235*, 251, 257, 273
Anne, Princess (Princess Royal) 263, *263*, 328
anniversaries
  Jubilee Festival (1878) 83, *83*
  70th (1897) 134
  Centenary (1927) 173–8, *173*, *177*
  sesquicentenary (1978) 244, 263–4, *263*
  160th (1986) 254
  Students' Union centenary (1993–94) 285

bicentenary (forthcoming, in 2026) 325
Annual Report 54, 89, 103, 251, 267
Anthropology 165, 214, 227, 240, 241, 256, 257
anti-apartheid 242
anti-vivisectionist movement 95, 145–8, *148*
anti-war movement 195
Applied Mathematics 112, 115, 142, 166, 167, 168, 201
Applied Statistics 151
Archaeology 105, 122–5, 192–3, 227, 262, 295; *see also* Archaeology, Institute of; Egyptology; Petrie Museum
Archaeology, Institute of 193, 227, 258–62, *258*, 313
Architectural Design 211, *212*; *see also* Architecture; Bartlett School of Architecture
  Architecture 69, *69*, 81, 159, 295, 326
  evacuation during Second World War 202, 207
  King's, merger with Department of Architecture (1911) 152
  Professors of 178, 211, 212
  see also Bartlett School of Architecture
Arena Centre for Research-based Education 314
argon, discovery of 109
Armistice Day (1922) 157, 195
Art Museum 315, *315*
art/artworks 89, *89*, 229, 297, 303, *308*, 312; *see also* Flaxman Gallery; History of Art; Slade School of Art
Arthur, Prof. Michael 6, 7, 295–7, *296*, 301, 307, 310, 311, *311*, 324, 325
Arts and Humanities, Faculty of 295, 308, 320
Arts and Sciences (BSc) 314
Arts, Faculty of 91, 117, 168, 203, 225–31, 286, 301; *see also* Arts and Humanities, Faculty of; Slade School of Art; *see individual subjects*
Ashbee, Charles Robert 320
Assembly of Faculties (1962) 226
Association of University Teachers (AUT) 244, *244*, 266
Astor College 263
Astronomy 239, 239
ASU (Academic Services Unit) 267
Athena Swan Award 324
Audley-Charles, Prof. Michael 257
Austin, Prof. John 43
Austin, Sarah 35, 42, 43
Australia 311, 312
Ayer, A. J. 214

Bagehot, Walter 39, 73, 76
Baker, Ian 255, *265*
Bangor 202, *202*, 203, 210
bank, on campus 159
Banks, Sir Joseph 41

Barlow, H. C. 117
Barnicot, Prof. N. A. (Lord Holford) 214
Bartlett Building (later Pearson Building) 114, 152
Bartlett School of Architecture *207*, 236, 320, 326, 328, 330
Bartlett, Sir Herbert 152
Battersea Park (Brown Dog statue) 148, *148*
Bayliss, William 145–8
Bazaar and Fête (1909) 148, *149*, 149
Beadles 55, 141, 157, 198–9, 202, 203, 223, 285, *285*
Bedford College 170, 257–8
Bedford Way 232
Bedford, Duke of 178
Beesly, Prof. E. S. 70, 112, 116
Behaviour Change, Centre for 303
Bell, Alexander Graham 192
Bell, Alexander Melville 192
Bell, Prof. Sir Charles 36, *37*, 47, 57
Bellot, Prof. G. Hale 90, 173
benefactions
  building projects, finance of 70, 79, 82, 152–3, 159, 178, 186, 224–5, 232, 236, 252
  Chairs, finance of 57, 79, 122–3; *see also* Quain Chairs/Professors library, to the 55, 57, 144
  see also fundraising; *and under individual names*
'Bentham Bungalow' 210
Bentham Hall 232
Bentham House 231, 330
Bentham, Jeremy 13–14, *13*, 55, 107
  'Auto-Icon' of 13–14, *14*, 208, 296
Benthamism/Benthamites 16, 20, 107, 116
bequests *see* benefactions
Bernard Katz Building 270, *270*
Bertillon, Alphonse 113
Beveridge, William 178
Billett, Prof. Harold 251, *251*
Biochemistry 165
Bioengineering Centre 258
Biology 196
Biology as Applied Medicine 271, 273
Biomedicine 282, 303, 307, *307*, 319
Biometrics 100, 196, 198; *see also* Statistics
Biometrika 112
Biophysics 165, 196, 237, *237*
Birkbeck Laboratory 68, *68*, 69
Birkbeck, George 20, 68
Biscoe, Prof. Tim 267–8, 275
Bishop, Prof. R. E. D. 237
Blakeney Point, Norfolk (later Francis Wall Oliver Research Centre), field trips to 102, *103*
'Bloomsbury masterplan' 326
Bloomsbury Science Library *see* D. M. S. Watson Library
Bloomsbury Theatre (previously the Collegiate Theatre) 266, 267

Bomberg, David 121
bonfires 134, 171–3
Bonn, University of 14
Bonney, Prof. T. G. 114–15
Bonnington, Kristina Clackson 289
Botanical Theatre 50
Botany 41, 50, 100–101, 151
Bouche d'Erquy, field trips to 101, 101
Bowles, David 267
Boyd, Prof. Sir Robert 211, 213, 239
Boyle, Lord 255
Bragg, Lawrence (later Sir) 166
Bragg, Prof. Sir William 164, 165–6
Brain Sciences, Faculty of 277, 195, 321
Breakthrough Prize in Life Sciences 321, 321
Brewer, Dr Dame Nicola 311, 312
Brewin, Prof. Chris 297
Bristol, University College 108
British Academy 324
British Association 115, 165
British Association for the Advancement of Science 213
British Museum 41–2, 82, 122, 192, 271
British Postgraduate Medical Federation 275–7, 280
British Psychological Society 187
Brougham, Henry 13, 13, 15–17, 15, 19–20, 22, 24, 28, 67
Brown, Prof. Frederick 118, 118, 121
'Brown Dog Affair' 145–8, 148
Browne, Annie Leigh 90
Browne, Thomazine Mary 90
Brundrett, Jonathan 70
Built Environment, Faculty of 236;
   see also Architecture
Burdon Sanderson, Prof. John S. 94–7, 95
Burt, Prof. Sir Cyril 191, 191
Butler, Prof. A. J. 117
Butler, Prof. H. E. 183
Butler, Reg 229, 230

Caddick, Prof. Stephen 308
Cairnes, Prof. John Elliot 89
Cambridge 202, 202, 207
Cambridge, University of 13, 17, 21, 25, 65, 75, 82, 94, 127, 293
Campbell Hall 232
Campbell House 323
Campbell, Thomas 13, 13, 14–15, 14, 17, 19–20, 24
campuses/sites
   Bloomsbury estate 23–4, 184, 185–6, 285, 301, 322, 325, 326–30, 330; see also under individual building names
   Canary Wharf 330
   evacuation from London (in Second World War) 201–8, 202, 203
   Olympic Park, Stratford (UCL East) 297, 299, 325, 330, 332, 334
   see also accommodation, student; overseas collaborations/partnerships; UCL Academy, Camden
Canary Wharf 330

Cardiff 202, 202, 208
Carey Foster Physics Laboratory 201
Carey Foster, Prof. G. 89, 90, 93–4, 94, 104, 106, 139
'Carey Foster Bridge' 93
Carmarthen Square 23–4
Carnegie Corporation 319
Carnegie, Andrew 145, 186
Carpenters Estate, Stratford (campus proposal) 323, 330
Carrington, Dora 121
Casson, Sir Hugh 264, 264
Castillejo, Prof. L. 211, 213
Centenary see anniversaries
Centenary Appeal 173, 178
Central Collegiate Building 225, 226
Centre for Biodiversity and Environment Research (CBER) 102
Centre for the Study of the Legacies of British Slave-ownership 307
CERN, Geneva 239, 281
Certificates of Honours 49, 50
Chadwick Chairs 107
Chadwick Laboratory 107
Chadwick Trust 107–8, 159
Chadwick, Prof. Osbert 107
Chadwick, Sir Edwin 107
Chambers, Prof. R. W. 143–4, 193, 210
Chatterjee, Helen 317
Chemical Engineering 184, 185–6
Chemical Society 68
Chemistry 41, 67, 68, 68, 80, 83, 91, 94, 108–10, 110, 151, 152–3, 154
   buildings/accommodation for 159, 225, 235–6, 235
   laboratories 67, 68, 68, 152–3, 154, 236
   Professors of 213, 216
Chen Futao 294
Chesterton, G. K. 177–8
Child Health, Institute of (ICH) 275–7, 277
China 294, 310–11
Chinese language 311
Christopher Ingold Laboratories 236
Church, Prof. Revd A. J. 116
Cippico, Prof. Antonio 170
City and Islington Sixth Form College 317
City University (later City, University of London) 301
Civil Engineering 66, 67, 105, 108, 168, 314
Clark, Prof. A. J. 165
Classical Archaeology 122
Classical Studies, Institute of 227
Classics, teaching of 125, 159; see also Classical Studies, Institute of
Clement-Jones, Lord Tim 294
Clifford, Prof. W. K. 115
Clinical Sciences, Faculty of 258
Clinical Surgery 71, 127
Clough, Prof. Arthur Hugh 70
CND 241–2
co-education 89, 90
Coates, Dora Meeson 121
Cobban, Prof. Alfred 229
Cohn, Prof. P. M. 258
Coker, Prof. E. G. 167–8, 167
Coldplay 232, 284

Coldstream Report 229
Coldstream, Sir William 223, 228, 229
Coleridge, Samuel Taylor 49, 75
Coleridge, Stephen 145
College Committee 142, 152, 242;
   see also Council
College Hall, Byng Place 89, 90
College Servants 198–9, 199, 200; see also Beadles
College Song Book 171
Collegiate Theatre (later the Bloomsbury Theatre) 266, 267
Collet, Collet Dobson 74
Collie, Prof. J. Norman 110, 111, 111
Collins, Prof. Susan 325
Colquhoun, Prof. David 241, 289, 289
'Committee for UCL' website 289, 289
Commonwealth Fund Professor of American History 229
Communications Research Centre 192
Comparative Anatomy 36, 236, 237
Comparative Grammar 51
Comparative Law 43
computers/computing 227, 229, 284, 308, 309
Comte, Auguste 91, 116
Confucius Institute 311, 330
'Connected Curriculum' 314
Conolly, Prof. John 36, 47, 187
Conservation 102
Conservative Society 195
Constance Gore-Booth see Markievicz, Countess
Constitution Unit 286, 287
Constitutional History 168, 169
Corfiato, Prof. H. O. 207, 211, 212, 224
Corfield, Prof. W. H. 107
Council
   original 20, 21, 35, 36, 65, 79, 139
   post-1977 242, 251, 254, 255, 283, 301
   see also College Committee
Course Unit system 227
Cox, Anthony 186
Cox, Revd Dr. Francis Augustus 20, 21, 24, 54, 54
Crabb Robinson, Henry 13, 13, 75–6, 76, 116
Crabtree, Joseph
Creed, Martin 286
Cricket Club 130
Criminal Law Commission 43
Cripps, Stafford 151, 151
'Cripps Cottage' 210
Cruciform Building (UCH) 127, 279; see also University College Hospital (UCH)
Cruciform Hub 301
Cruikshank, George 22
crystallography 166
Culture and Society (SELCS) 295
Currie, Sir Donald 140–1, 142
'Cut the Rent' campaign 323, 323

D. M. S. Watson Library (later Bloomsbury Science Library) 258
D. M. S. Watson Library (previously

National Central Library) 186, 258
D'Oyly, Revd Dr George 48
Dale, Prof. Thomas 42
Dante studies 117
Darby, H. C. 214
Darwin, Charles 36, 112, 198
Davies, Geraldine 318
Davies, Prof. Wendy 286, *286*
Davis, Prof. David D. 36
De Morgan, Prof. Augustus 39–41, *40*, 47, 55, 65, 93, 106
degrees, awarding of 49, 65, 73, 89, 168, 227, 301; *see also* Certificates of Honours; graduation ceremonies
dementia research 321
demonstrations, student 47, 194, 323, *323 see also* protests, student
Denman, Maria 76
Development Office 267, 283; *see also* fundraising
Dickens, Charles 59
Dickinson, Thorold 229
discrimination 242; *see also* gender equality
diversity 317, 324
Dobson, Edward 74
Doctoral School 301
Donaldson, Prof. Thomas Leverton 69, *69*, 70, 71, 178
Donnan, Prof. F. G. 152
'Donnan membrane equilibrium' 152
Douglas, Prof. Mary 240, *241*
Douie, C. O. G. 183
Downing College, Cambridge 25
Downing, Edith Elizabeth 121
Dr William's Library (previously University Hall) 69–70, 71, 76
dramatic productions 267
Dramatic Society 196
Drapers' Company 112–13, 135, 159
Drummond, Prof. J. C. 165
Dutch 257–8

Earth Sciences (previously Geological Sciences) 257; *see also* Geology
Eastman Dental Clinic 279–80
Eastman Dental Institution 279–80
Eastman, George 279
Ecology, studies in 102
Economic Law 231
Economics 43, 116, 315; *see also* Political Economy
Edinburgh School of Arts (now Heriot-Watt University) 46
Edinburgh, University of 17, 18, 36, 41, 55, 72
Education Studies 315
Education, Institute of 191, 295, 300, 311, 318, 319–20, 320
Education, Professors of 319; *see also* Education, Institute of
Edwards, Amelia 123
Egyptology 123, *123*–5, *124*, 186, 227
Eisai Research Laboratory 270
Elderton, Ethel 113
Electrical Engineering 105–7, *106*, 142
Electrical Technology 105–7, *106*

Electronic Media in Fine Art, Centre for 286
Elizabeth Garrett Anderson Centre for Women's Health 324
Elizabeth II, Queen of England 265, *265*
Elizabeth, HM The Queen Mother 263
Elliot Smith, Prof. Sir Grafton 159–65
Elliotson, Prof. John 58, 59, 187
Embryology 159
Emery, Prof. W. B. 227
Energy Institute 303
Engineering 66–7, 103–5, *104*, 169, 185, 237, 308, 314–15
 buildings/accommodation for 159, 224, 225, 252, 330
 evacuation during Second World War 208
 partnership with University of South Australia 313
 see also Chemical Engineering; Civil Engineering; Electrical Engineering; Mechanical Engineering; Municipal Engineering; Ocean Engineering
Engineering Laboratory 104–5, *104*
English History 169
English Language and Literature 35, 42, 70, 89, 125, 186, 192, 223, 240, 314
 printing press 214, *218*
 Professors of 192, 240, 257, 258
 see also Survey of Spoken English
English Literature *see* English Language and Literature
enterprise activities 90, 296, 308, 310
Environmental Studies, Faculty of 236; *see also* Bartlett School of Architecture; Conservation
environmental sustainability 327, 330
Equal Opportunities, Committee on 256
Equality, Diversity and Inclusion Strategy 2015–2020 324
Erichsen, Sir John 101, 127
ether 71, 72, 92
Ettlinger, Prof. Leopold 229
Eugenics 112–14, *113*, 167
Eugenics Laboratory 113, 142
Eumorfopoulos, N. 213
European Institute 303
European Languages, School of 295; *see also under individual languages*
European Organisation for Nuclear Research *see* CERN, Geneva
European Union 297–9
Evans, Prof. Charles Lovatt 165
Evans, Sir Ifor (Lord Evans of Hungershall) 13, 183, 223–4, *223*
Ex-Service Students' Association 157
Experimental Physics 93
Experimental Psychology 187, 190
Faithfull, Leila 208

Farinelli, Prof. Antonio 117
fascist movement 170
fees *see* tuition fees
Festival of Culture (previously Festival of the Arts) 308
field trips 102, 103, *103*
Fielden Chair of French 227
Film Society 217
film, study of 229
Filon, Prof. L. N. G. 166, 167–8
First World War 152, 153–6, *153*, 169
 memorials to 156, 157, *157*, 178
Flaherty, Miss 59
Flaxman Gallery 13, 75, 76–7, *78*
Flaxman, John 75
Fleming, Prof. Ambrose 106–7, *106*
'flipped lecture' 314
Florence, Mary Sargent 121
Flowers, Lord 257
Flugel, Prof. J. C. 190
Forde, Prof. Daryll 214, 227
Foster Court buildings (later Malet Place) 186, 189, 210, 325
Foster, G. C. 90
Foster, Prof. Michael 94
Foster, Sir Gregory 139–40, *139*, 141, 183–5, 192
Foundation Play and Dance 171
Foundation Week 134, 171, 226
Fownes, Prof. George 68–9
Foxwell, H. S. 116
Frances Gardner House 285
Francis Crick Institute 307, 307
Francis Wall Oliver Research Centre 102, 103
Freemedic PLC 267
French 41, 213, 215
 Fielden Chair 227
 see also Modern Foreign Languages
Frith, Prof. Uta 324
Front Quadrangle 107
 architecture 159, 210, 263, 264, *264*, 299
 use for events 134, 170, *148*, *149*, 149, 173, 226, 322
Fulbrook, Prof. Mary 307
funding, sources of 297–9
 charitable foundations 254, 283, 303–7
 donations 145, 148, 196; *see also* philanthropy
 government 110, 117, 178, 186, 235, 244, 252, 273–5, 279, 283, 308
 industry 168, 185, 225, 254, 267, 283, 308
 research councils 254, 283, 307, 308, 320–1
 see also benefactions; fundraising; grants; *and under individual names*
fundraising 148, 149, *149*, 224–5, 267, 279, 283, 310
 Centenary Appeal 173, 178
 Sesquicentenary Appeal (1981) 263–4, *263*
 see also rags
Furnivall, F. J., undergraduate in 1842 65
Gaitskill, Hugh 183, 195–6, *195*

Galiano, Prof. Antonio Alcalá 42
Gallyer, Marilyn 267
Galton Collection 114, 115, 315
Galton Laboratory 113, 114
Galton, Francis 100, 112, 113, 114, 115, 190
Gardner, Prof. E. A. 122–3
Garrett Anderson, Elizabeth 278, 279
Garwood, Prof. E. J. 142
Gatsby 307
Gatsby Computational Neuroscience Unit 307
gay rights campaign (1970s) 242
'Gay Soc' 242
Geikie Cobb, M. M. 152
gender equality 255–6
gender pay gap 256
General Certificates 49
General Library *see* Library
Genetics 114, 198
    Professors of 198, 271, 273
Genn, Dame Hazel 330
Geography 55, 186, 214
Geological Museum 78–9
Geological Sciences 257; *see also* Geology
Geological Society 41, 46–7
Geology 41, 78–9, 114–15, 122, 142, 151, 257
George V, King 173–7, 173
German 41, 42, 170
Giessen 68, 92
Gilliand, Margaret 152
Glasgow University 72
Global Citizenship Programme 313
Goldsmid House 232
Goldsmid, Frederick 48
Goldsmid, Isaac Lyon 19–20, 19
Gombrich, Prof. Sir Ernst 229
Goodman, Lord 163
Gordon Square 223
    Institute of Archaeology building 258
    University Hall 69–70
Gordon Street 184, 330
    Bartlett Faculty building (2016) 326, 328, 330
    Bloomsbury Theatre
    Chemical Engineering laboratories (1931) 185–6
    Chemistry Building (1969) 235
    London Centre for Nanotechnology 326
    student accommodation 232
    Student Centre 301
    Students' Union building 134, 135, 217, 235
Gordon, Douglas 286
Gormley, Antony 286
government
    cuts to education spending 235, 244, 244, 252
    as a funding source 110, 117, 178, 186, 235, 244, 244, 252, 273–5, 279, 283, 308
    war damage compensation (Second World War) 224
Governors 79
Gower Socialist Society 193

Gowing, Prof. Sir Lawrence 271, 272
Graduate School 275, 301
graduation ceremonies 199, 275, 275, 300
Graham, Prof. Thomas 67–8, 67
Grammar *see* Comparative Grammar
Grand Challenges programme 302–3
Grant Museum (previously Anatomy and Zoology Museums) 57, 96, 100, 315, 316
Grant, Prof. Robert E. 36–8, 38
Grant, Prof. Sir Malcolm 293, 293, 294, 295, 296, 298, 308, 314, 317
grants 110, 177, 224, 252, 273, 275, 279, 283, 308, 324
    for ex-service students 157
    for research 117, 283, 302
    student 232
    see also tuition fees
Granville, Earl 83
Graves, Prof. J. T. 55
Great Hall 26, 27, 28, 51, 59, 69, 70, 173, 177, 178, 201
Great Ormond Street Hospital for Sick Children 275, 277
Great War *see* First World War
Greek 42–3, 125
Green Paper (2004) 293
Green, J. R., Mrs 125
Grote Professor of Philosophy of Mind and Logic 79, 187, 190
Grote, George 20, 79, 116
Grote, Harriet 78, 79
Grove, Eleanor 90, 91
Gustave Tuck Theatre 178, 178, 201
Guttmann Health and Wellbeing Centre, Stratford 330

Haileybury College, Hertfordshire 25
Haldane Room 198
Haldane, Prof. J. B. S. 196, 198, 208
Hall, Prof. Catherine 307
Hall, Edna Clarke (née Waugh) 121
Hall, Rachel 267
Halliday, M. A. K. 192
halls of residence 69–70, 71, 89, 232; *see also* accommodation, student; *and under individual buildings*
Hanwell Lunatic Asylum 36
Hardy, Prof. John 321, 321
Harris, Col. H. J. 183
Hawkins/Brown architects 328
Hawkridge House 323
Hazell, Prof. Robert 286, 287
Heath, Prof. Christopher 126, 127
Hebrew and Jewish Studies 178
helium 111
Here East, Olympic Park, Stratford 330
Heriot-Watt University *see* Edinburgh School of Arts
Higher Education Academy 314
Higher Education Funding Council for England (HEFCE) 275, 279, 283, 308
Hill, Prof. A. V. 164, 165, 196
Hill, M. G. M. 167
Hirobume, Ito 92–3, 92

Hirst, Prof. T. A. 93
Histology 159
Historical Association 168
Historical Research, Institute of 168
History 55, 116, 168–70, 169, 173, 227–9, 228
    Professors of 213, 217, 228, 286, 286
History of Art 229
History of Medicine 165
History, School of 168
Hodgkinson, Prof. Eaton 66
Holdsworth, W. S. (later Sir) 168
Holford, Lord *see* Barnicot, N. A.
'Honours' degrees 168
Hopkins, Prof. Colin 321
Hoppus, Prof. J. 79
Horizon 2020 programme 302
hormones 145
Horner, Leonard 45–7, 46
Horsley, Prof. Sir Victor 126
Houlihan, Lori 310
housekeepers 198
Housman Room 289
Housman, Prof. A. E. 125–7, 126, 178
Housman, Laurence 196
Howard-Jones, Ray 208
Human Communication Science 275
Human Genetics and Biometry 114
humanities 125, 196; *see also* Arts and Humanities, Faculty of; Humanities and Social Sciences; *and under individual subjects*
Humanities and Social Sciences 281, 301
Hume, Joseph 21, 55
Humphreys, Prof. R. A. 227
Huntington Disease Centre 307
huts, postwar 210, 226, 264
Huxley, Julian 114
Huxley, Prof. Sir Andrew 236, 237
Huxley, T. H. 94, 95, 115
Hygiene 81, 107, 108
Hygiene and Public Health 81, 107
Hygiene and Tropical Medicine, School of 107
Hyman, Miriam 297

Ifor Evans Hall 232
Imperial College 301, 307
    proposed merger with UCL 287–9, 293
    Translation Studies Unit 320
Imperial War Museum 156
inert gases, discovery of 109, 109, 111
Ingold, Prof. Sir Christopher 213
Inner Temple 43
Inoue, Bunta 92, 93
Institute of Advanced Studies in the Humanities and Social Sciences (IAS) 301
Integrated Engineering Programme (IEP) 315
intelligence, measuring/testing 190, 190, 191
Inter-Union Standing Committee 171
Intercollegiate Suffrage Society 152
International Air Law 231

International Centre for Chinese Heritage and Archaeology 310
International Society 193
International Student Service (ISS), Co-operating Committee of 196
international students 92–3, 92, 196, 242, 252, 270, 270, 300, 311
'It's All Academic' 310, 311
Italian 41, 117, 170, 258
iTunes 314

James Lighthill House 285
Japan 92–3, 92, 270, 270
Jaray, Tess 241
Jarratt, Sir Alex 266
Jeaffreson, J. W. 213, 215
Jenner, Prof. Sir William 127, 275
Jessop, H. 100
Jessop, H. J. 168
Jevons, Prof. W. Stanley 39, 116, 117
Jewish Historical Society 144, 178
Jex-Blake, Sophia 278, 278
Jill Dando Institute of Crime Science 286–7
Jodrell Professor of Zoology and Comparative Anatomy 236, 237
Jodrell Professors of Physiology 145, 165, 236, 237, 275
Jodrell Professors of Zoology 187, 236, 237
Jodrell, T. J. Phillips 95, 99
John Dodgson House 285
John, Augustus 120, 121, 121
John, Gwen 120, 121
Joint Infrastructure Fund (JIF) 282
Jolowicz, Prof. H. F. 170
Jones, Prof. Daniel 192
Jones, Prof. Steve 271, 273
journalism 74
Jurisprudence 43, 55, 229

Kalmus, Prof. Hans 196
Kathleen Lonsdale Building 153, 264, 330
Katz, Prof. Sir Bernard 237, 237
Kazakhstan 311, 313
Kennedy, Prof. Alexander 103–5, 103, 106, 112
Ker, Prof. W. P. 125, 143, 178
Kew Gardens *see* Royal Botanic Gardens, Kew
Key, Prof. Thomas Hewitt 51, 51
Keynes, John Maynard 114
King's College, Cambridge 25
King's College, London 42, 59, 65, 72, 142, 152, 307
tradition of rivalry with UCL 47–8, 49, 170, 171

laboratory facilities 67, 68, 68, 81, 93, 95, 99–100, 99, 101, 104, 107, 109–10, 201, 208; *see also under individual entries/subjects*
Labour Party/movement 116, 195
Ladies Sanitary Association 78
Ladysmith night (1900) 133, 134, 135
Lancaster, Lilian 122
Langton Close 284–5
Langton, Alfred 285
Language Centre 270, 271

Lankester, Prof. E. Ray 99, 99, 100, 186
Lansdowne, Lord 65
Lardner, Prof. Dionysius 38–9, 38, 39
Laryngology and Otology, Institute of 262
Lasdun, Sir Denys 319–20, 320
Latin 43, 51, 70, 116, 183
Latin America Studies, Institute for 227
Latin American History 227
Law Society 43, 74
Laws, Faculty of 43, 116, 170, 229–30, 231, 231, 317, 330
Laycock, Prof. Gloria 287
league tables/ranking systems 295, 300, 313
Leatherhead 202
lecture theatres 26, 50, 178, 178
Lee, Alice 113
Leeds, University of 295
Legros, Prof. Alphonse 118, 118
Leonard Wolfson Experimental Neurology Centre 307
Lesbian, Gay, Bisexual, Transgender and Queer Equalities and Advisory Group (LEAG) 324
Levinsky, Roland 277
Lewis building 270
Lewis, Hayter 80, 81, 82
Lewis, Sir George Cornewall 39–40
'Liberating the Curriculum' small grants 324
Library 26, 27, 54–5, 54, 67, 69, 70, 81, 143–4, 159, 210, 211, 301
Arts 144
bequests/donations of books to 55, 57, 144
bomb damage (1940) 201, 208, 210
evacuation during Second World War 208
Science 144, 208, 258
see also under individual names
Liebig, Baron Justus von 41, 68, 91–2
Life Governors 79
Life Sciences, Faculty of 275, 295, 319, 320, 321, 321
Lighthill, Prof. Sir James 251–2, 252, 255, 263, 264, 266, 285
Lindley, Prof. John 41, 65, 100
Linguistics 192
Lister, Prof. Joseph 71, 72
Liston, Prof. Robert 70, 71–2, 72
Literary & Philosophical Society 74
'Little Plays of St Francis' 196
Liverpool University 185
Llewellyn Smith, Prof. Chris (later Sir) 281–2, 282, 283
Lloyd, E. 152
Lodge, David 223
London Centre for Nanotechnology 326
London Day Training College (later Institute of Education) 319
London Ladies' Educational Association 89–90
London School of Economics (LSE) 116
London School of Medicine for Women 278, 278, 279

London University Examiner 74
London, University of 65, 66, 139, 178, 232, 273, 301, 320
Vice-Chancellors of 79, 166, 167, 173, 185, 251, 258
London, University of, constitution of
reform (1858) 79
incorporation of UCL into (1905) 135, 140, 142
Act of Parliament (1926) 242
UCL devolves from (1977) 142, 242, 242–4
Act of Parliament (1978) 251
restructuring (1978–85) 257–8
restructuring (1994) 275
University of London Act (2017) 301
Long, Prof. George 42–3, 47
Lonsdale, James 15
Lonsdale, Prof. Kathleen 153, 166, 213, 216
Lucas, E. V. 130

Macaulay, Charles 48
Macaulay, Selina 35
Macaulay, Thomas Babington 29
Macaulay, Zachary 20, 20
Maccoll, Prof. Allan 244
Machinery 67
Machinery Museum 67
Maconochie, Prof. Alexander 55
Malden, Prof. Henry 51, 65
Malet Place (previously Foster Court) 186, 325
Management, School of 330
Manchester Museum 125
Maple, Sir John Blundell 127, 134
Marconi 106
Margaret Murray Room 241
Markievicz, Countess (née Constance Gore-Booth) 152
Marks, Lord 225
Marshall, John 77
Martin, Prof. G. T. 227
Martineau, Prof. James 41
Marx, Karl 116
Marxism 193
Mary, Queen (wife of George V, b. Princess May of Teck) 173, 173
Masaryk, Tomáš 280, 281
mascot *see* Phineas Maclino
Massey, Prof. Sir Harrie 211, 213, 239, 239
Materia Medica, Anthony Todd Thompson, Prof. of, at Edinburgh University 36
Mathematical Physics 93
Mathematics 39, 93, 167, 211–13, 213, 258, 314; *see also* Applied Mathematics
Matthews, Sir Peter 255
Maudsley Hospital 36
Maudsley, Prof. Henry 36
Mawer, Sir Allen 184, 185, 192, 193, 210
Max Rayne Foundation 229, 232
Max Rayne House 232
McCulloch, Prof. J. R. 43, 45
McDougall, William 190

Mechanical Engineering 66, 107, 168, 237, 251, 258
Mechanical Technology 105
Medawar, Prof. Sir Peter 236, 237
Medical Research Council (MRC) 307, 320–1
Medical School *see* University College Hospital Medical School (UCHMS)
Medical Sciences, Academy of 273
Medical Society 74
Medicine
   awarding degrees in 65, 278
   students of 74, *74*, 90, 101, 156, 301
   teaching of 35, 36, 55–7, 95, 96, 111
   women studying 90, 278, *278*, 279
   see also Biomedicine; Medical Faculty; surgery
Medicine for Women, School of 90
Medicine, Faculty of 36, 47, 57, 59, 72, 127, 237, 295
   evacuation during Second World War 202
   see also History of Medicine; University College Hospital Medical School (UCHMS)
Medieval Archaeology 192
Megaw, Eleanor 217
memorials 297; *see also* war memorials
Mental Philosophy and Logic 41
Merlet, Prof. P. F. 41
mesmerism 59, 72
Middlesex Hospital 36
Middlesex Hospital Medical School 262, 263
Midwifery and Diseases of Women and Children 36
Mill Hill Observatory 167, 239, *239*
Mill, James 20, *20*, 48
Mill, John Stuart 43
Millington, Prof. John 66
Mirsky, D. S. 280
Mocatta Collection 144, 178, 208
Mocatta Library 144, *144*,178, 208
Mocatta, Frederick 144, *144*
Modern Languages 35, 41, 192, 295; *see also under individual languages*
'Modernising UCL' (White Paper, 2007) 293
Molecular and Cellular Neuroscience Laboratories 326
Momigliano, Prof. A. D. 196, 228, 229
Moncrieff, Prof. Alan (later Sir) 277, *277*
Montgomery, Dr Stephen 267
'moodle' 314
Moore, Edward 117
Moorfields Eye Hospital 275
Morison, Rosa 90, *91*, 152
Morley, Prof. Henry 70, 89, 90–1, *91*, 112
'morning women' (cleaners) 198
Morris, John 78
Moynihan, Rodrigo 235
MRC Laboratory for Molecular Cell Biology 320–1, 324
MRC Prion Unit 321

Municipal Engineering 107, 108
Municipal Hygiene 107
Murison, Prof. A. F. 170
Murray, Margaret 124, 125, 152
museum and library studies 313
Museum of Natural History 26, 27
Music Society 267

Nash, Paul 208
National Anti-Vivisection Society 145
National Central Library (later D. M. S. Watson Library) 186
National Gallery, London 25–6
National Hospital for Neurology and Neurosurgery 277, *277*
National Hospital's College of Speech Sciences 275
National Institute for Medical Research 307
National Portrait Gallery 271
National Student Survey (NSS) 313
National Trust 102
National Union of Students (NUS) 171
Natural Philosophy 38, 39, 93
natural selection, theory of 100
NatWest Bank, College branch of 159
Nazarbayev, University of, Kazakhstan 311
Neale, Prof. Sir John 213, 217
Nettleship, Ida 121
Neurology, Institute of 277, *277*, 307, 321
neuroscience 277, *277*, 303, 305, 307, 326
Nevinson, Christopher 208
New English Art Club 118
New Phineas 202, *203*
Newcastle University 185
Newman, F. W. 70
newspapers/magazines *see under individual titles*
Newton, Prof. Charles 122
Nobel Prize winners 109, *109*, 164, 165, 166, 196, 236–7, *236*, 237, 321, *321*
Norfolk, Duke of 20
North London Hospital 57, 59; *see also* University College Hospital
nuclear research 239, 281
Nunn, Percy 319

O'Keefe, Prof. John 321, *321*
object-based learning (OBL) 317
Ocean Engineering 239
Old Students' Association 130
Oliver, Prof. Daniel 100–101
Oliver, Prof. Francis 100, 101–2
Olympic and Paralympic Games (2012) 297, *297*; *see also* UCL East
Olympic Park, Stratford *see* UCL East
'open access' 308
operas 267
Ophtalmology, Institute of 275
Oration 134
Organic Chemistry 110
Oriental Literature 45
Ormsby, Prof. M. T. M. 159

Orpen, William 121, 139
Orthopaedics, Institute of 262
Out@UCL network 324
overseas collaborations/partnerships 311–13, 312; *see also* international students
Oxford 202, *202*, 208
Oxford, University of 13, 17, 21, 65, 75, 82, 94, 100, 114

Padfield, Deborah 303
Palaeobotany 103
Palaeontology 186
Panizzi, Prof. Antonio 41–2, 47
Papyrology 227
Parkes, Prof. Edmund 107
Pasmore, Victor 229
'passing in rule' 90, 152
Patent Office Museum 67
Pathology Collection 315
Pattison, Prof. Granville Sharp 41, 43, 47
Pearson Building (formerly Bartlett Building) 114, 254, *254*; *see also* Bartlett Building
Pearson, Prof. Egon S. 211–13, 214
Pearson, Prof. Karl 112–13, *112*, 152, 159, 167, 190
Peking University (PKU) 310–11, 313
Penrose, Prof. Lionel 114
Perivale (sports grounds/facilities) 149
Petrie Museum 123, 256, *257*, 315
Petrie, Prof. W. M. Flinders 123, *123*, 124, 125
Pewterers' Gate 184
Pharmaceutical Society of Great Britain 318–19, *318*
Pharmacology 159, 165, 219, 240–1
Pharmacy, School of 318–19, *318*
philanthropy 144, 196, 310, 311; *see also* benefactions
Philosophy 41, 79, 116, 142, 187, 190, 213–14; *see also* Natural Philosophy
Philosophy of Mind and Logic 79, 187, 190
Philosophy, Politics and Economics 315
Philpott, S. J. F. 190
Phineas Bar 134, *135*
Phineas Maclino 134, *135*, 171
Phonetics 191, 192, 208
photoelasticity 167–8, *167*, 237
Photogrammetry and Surveying 237
photography *see* X-ray photography
Physical Anthropology 214, 227
Physics 80, 89, 93–4, 159, 165–6, 201, 239
   academics/teaching staff 165–6, 213
   evacuation during Second World War 208
Physiological Society 95
Physiology 83, 94, 95–7, 145, 159, 165
   Professors/teaching staff 145, 165, 236, 237, 275
   see also Anatomy and Physiology
Physiology, Institute of 145, *147*
Pi (newspaper) 214, 219, 242, 322

Pi Media 322
Place Names Survey 192
Platt, Prof. Arthur 125, 127
playing fields see sports/athletic facilities
Plimmer, Prof. R. H. A. 165
Poldu, Cornwall 106
Political Economy 43, 116, 117, 195
Political Science 315
Pollard, Prof. A. F. 168–70, 169
Pollardian 170
Poole, Prof. R. S. 122
Poore, Prof. G. Vivian 134
Population Health Sciences 295
Porter, Prof. A. W. 166
porters 198
postgraduate students/courses 102, 165, 186, 229, 239, 263, 275–7, 286, 300, 311, 320
Potter, J. P. 47, 65
Potter, Prof. Richard 65, 78, 93
Poynter, Prof. Edward 82–3, 89
Practical Chemistry 68–9, 91
Practical Physiology 94
Price, Prof. David 302, 302
Priebsch, Prof. Robert 170, 208
Prion Diseases, Institute of 321
Professorial Board (later Academic Board) 142, 196, 244, 244
   student representation on 242, 244
Professors/teaching staff
   female 90, 91, 102–3, 151–2, 213, 216, 217, 240–1, 241, 255–6, 319, 324–5
   founding members 35–45, 47
   developing media profiles 271–3, 272, 273
   from minority ethnic groups 324
   payment of 116–17, 134, 168, 170, 256
   see also under individual names
'proprietors' 21, 21, 24, 49, 79
protests, student 148, 195, 241–2, 244, 322, 323
Provosts 139–40, 139, 183–4, 192, 210, 223, 235, 235, 251–2, 251, 252, 255, 266, 266, 281, 293, 293, 295
Psychological Laboratory 142
Psychology 142, 187–91
   Professors of 190–1, 190, 191
Psychopharmacology 240–1
Public Engagement Unit 308
public health 107; see also Hygiene and Public Health
Public Policy, School of 286
Pugin, Augustus 28
Punnett, Margaret 319
Pure Mathematics 167
Pye, Dr David (later Sir) 210, 223

Qatar 311–13
Qatar Foundation 311
Quain Chairs/Professors 43, 57, 143, 143, 166, 192
Quain Fund 57, 102, 117
Quain, Prof. Jones 57
Quain, Prof. Richard 57, 102
Quain, Sir John Richard 57
Queen Mary College 257

Quirk, Prof. Sir Randolph (later Lord) 240, 257, 258

Race Equality Charter Bronze Award 324
racism 114, 242
radio 106
radioactivity 166
radon 111
rags 171–3, 173, 177
Ramsay Hall 232, 232, 284
Ramsay Memorial Laboratory of Chemical Engineering 184
Ramsay, Prof. William 108–10, 108, 109, 110, 111, 151, 185
Ramsey, A. C. 78
Rayleigh, Lord 109
Reading Room Society 90
Refectory 134, 151, 194, 210, 225, 225
refugees (academics/scholars) 41, 196, 229
religion/religious teaching 17–18, 21, 29, 48, 70, 79, 217
rent strikes (2015) 323, 323
Research Assessment Exercise (RAE) (2008) 302
Research Councils UK (RCUK) 308
Research Excellence Framework (REF) (2014) 302
research programmes 144–5, 302–3, 308
   funding for 117, 145, 148, 275, 282, 283, 302
   see also funding, sources of; grants; under individual subject entries
research staff/students 254, 275, 301, 308
Retired Professors Fund 117
Ricardo, David 43
Richardson, Prof. Sir Albert E. 77, 178, 184, 186, 207, 211, 211
Rivers, W. H. 187
Roberts, Dr Sir Derek 266, 266, 281, 283, 287, 301
Robertson, Prof. Croom 112, 116
Robertson, John G. 170
Robinson, James 71
Rockefeller Building 156, 178
Rockeller Foundation 159, 165, 186
Roehampton 258
Rogers, Prof. C. A. 211, 213
Rogers, Claude 229
Roman Law 170, 230
Roper, J. T. 190
Roscoe, Sir Henry 39
Rosen, Prof. F. A. 43–5, 47
Rothamsted 202
Rothenstein, Sir William 118, 208
Royal Academy 156, 271
Royal Albert Hall 241, 275
Royal Botanic Gardens, Kew 41, 100–101
Royal Corps of Naval Constructors 237–9
Royal Free Hospital 71, 279, 280, 301
Royal Free Hospital Medical School 71, 278–9, 280
Royal Free Hub 301
Royal Geographical Society 55

Royal Institute of British Architects (RIBA) 69
Royal National Orthopaedic Hospital 263
Royal National Throat, Nose and Ear Hospital 263
Royal Naval College, Greenwich 239
Royal Society 41, 57, 92, 167, 213, 273, 324
royal visits 173–7, 173, 263, 263, 265, 265
RUMS (Royal Free, University College and Middlesex Medical Students Association) 322, 322
Ruskin Drawing School, Oxford 208
Ruskin, John 82
Russell Group of Universities 293, 295
Russell, Lord John 65
Russian 280
Russian and Soviet Law 231
Rutherston, Albert 208

Sadler's Wells 330
Sainsbury Wellcome Centre for Neural Circuits and Behaviour 303–7, 305
Sainsbury, David 307
Sakurai, Joji 93
salaries, academic 116–17, 134, 168, 170, 244, 256, 266, 283, 323; see also Professors/teaching staff
Samuel, Lord 225, 232
Sanchez, Jose, 'Bloom' 297
Sandoz Institute for Medical Research 264
Satow, Ernest 93
Saville, Richard 242
Scandinavian Studies 125, 170, 186, 192, 193
Schafer House 285
Schäfer, Prof. E. A. (later Sir Edward Sharpey-Schafer) 94, 130–4, 285
Scharf, George 57
School of Energy and Resources Australia 311
School of Life and Medical Sciences (SLMS) 295
School of Oriental and African Studies (SOAS) 45
Schwabe, Prof. Randolph 208
Science
   degrees in 79
   teaching of 78, 80, 91–2, 93, 94, 99–100
Science Museum 67
Science Research Investment Fund (SRIF) 282
Science, Faculty of 92
sculpture 228, 229, 230, 312; see also Flaxman Gallery; Slade School of Art
Seaton, Prof. M. J. 211, 213
Second World War 165, 196
   bomb damage 77, 93, 144, 178, 183, 186, 201, 201, 208, 208, 210
   evacuation of college 201–8, 202, 203
   memorials 210
   postwar reconstruction 210–17, 226, 264

war damage compensation 224
Seeley, Prof. Sir John 116
Senate (later Professorial Board) 47, 139, 142; see also Professorial Board
Senate House 178, 280
Sesquicentenary Appeal (1981) 263–4, 263
Seton, Walter 139–40, 140, 148, 151, 183, 196
shareholders see 'proprietors'
Sharpe, Samuel 81, 117, 143
Sharpey-Schafer, Sir Edward see Schäfer, E. A.
Sharpey, Prof. William 55–7, 56, 94, 159
Shaw, Batty 141
Shaw, Benjamin 23
Sheffield 202, 202
Shenley (sports grounds/facilities) 235
Shepherd, George Sidney 59
Shoolbreds Mews 186, 189
Sickert, Walter 121, 122
Simpson, Prof. F. M. 163
Simpson, Henrietta 308
Sisson, Prof. C. J. 193
Slade School of Art 82–3, 82, 118–22, 177–8, 228, 229, 230, 244, 286
  Antique Room 228
  evacuation during Second World War 208
  female students 89, 118, 120, 121, 122, 152
  memorial (First World War) 156, 157
  Professors/teaching staff of 13, 82–3, 118, 156, 228, 229, 241, 271, 272, 325
Slade, Felix 82
slavery, legacies of see Centre for the Study of the Legacies of British Slave-ownership
Slavonic and East European Studies, School of (SSEES) 280, 281, 326, 327
Smith, Prof. A. H. 192
Smith, Prof. Anthony 314
Smith, Prof. H. S. 227
Smith, John 23
Smith, Winifred 90, 102, 152
Smyth, Prof. Rosalind 277
Social and Historical Sciences, Faculty of 286, 320
Social Anthropology 227, 240, 241
social sciences 116; see also Humanities and Social Sciences; and under individual subjects
socialism 195
Societies (for students) 74, 90, 130, 157; see also Union; Women's Union Society (WUS); and under individual entries
Society for the Diffusion of Useful Knowledge 43
Society for the Protection of Science and Learning see Academic Assistance Council
Somerset House 48
South Cloisters 157, 157, 208
Southampton 202

Southampton, University of 295
space research 167, 239, 239
Spanish 42
Spanish Civil War 195
Spearman, Prof. Charles 190, 190
Speculative Society 36
speech 192
speech therapy 275
Spencer, Stanley 121, 208
Spurway, Helen 198
Spyer, Prof. Mike 308
Squire, William 72
SSEES Building 326, 327
St John's College, Cambridge 114
staff, non-academic 198–9, 199, 200, 235, 244, 323; see also Beadles
Stanstead Bury 202, 208
Starling, Prof. Ernest 145–8, 159, 165
Statistics 112, 116, 151, 159, 211–13
Steer, Wilson 118
Steinberg, Prof. Hannah 217, 219, 240, 255, 256
Stephenson, Dr Bill 258
stewards 198
Stopes, Marie 101, 103, 114, 115, 152
Stratford
  Carpenters Estate (campus proposal) 323, 330
  Guttmann Health and Wellbeing Centre 330
  new UCL campus at, see UCL East
Student Central 301
Student Health Service 236
Student's Song Book 171, 213
Students' Handbook 232, 232
Students' Union see Union
students 74, 75
  enrolments 43, 45, 47, 48, 59, 73, 110, 116–17, 153, 202, 231, 263, 284, 299–300
  fees paid by 43, 45, 49, 252; see also tuition fees
  from overseas 92–3, 92, 196, 242, 252, 270, 270, 300, 311
  from state schools 317
  studying abroad 313
  see also accommodation, student; Union; women, admission of
suffrage movement 90, 152
Sully, Prof. James 187
surgery 70–2, 127
Survey of English Usage see Survey of Spoken English
Survey of London 320
Survey of Spoken English (later Survey of English Usage) 239–40, 240
Sussex, Duke of 24, 264
Swansea 202, 202
Swinnerton-Dyer, Sir Peter 257
Sykes, Sir Richard 287
Sylvester, Prof. J. J. 74–5
Syme, James 72

Tate Gallery 271
Tattersall, Arthur 242
teaching
  quality of 313–14
  style/methods 48–9, 93, 94, 99–100, 107, 228, 314
Teaching Excellence Framework (TEF) 314
teaching staff see Professors/teaching staff
technology 105–7, 106, 267, 310, 314, 326; see also computers/computing
telephone, invention of 192
terrorist attacks (2005) 297
theology, teaching of 70; see also religion/religious teaching
thermionic valve 106–7, 106
Thomas, Ethel 102
Thompson, E. H. 237
Thompson, Prof. Sir Henry 127
Thomson, Prof. Anthony Todd 36
Tian Xiaogang 294
Todd, Margaret G. 278
Tomlinson Report 279
Tonks, Prof. Henry 13, 13, 76–7, 109, 118, 118, 121, 122, 156
Tooke, William 21
Tots and Quots 195
Town Planning 214
translation 320
Translation Studies, Centre for 320
Trinity College, Cambridge 42
Tübingen, University of 217
Tuck, Gustave 178, 178
tuition fees 284, 314, 322
Turner, Prof. Edward 41
Turner, Prof. Sir Eric 227, 228
Tutor to Women Students 217
Tyrwhitt, Ursula 121

UCL Academy, Camden 316, 317–18
UCL BioMedica (later UCL Business (UCLB)) 267, 308–10
UCL Business (UCLB) (previously UCL BioMedica) 267, 308–10
UCL Culture (previously UCL Museums and Collections) 315–17
UCL East (Olympic Park, Stratford) plans for new campus in 297, 299, 325, 330, 332, 334
UCL Medical School see University College Hospital Medical School (UCHMS)
UCL Museums and Collections see UCL Culture
UCL NEWS 267
UCL Partners 303
'UCL Past and Present' (1977) 244
UCL Press 308
UCL Public Policy 308
'UCL 2034' strategies 296–7, 310, 311, 313, 314
UCL Universe 267
UCL Ventures 267
UCL Women 324
UCLH NHS Foundation Trust 277, 303
UCLi (UCL Initiatives) 267
Union 130–4, 131, 149, 173, 210, 217, 285–6, 322–3
  joint men/women 151, 171, 217, 219
  men's 130, 217, 219

accommodation/
building 134, 135, 151, 151, 195, 217, 235
women's 90, 149, 151, 151, 152, 210, 217, 218, 219
Union Magazine 114, 131, 151
United States Studies, Institute for 227
Universities Funding Council (previously UGC) 273
University College Gazette 134
University College (Transfer) Act (1905) 135
University College and Middlesex School of Medicine (1987) 258, 262–3
University College Hall, Ealing 151, 157
University College Hospital (UCH) 57, 59, 70–2, 126, 127, 127, 152, 279, 302
University College Hospital Medical School (UCHMS) 140–1, 141, 142, 244, 258, 278, 279
University College London (UCL)
aerial view of 158
construction of 24, 26–8; *see also* University College London (UCL), architecture of
finances of 20–1, 24, 45, 55, 59, 134–5, 235, 252–4, 252, 273–5, 282, 297–9; *see also* benefactions; funding, sources of; fundraising
foundation of 13–23, 20, 24, 24, 28, 31
founding principles of 14–16, 21, 28, 41, 196, 293
international strategy 310–13
as 'London's Global University' 293, 294, 296
opposition to 28–9, 28
overseas collaborations/ partnerships 311–13, 312
plans of 13, 23, 25, 163, 184
teaching style/ methods 48–9, 93, 94, 99–100, 107, 228, 314

see also campuses/ sites; Council; *and under individual departments*
University College London (UCL), architecture of 24, 26–8, 158
Dome 26, 28, 35, 59, 77, 201
Gower Street entrance 263–4, 264
lecture theatres 26, 50, 178, *178*
main façade 31, 45
North Wing 26, 27, 28, 45, 80, 82–3, *82*, *83*, 85, 97, 186
original designs for (Wilkins) 25–6, *25*, 27, 45, 80, 178
Portico 26, 28, 35, 76, 78, 134, 141, 157, 264
South Wing 26, 27, 28, 45, 80, *80*, 81, 81, 83, 114, 142, 190
see also under individual departments and building names
University College London (UCL), constitution of 21–3, 49
Deed of Settlement (1826) 20–1, *21*, 242
Royal Charter (1836) 23, 65, *65*
Act of Parliament (1869) 79, 242
Act of Parliament (Transfer Act, 1905) 135, 242
University of London, incorporation into (1907) 135, 140, 142
Royal Charter (1977) 142, 242, 242–4
Act of Parliament (1978) 251
proposed merger with Imperial College (2002) 287–9, 293
University College Magazine 171, *193*, 196
University College School 51, *51*, 80, 81, 140, 141, 267
University College Society 90, 130; *see also* Union
University Grants Committee (UGC) 224, 252, 273
University Hall (later Dr William's Library) 69–70, 71, 76
University of London Union 171, 301
University of the Arts London 330

Urology, Institute of 262

V&A Museum, London 330
Ventris, Michael 227
Vignoles, Prof. Charles Blacker 66, 67
Virginia, University of 16, 17, 42, 51, 75
Voluntary Aid Detachment (VAD) 156
Voluntary Services Unit 322
von Mühlenfels, Ludwig 41, 42

Wadsworth, Edward 121
Waley-Cohen, Sir Bernard 342–4
Walker, Ethel 121
Wallace-Dunlop, Marion 152
Wallis, Henry 124
war artists 156, 208
war memorials 156, 157, 157, 178, 210
Warburg Institute 229
Waterhouse, Alfred 127
Wates Foundation 236
Wates House ('The Bartlett') 236, 326
Watson, Prof. D. M. S. 186, 187
Waugh, Edna *see* Hall, Edna Clarke
Webster, T. B. L. 227
Webster, Prof. Thomas 78
Weldon Professor of Biometrics 198
Weldon, Prof. W. F. R. 100, 112
Welfare Committee 242
Wellcome Trust 307, 308
Wells, Prof. G. P. 195
West End Hospital for Nervous Diseases 275
West, Charles 275
Westfield College 262
Wheeler, Adrian 143
Wheeler, Sir Mortimer 139
White Papers (2004/2007) 293
White, Prof. John 229, 270
Whiteread, Rachel 286
Whittington Hub 301
Widening Participation strategies 316, 317
Wilkins Building 301, 330
Wilkins Terrace 330, *330*
Wilkins, William 13, *13*, 25–6, *25*, 27, 45, 80, 178
Wilks, John 208
Williams, Prof. E. C. 185
Williams, Shirley 244
Williamson, Prof. Alexander 69, 91–2, 92, 93, 109, 112
Wilson, D. M. 192
wireless (long-distance) 106

Woledge, Prof. Brian 227, 241
Wolfson Foundation 225, 279, 307
Wolfson Trust 236
Wolpert, Prof. Lewis 271–3, 273
women
admission of 47, 77–8, 89–90, 102–3, 127, 171, 284
first Professor 213, 216
teaching staff 90, 91, 102–3, 151–2, 217, 240–1, 241, 255–6, 319, 324–5
and the war effort (First World War) 156
and the war effort (Second World War) 210
see also women's rights; Women's Union Society (WUS)
women's rights 74, 90, 152; *see also* suffrage movement
Women's Union Society (WUS) 90, 149, 151, *151*, 152, 218, 219
Wood, Orson 208
Woodcroft, Bennet 67
Worldwide Universities Network 295
Worton, Prof. Michael 315, 316, 317
Wren, Sir Christopher 184
Wundowa, Gladys 297
Wyatt, Digby 82
Wyndham Lewis, Percy 121, *121*, 208

X-ray photography 111, 111
X-rays 111, 166

Yale–UCL Collaborative 313
Yates Archaeological Library 123
Yates, James 79, 122
Young, Lord 282–3
Young, Sir Frank 165

Zakrzewska, Prof. Joanna 303
Zoology 83, 97–9, 99, 186, 189
Professors of 187, 236, 237
Zoology Museum 100; *see also* Grant Museum